C0061 74525

D1187706

Scourge of Henry VIII

Scourge of Henry VIII

The Life of Marie de Guise

Melanie Clegg

PEN & SWORD
HISTORY

First published in Great Britain in 2016 by
PEN AND SWORD HISTORY
an imprint of
Pen and Sword Books Ltd
47 Church Street
Barnsley
South Yorkshire S70 2AS

Copyright © Melanie Clegg, 2016

ISBN 978 1 47384 838 2

Th~~~~~~~~~~~~~~~~~~~

as the author ~~~~~~~~~~~~~~~~~~ :ordance
with t ~~~~~~~~~~~~~~~~~~~~ 3.

A CIP recor ~~~~~~~~~~~~~ Library
All rights re ~~~~~~~~~~~~~ uced or
transmi ~~~~~~~~~~~~~~~~ : or
mech ~~~~~~~~~~~~~~~~~~~ r
by any ir ~~~~~~~~~~~~~~~~ hout
p ~~~~~~~~~~~~~~~~~~~~~

Glasgow Life Glasgow Libraries	
EA	
C 006174525	
Askews & Holts	31-Aug-2016
941.105092 H	£19.99

by CPI Group (UK) Ltd, Croydon, CR0 4YY

Typeset in Times New Roman by
CHIC GRAPHICS

Pen & Sword Books Ltd incorporates the imprints of Pen & Sword
Archaeology, Atlas, Aviation, Battleground, Discovery,
Family History, History, Maritime, Military, Naval, Politics, Railways,
Select, Social History, Transport, True Crime, Claymore Press,
Frontline Books, Leo Cooper, Praetorian Press, Remember When,
Seaforth Publishing and Wharncliffe.

For a complete list of Pen and Sword titles please contact
Pen and Sword Books Limited
47 Church Street, Barnsley, South Yorkshire, S70 2AS, England
E-mail: enquiries@pen-and-sword.co.uk
Website: www.pen-and-sword.co.uk

Contents

Dramatis Personae 6

Chapter 1   The Death of a King 10
Chapter 2   One for All 13
Chapter 3   Dynastic Ambitions 28
Chapter 4   Mademoiselle de Guise....................................40
Chapter 5   The Auld Alliance 53
Chapter 6   A Farewell to France.......................................67
Chapter 7   Queen of Scots 80
Chapter 8   The Baby Princes 94
Chapter 9   Solway Moss..106
Chapter 10   The Little Queen 119
Chapter 11   The Rough Wooing...132
Chapter 12   The Defence of the Realm 147
Chapter 13   The Homecoming 160
Chapter 14   Queen Regent 174
Chapter 15   And Still it Stands...188

Afterword 200
Bibliography..202

Dramatis Personae

FRANCE

The Lorraines

Philippa de Guelders, Dowager Duchesse de Lorraine (Marie's paternal grandmother, matriarch of the family)

Antoine de Lorraine, Duc de Lorraine (Marie's paternal uncle)
Renée de Bourbon, Duchesse de Lorraine (Antoine's wife, Marie's aunt)
François de Lorraine (Marie's cousin and betrothed of Anne of Cleves)
Anna de Lorraine (Marie's cousin)

Jean de Lorraine, Cardinal de Lorraine (Marie's paternal uncle, King François' closest friend)
Louis de Lorraine, Comte de Vaudémont (Marie's paternal uncle)
François de Lorraine, Comte de Lambesc (Marie's paternal uncle)

Claude de Lorraine, Duc de Guise (Marie's father)
Antoinette de Bourbon, Duchesse de Guise (Marie's mother)

Marie de Guise (eldest daughter of the Duc de Guise)
Louis d'Orléans, Duc de Longueville (Grand Chamberlain of France and first husband of Marie de Guise)
François d'Orléans (eldest son of Marie and Louis)
Louis d'Orléans (second son of Marie and Louis)

François de Guise, Duc de Guise (Marie's eldest brother)
Charles de Guise, Cardinal de Lorraine (Marie's brother)
Claude de Guise, Duc d'Aumale (Marie's brother)
Louis de Guise, Cardinal de Guise (Marie's brother)

DRAMATIS PERSONAE

René de Guise, Marquis d'Elbeuf (Marie's brother)
Louise de Guise, Duchess of Arschot (Marie's eldest sister)
Renée de Guise (Marie's sister)
Antoinette de Guise (Marie's sister)

The Bourbons
Marie de Luxembourg, Dowager Comtesse de Vendôme (Marie's
  maternal grandmother)

Charles de Bourbon, Duc de Vendôme (Marie's maternal uncle)
Marie de Bourbon (his eldest daughter, Marie's cousin, prospective
  bride of James V)

Charles de Bourbon, Duc de Bourbon (Constable of France and
  brother of Marie's aunt Renée)
Suzanne de Bourbon, Duchesse de Bourbon (his wife, a relative of
  Marie's mother and niece of Charles VIII of France)

The Valois
Louise de Savoie, Dowager Duchesse d'Angoulême (a relative of
  Marie's mother)
Marguerite d'Angoulême, Queen of Navarre (her daughter)

François I (Louise's son, King of France and close friend of Marie's
  father and uncle Jean)
Claude de France (his first wife, daughter of Louis XII of France)
Eleanore of Austria (his second wife, sister of Emperor Charles)

Princesse Madeleine (King François' eldest surviving daughter, first
  wife of James V of Scotland)
Princesse Marguerite (King François younger daughter)
The Dauphin François (King François' eldest son)

Henri, Duc d'Orléans (King François' second son, later to become
  Henri II)

Catherine de' Medici, Duchesse d'Orléans (Henri's wife, cousin of
Pope Clement VII)

François de Valois (son of Henri and Catherine, future husband of
Mary Queen of Scots, later to become François II)

Elisabeth de Valois (eldest daughter of Henri and Catherine, best
friend of Mary Queen of Scots, prospective bride of Edward VI.)

Charles de Valois (second son of Henri and Catherine, godson of
Marie de Guise and future Charles IX.)

Diane de Poitiers, Madame de Brézé (mistress of Henri II and friend
of the Guise family)

Louise de Brézé (Diane's daughter and future wife of Marie's
brother François de Guise)

SCOTLAND

James V (King of Scotland, Marie's second husband and nephew of
Henry VIII of England)

James Stuart, Duke of Rothesay (eldest son of James and Marie)

Robert Stuart, Duke of Albany (second son of James and Marie)

Mary Stuart (daughter of James and Marie, Queen of Scots and
France, wife of François II of France)

James Stewart, Earl of Moray (illegitimate son of James V)

Queen Margaret Tudor (James' mother and sister of Henry VIII)

Archibald Douglas, Earl of Angus (Margaret's second husband,
James V's former regent and a terrible trouble maker)

Lady Margaret Douglas (daughter of Margaret and Archibald, half
sister of James V and favourite niece of Henry VIII)

ENGLAND

The Tudors

Henry VIII (King of England, uncle of James V, prospective bridegroom of Marie and a thorn in everyone's side)

Anne Boleyn (his second wife and mother of his daughter Elizabeth)

Jane Seymour (his third wife and mother of his son Edward)

Anne of Cleves (his fourth wife, former betrothed of Marie's cousin François)

Catherine Howard (his fifth wife)

Edward VI (Henry VIII's son by Jane Seymour and a prospective husband for Marie's daughter)

Mary I (Henry VIII's daughter by Catherine of Aragon)

Elizabeth I (Henry VIII's daughter by Anne Boleyn)

Edward Seymour, Earl of Somerset (Jane Seymour's brother and Lord Protector of her son Edward VI)

Chapter 1

The Death of a King
December 1542

The windows of Linlithgow Palace, an imposing royal residence with the look of a French château about 17 miles to the west of Edinburgh, were shrouded in darkness as the messenger, dressed in the scarlet and gold livery of the Stuart royal family, rode through the gates and dismounted from his horse in the courtyard. He had ridden through the snow and sleet of a wintry night from Falkland Palace, another royal residence over 40 miles away, and was in no mood to do anything other than bark an order to be taken directly to the Queen, who was recovering from childbirth and asleep in her sumptuous rooms overlooking the loch.

As he raced up the stone staircase to the royal apartments, the messenger would have been aware of the shocked faces of the courtiers and servants who had tumbled out of bed as soon as word went round that news had arrived from Falkland, where the King lay mortally ill. After his resounding defeat at the Battle of Solway Moss by the forces of his uncle Henry VIII twenty days earlier, the King had either been felled by dysentery or by an emotional breakdown. The arrival of an official messenger so late at night was not suggestive of good news and they would have watched him nervously as he made his way through the rooms of the royal apartments, with their tapestry covered walls, intricately painted ceilings and polished and gilded wood panelling, to the Queen.

Marie de Guise, Queen of Scotland, an unusually tall woman in her late twenties, with long chestnut red hair and clear grey eyes, would have been woken by her ladies-in-waiting as soon as news of the messenger's arrival reached her rooms, and it is likely that she hastily dressed and received him beside the blazing fire in her closet, surrounded by her household and with her infant daughter, just 6 days old and named Mary after both her mother and the Virgin Mary, upon whose feast day she had been born.

As expected, the news from Falkland Palace was not good. In fact, it was disastrous. James V, the 30-year-old King of Scotland, had died a few hours earlier of his fever, raving to the very end about his ignominious defeat and lamenting the fact that he had no legitimate sons to succeed him. The tiny baby, less than a week old, who lay asleep in her beautifully carved wooden crib at the side of Marie de Guise, was now Queen of Scotland.

As the now Dowager Queen listened carefully to the messenger's report of her husband's final hours, her mind would have been working fast, weighing up the unenviable situation that she now found herself in. Although she and her husband were more or less estranged, she must have felt sorrow for a life prematurely snuffed out, thankful for the happiness they had shared at the beginning of their marriage and profound regret for the loss of his support.

However, regardless of whatever she felt privately, it was not in the nature of Marie de Guise, strictly raised by those austere great ladies, her mother Antoinette de Bourbon and grandmother Philippa of Guelders, to lose control of her emotions. After thanking the messenger, she would have retired further into her rooms to take proper stock of what lay ahead, while snow fell outside her windows and covered the great park that surrounded Linlithgow, further isolating it from the world.

Once safely ensconced in private with the infant Queen and her most trusted attendants, many of whom had come with her from France in the spring of 1538, Marie would have considered her next move, only too aware of the storm clouds brewing beyond the thick stone walls of Linlithgow. As far as royal successions went, this one involved the worst possible scenario for an already beleaguered Scotland: instead of the desired adult male heir, the new ruler was both an infant and female which, in the sixteenth century, was considered an ominous and undesirable combination.

There was an unfortunate precedent too in the fact that her dead husband had succeeded to his own father's throne in similar circumstances at just 17 months old after James IV had been slaughtered, along with thousands of Scottish soldiers, by the forces of his brother in law, Henry VIII, at Flodden. His mother, Margaret Tudor, had learned the news of her husband's death in the very same rooms at Linlithgow, but there, Marie de Guise determined, the similarity between their situations would end. The feckless Margaret had quickly proved herself to be an inadequate regent for her infant son, having fled back to her brother in England within two years of her husband's death, leaving her son behind.

As she shivered in her fur-lined robes and stared out across the snow covered landscape, it no doubt crossed Marie's mind that, according to the terms of the marriage contract, she was now free to return to France and her own close-knit family, which included her beloved 5-year-old son, the Duc de Longueville, product of her first marriage. However, tempting though this idea might have been, she resolutely pushed it from her mind. From now on, her place was in Scotland with her baby daughter, who could not possibly be entrusted to the Scottish nobles, whom Marie already suspected would not waste an instant before brokering a deal with the hostile English.

After all, it was too convenient that the heir to the English throne, Edward, Prince of Wales, was, at just 5 years old, close enough in age to the baby Queen of Scotland to be considered an eligible contender for her hand. Marie was no fool and it would have occurred to her that as soon as the news of her husband's untimely death arrived in London along with the news of his defeat in battle, the indomitable Henry VIII would start moving heaven and earth in order to secure the little Queen for his son and by extension, Scotland for himself.

However, if he thought that the widowed Queen Marie was going to be a pushover like his sister Margaret had been during her own brief period of regency thirty years earlier, he had underestimated her. It would not take long, however, before events showed him that here, in this member of the noble Lorraine family, was an opponent worthy of respect and it was not for nothing that her personal emblem was a crown set on top of a rock surrounded by a turbulent sea, surmounted by the motto '*Adhuc stat*' – 'And yet it stands'.

Chapter 2

One for All

Squabbles over succession were not unusual within Marie's family – after all, her great-great-grandfather, Good King René d'Anjou, had famously squandered his family's fortune on pursuing his claim to the thrones of Naples and Jerusalem, while his youngest daughter, Marguerite, as the wife of Henry VI, became one of the main protagonists in the dynastic row commonly known as the Wars of the Roses. However, it was not from the formidable firebrand Marguerite, but rather from her meek and more dutiful elder sister, Yolande, Duchesse de Lorraine, that Marie would claim descent.

The 1445 marriage of Yolande d'Anjou and her cousin, Frédéric, Comte de Vaudémont, put an end to yet another dynastic argument over the fate of the vast Duchy of Lorraine, which had been fought over by the young couple's respective fathers for years and was currently held by the bride's mother, Isabelle. However, when Yolande inherited the duchy in 1473, she immediately passed it over to her pugnacious and extremely ambitious 22-year-old son, René, whom she felt was better equipped to deal with the predatory advances into their territory of both Louis XI and Charles the Bold, Duke of Burgundy.

René's subsequent attempts to secure his Lorraine inheritance embroiled him in a long and arduous conflict with Louis and Charles, which at one particularly low point in November 1475, lost him his capital city of Nancy, the very heartland of the Lorraine territory. However, the war eventually ended in triumph for René after his forces defeated and killed Charles of Burgundy in the battle to regain Nancy in 1477. Although his dispute with King Louis would grumble on for a few more years, this victory against the powerful Duke of Burgundy would serve to boost and underline the previously rather tenuous prestige of the Lorraine family, and also secure what had hitherto been an unstable inheritance.

Of course, after securing the family lands, it was inevitable that the victorious René's thoughts, like those of many a conquering hero, should immediately turn to founding a robust dynasty to inherit the fruits of his labours. After the annulment of his first childless marriage to Jeanne d'Harcourt, Comtesse de Tancarville, René took as his second wife Philippa of Guelders, the twin sister of the Duke of Guelders. A noblewoman of impeccable lineage, Philippa of Guelders also had crucial dynastic links to the French kings, the dukes of Burgundy, the kings of Scotland (her aunt Mary had married James II of Scotland) and also the Hapsburg emperors, who coveted her family's vast domains in the Netherlands and would eventually take them over after the death of her brother.

This exceedingly grand marriage took place in Orléans on 1 September 1485 and formed the basis of the new, much stronger and less vulnerable Lorraine dynasty, which would go on to dominate European politics for the next 300 years thanks to a mixture of charm, cunning, judicious marriage and single-minded ambition, eventually becoming Holy Roman Emperors themselves in the eighteenth century.

While their eldest son, Antoine, inherited the duchy of Lorraine in December 1508 following the death of his father in a hunting accident, it was with the fortunes of her second son, Claude – the future father of Marie de Guise – that Philippa most interested herself; he was acknowledged by the rest of their family, with some resentment, to be her favourite child. Certainly, there was concern over the legitimacy of Antoine, the elder Lorraine boy, because his father's first wife, Jeanne, was still alive and well at the time of Antoine's birth. The Papal bull that formally ended the first marriage did not arrive in France for several years, although fortunately, it did materialise before Claude was born.

Born on 20 October 1496 at the Château de Condé, in what is now modern day Custines, Claude de Lorraine, Comte de Guise, was the epitome of the accomplished, charming and erudite Renaissance nobleman, equally at home on the ballroom as he was on the battlefield. He demonstrated courage and skill at war and on the jousting and hunting fields and was also known for his enjoyment of more decorous courtly pursuits like music, tennis, gambling and dancing. However, his unusual height and fair-haired good looks, which would be inherited by both his daughter and granddaughter Mary, Queen of Scots, gave rise to malicious whispers around court that the Lorraine family were more Germanic than French.

Thanks to his own experiences of battling for Lorraine, Claude's father was all too aware of the issues that a disputed inheritance could provoke and so he determined to ensure that his own affairs were fully in order before he died. His will, therefore, divided his property between his two elder sons; Antoine inherited Lorraine, while Claude was to receive the sizeable family lands in France, which included Guise, Aumale, Mayenne, Joinville, Elbeuf, Lambesc and a whole host of other fiefdoms. To ensure that there could be no doubt about the younger boy's right to hold territory in France, and no opportunity for him to attempt to seize his elder brother's lands using the doubts about his legitimacy as an excuse, he decided that 9-year-old Claude and his younger brother, Jean (who had been earmarked for a career in the church and was, in fact, made Bishop of Metz at the age of 7), should be raised as naturalised French men by their mother's cousin, Louise de Savoie, Duchesse d'Angoulême, at her court at Blois in the Loire Valley. The two youngest Lorraine boys, Louis and François, would have to fend for themselves.

This happened to be a fortuitous arrangement in more ways than one because Louise's son, François, who was two years older than his cousin Claude, was heir presumptive to the French throne should Louis XII die without any legitimate sons. As might have been expected (and as the ambitious René and Philippa very probably hoped), the boys became close friends, bonding over their mutual love of jousting and hunting and sharing the same charming, chivalrous manners. When François took up residence with the court in Paris, it was naturally assumed that Claude would accompany him and it was here that he really began to make his mark, impressing everyone with his sporting prowess and friendly. It was even rumoured for a while that he might be engaged to Louis XII's younger daughter, Renée, but this seems unlikely to have been true.

François, Duc d'Angoulême, had been betrothed to Madame Claude, the eldest daughter of Louis XII and Duchess of Brittany in her own right, since 1506; the match being seen as a way of keeping her enormous inheritance as part of France and of strengthening François' own claim to the throne, Madame Claude herself being unable to inherit due to the Salic Law, which stipulated that the French crown could only be passed on to male heirs.

In 1512, when the 16-year-old Claude de Lorraine first arrived at court, the marriage still seemed to be quite far off due to the youth of the bride to be, but François still paid courtesy visits to his affianced in her apartments in the Hôtel de Tournelles in the Marais district of Paris. It was during one of these visits, while loitering around the Princess' apartments as he waited for his friend, that Claude first met the 19-year-old Antoinette de Bourbon, daughter of the Comte de Vendôme and Princesse Marie de Luxembourg, Comtesse de Saint-Pol.

Antoinette was not a beauty, but she was pleasing to look at with long auburn hair and sharp blue eyes and was also strong willed, intelligent and affectionate. Although her dowry of 40,000 livres was rather on the small size, her lineage was more impressive even than that of Claude's intimidating mother, Philippa of Guelders, with close links to several royal and notable families across Europe and a line of descent from Saint Louis himself, as well as several Holy Roman Emperors on her mother's side of the family. Furthermore, her great aunt Charlotte de Savoie had been married to Louis XI, while another, Bona, was married to the Duke of Milan and her great grandmother, Anne of Cyprus, Duchesse de Savoie, claimed descent from the infamous Melusine de Lusignan, who was allegedly able to transform into a sort of mermaid when she came into contact with water. Marriage to Antoinette de Bourbon would mean marrying into royalty.

It was a dazzling match for an ambitious young nobleman and Claude apparently wasted no time in urging his friend François to use all his influence to seal the deal, keenly aware that as the younger son of a family, and despite the efforts of his father, he would never be regarded as entirely French and might not be as tempting a prospect to his future in-laws as might be hoped. However, all went to plan and Claude and Antoinette were married in front of the royal family and all of the court on 9 June 1513, in a splendid ceremony at the beautiful royal church of St Paul in Paris.

Although the new Comte and Comtesse de Guise were great favourites at court, the latter at least seems to have preferred country living and was keen to set herself up as chatelaine of her husband's estates. While her formidable mother in law, Philippa of Guelders, kept a tight control on the Lorraine family domains, the young couple were unable to set up home at Joinville, which would otherwise have been their main seat, and took up residence in the charming town of Bar-le-Duc in northern France instead. It was in the medieval fortress there on 20 November 1515, that their first child, a daughter, was born. The baby was baptised Marie twelve days later in the château chapel with her two grandmothers, Philippa of Guelders and Marie de Luxembourg, who were both present at her birth, standing as godmothers, while her uncle Jean, the Cardinal de Lorraine, acted as godfather.

During the sixteenth century, childbirth was regarded as a great female mystery and a time when women would retreat to a hushed feminine world to await the arrival of their baby, attended only by close female family members, maid servants and midwives. Male doctors would be admitted only in emergencies and even the baby's father would find himself excluded until his child was safely born, relegated to a lengthy and tense waiting game elsewhere. However, while Claude was almost certainly close at hand for his wife's subsequent labours, unfortunate circumstances meant that he was far away in Italy when she gave birth to his first child.

Claude's great friend, François, had succeeded his father-in-law, Louis XII, as King of France at the start of 1515 and immediately concentrated his efforts into reviving the old French claim to the Duchy of Milan, which had fallen under the control of the Swiss. As one of the new King's most trusted companions, Claude was naturally expected to accompany him when he invaded Italy in the autumn of that year, even though his wife was expecting their first child. At first all went well and Antoinette, anxiously waiting at Bar-le-Duc for news of her husband, would have been much cheered by the positive news that filtered back to France about the French army's military successes as they progressed across the Alps and through the hostile Italian countryside.

After a daring French capture of the fearsome Papal commander, Prospero Colonna, along with 300 of his men, François offered to come to terms with the Swiss, offering them a large financial inducement and the promise of future military support if they would agree to his occupation of Milan. Although a treaty was duly agreed, some Swiss leaders were unhappy with such an easy capitulation to the hated French and so planned an attack near Marignano, which occurred with devastating ferocity on the 13 September 1515.

The battle that followed was to result in a great and unquestionable victory for the French, but it came at a heavy price. There were tremendous casualties on both sides, including François, Duc de Chatellerault, younger brother of the Duke of Bourbon and brother-in-law of Claude's elder brother, Antoine, who had married Renée de Bourbon at Amboise in June of that year. For a while, it was feared that Claude de Guise, who had taken charge of his uncle the Duke of Guelders' famous Black Band of terrifying German *landsknechts*, had also perished in the chaos and bloodshed of Marignano. He was eventually discovered by James Scott, a Scottish soldier, in the midst of the several thousand corpses that littered the field; lying trapped, grievously wounded and insensible beneath the weight of his dead horse and squire, Adam Fouvert, a loyal German boy who had flung himself on top of Claude to protect him and then died himself beneath the hooves of the relentless Swiss cavalry.

At first it looked as though Claude, who had been shot in the thigh by an arquebus and suffered over twenty different other wounds, including a broken arm, would probably die. However, under the careful ministrations of King François' own doctors, he began to make a rapid recovery. By the beginning of October, less than a month later, he was well enough to ride into Milan, albeit one handed as his broken arm was still in a white silk sling, as a conquering hero at the side of his King and at the head of a splendid procession.

Antoinette was naturally devastated when news of her husband's brush with death at Marignano filtered back to her at Bar-le-Duc, but she was made of stern stuff and, like most women of her station, had a firm and absolute faith in God so she applied herself with extra diligence to her daily devotions until she heard of his recovery. However, many months were to pass before he was able to return home to France and meet his new daughter, Marie, at a family reunion at his mother's château at Joinville. During his stay, he kept a vow he had made to St Nicolas when he thought he might die from his terrible injuries; donning full armour, he walked the twenty-five leagues to the Lorraine family basilica devoted to the saint, which had been built by his own father to give thanks for his victory against Charles of Burgundy.

Claude de Guise made it plain that he was absolutely delighted with his baby daughter who looked set to inherit his own striking auburn colouring, unusual height and charm. For her part, Antoinette, who otherwise strictly conformed to the behaviour expected from a woman of her high status, was also smitten with her baby and refused to entirely consign her to the care of nursemaids. Instead she oversaw her daughter's upbringing herself and kept her close in a way that many other mothers and children of their class must surely have envied. For the next four years at Bar-le-Duc, Marie was Claude and Antoinette's only child and revelled in having her beloved parents' attention entirely on herself.

The Guise's second child, born in February 1519, was a boy named François in honour of his godfather the King, and was destined to become the future Duc de Guise. More children were born at regular intervals after that: three daughters and seven sons (two of whom did not survive infancy). Later, in 1519, there was another great change to Marie's circumstances when her strong-willed and extremely devout grandmother, the 58-year-old Philippa de Guelders, announced her intention to withdraw from the world and devote her life to God.

Her sons, who had come to rely on her strength of character and shrewd management of their estates and affairs, were shocked by the news, although one suspects that her daughters-in-law felt rather more sanguine about the removal of their domineering mother-in-law. Perhaps it should not have been such a surprise to them though – Philippa's health had been declining for some time and she had become subject to headaches and heart problems, probably brought on by stress and which were naturally alleviated when she entered the much calmer atmosphere of the convent. Diligent as always, however, she returned to the seat of the Ducs de Lorraine at Nancy and made formal preparations, which involved dividing up her considerable lands between her sons. As expected, Claude received Joinville and was finally able to move there with his family and household shortly after the birth of his son.

The couple's third child, a daughter christened Louise in tribute to King François' mother, whose patronage had taken Claude to court as a young boy, was born at Joinville a year later. Once again Antoinette's mother, Marie de Luxembourg, acted as godmother to the new Guise baby at her baptism in January 1521, but as her other grandmother Philippa was already happily ensconced in her convent, it seems that it was her 5-year-old sister, Marie, who was entered into the records as 'Mademoiselle de Guyse', took over as godmother.

Sadly, very little remains of Joinville as it looked in the sixteenth century as it was demolished during the French Revolution, but from contemporary drawings we can see that it was a large and beautiful domestic castle, which perched high on a hill above the river Marne. Like a fairy castle in one of the exquisite books of hours that Antoinette was so fond of, it bristled against the skyline with a seemingly endless array of turrets, round towers and elegant spires, while at its heart was Jovin's Tower, a huge round tower that was said to date to Roman times. Surrounding the castle there were extensive gardens, said to be amongst the finest in France; there were also orchards, where exotic fruits such as oranges and pomegranates grew alongside more humdrum offerings such as apples and pears, and the family's vineyards, which stretched across the surrounding hilltops and down to the river.

There were also Claude's prized stables, which housed over a hundred fine horses as was only right for the Head of the Royal Hunt and a man of such renowned prowess at war and sport. Unusually for the time, he used his famous stables to make connections within the locality by providing riding apprenticeships to talented young horsemen, who would then go on to enjoy his continued patronage and, in return, serve him when called upon.

His children were also schooled in riding from an early age, as was expected for young people of their status. Marie, his eldest and some would say favourite daughter, would go on to become a notable horsewoman who would delight in the hunting opportunities offered by the wild Scottish landscape, possibly emulating the likes of Diane de Poitiers who never rode out without her own bird of prey on her wrist so she could indulge in a spot of hunting even when on the move.

The interior of Joinville was no less impressive than its beautiful surroundings, being richly decorated with all the luxuries that the Guise family could command in order to embellish their beloved home. Marie would have grown up in rooms filled with colourful tapestries, stained glass windows, paintings, statues, gold and silver plate and rich brocade, silk and velvet hangings. Even the very walls and ceilings were covered in painted designs and mottos, all devised to underline the noble descent and heritage of her family. There would have been music too because her father was a passionate music lover and patron of several musicians, most prominently Clément Janequin and Jacques Arcadelt, who left his tenure as choirmaster of the Sistine Chapel to become choirmaster at Joinville. Both musicians were renowned throughout Europe for their compositions, which included pieces commissioned to celebrate notable events in the Guise family, such as Claude's promotion to Head of the Royal Hunt, which inspired Janequin's piece *La Chasse;* or his eldest son François' successful defence of Metz in 1553, which was lauded in an intricate piece for five voices.

It was in the exquisitely decorated Joinville chapel, dedicated to Antoinette's ancestor St Louis, that the most beautiful music would have been heard as the family knelt at their devotions during the daily services. Both Claude and Antoinette were deeply devout, even by the religious standards of the day when most people believed unquestioningly in God. The chapel at Joinville, which was full of holy relics collected by Claude and his ancestors, was a prominent focus of daily life, where the whole household, (which amounted to over a hundred people and included two doctors and a surgeon,) would be gathered together every morning for Mass, which was conducted by their two priests, nine canons, four choristers and choirmaster that had been installed in the château as soon as they moved in. The Guise children were brought up to be as firmly devoted to God so Marie would have attended Mass alongside her mother and father from an early age, kneeling dutifully behind them with her growing band of brothers and sisters, all of whom were made to learn their catechism in early childhood. However, while the Guise family were well known for being almost fanatical in their devotion to the Catholic faith, we will see that Marie herself took a rather more moderate path during her time as regent of Scotland.

The other focal point of household life was the great hall of Joinville, where as was the custom, the Guise family dined on a dais at the far end, surrounded by their household and honoured guests. Here too, religion played its part, as Antoinette was a stickler when it came to the fasts ordered by the church and would insist that the entire household forgo meat on Fridays and strictly adhere to the fasts of Lent and Advent. Although sixteenth-century children were usually allowed extra rations of meat and butter and other otherwise forbidden foods during fasting periods, it is likely that Antoinette, if not Claude who was the more indulgent parent of the two, insisted that her own brood participate as fully as herself in preparation for the spiritual life they would be expected to lead as adults.

At other times, however, the food served at the Guise household was as lavish as the surroundings in which it was consumed. Dozens of cooks and their assistants worked hard in the Joinville kitchens to produce mouth-watering dishes for the household, which involved an array of different meats as well as fish, crab and game, all cooked with imported spices, butter and plenty of cream and cheese. The diet at the time was extremely rich and a typical meal would involve around sixteen different dishes so Marie would have been taught from an early age how to eat sparingly, selecting only a few items from the dishes of pies, tarts, roasted meats and flower-petal decorated salads placed in front of her. Spiced and honeyed wines were served throughout the meal and she would have been taught to exercise restraint here too, because drunkeness, especially in young women of good family, was much frowned upon. Besides, she would have wanted to save her appetite for the later courses of custard tarts, gilded gingerbread, sweetmeats, sugar plums, syllabub and, on special occasions, elaborate marzipan constructions designed to honour a special guest or event, perhaps one of her father's military victories or a family betrothal.

Then as now, the enjoyment of food was an important part of French culture. As with all noble families of this period, meal times at the Guise court were a formal affair, always starting with diners being summoned to table by the call of a hunting horn, to ceremoniously wash their hands in silver bowls of rosewater before the meal could begin. We can imagine Antoinette, with her formidable eye for detail, glancing around to ensure that nothing was overlooked and that the top table was strewn with sweet smelling herbs and flowers and each high ranking diner had their own plate, spoon, knife, goblet and sauce bowl, as well as a fresh loaf wrapped in a napkin and a flagon of wine. As with everything else at their court, Marie would have been schooled in table manners and taught how to properly place her napkin on her shoulder (to make it easy to wipe her fingers on it while eating), eat tidily with just her fingers and a spoon, using her knife to cut meat into small portions and spread pâté on bread, and being sternly reminded never to break wind, belch or commit other such unhygienic social solecisms.

On special occasions, the boat would be pushed out even further, and we have a wonderful description of a feast given in 1455 by René d'Anjou, Claude's great grandfather, who had wowed his guests with:

a centre-piece, which represented a green lawn, surrounded with large peacocks' feathers and green branches, to which were tied violets and other sweet-smelling flowers. In the middle of this lawn a fortress was placed, covered with silver. This was hollow, and formed a sort of cage, in which several live birds were shut up, their tufts and feet being gilt. On its tower, which was gilt, three banners were placed, one bearing the arms of the count, the two others those of Mesdemoiselles de Châteaubrun and de Villequier, in whose honour the feast was given.

Followed by a banquet that included such delicacies as 'a civet of hare, a quarter of stag which had been a night in salt, a stuffed chicken, and a loin of veal. The two last dishes were covered with a German sauce, with gilt sugar-plums, and pomegranate seeds.'

While the household ate, the Guise servants, in the distinctive crimson and yellow livery of the house of Lorraine, would serve the tables and stand behind the Comte and Comtesse's chairs, while underfoot there ran the family's dogs, yapping, barking and hoping for some delicious scraps to come their way. All of the family were fond of dogs, a trait that would be inherited by Claude and Antoinette's granddaughter, Mary Queen of Scots. Joinville was always full of Claude's favourite hunting hounds and the smaller lap dogs favoured by Antoinette, her ladies and her daughters; their sharp little claws skittering on the polished floors of the galleries and chambers or begging for treats beneath the dining tables.

Despite all the care and attention that was paid to the Guise families diet, their less fortunate peers were not forgotten either and Antoinette, who saw dispensing charity as an important and integral part of her faith, personally oversaw the daily distribution of alms to the poor, which included rations of peas and salt during Lent. The family's philanthropic efforts also extended to providing dowries to 400 poor girls who might not otherwise be able to marry honourably as well as paying for the education of a hundred promising, but otherwise disadvantaged, young scholars. Antoinette was often seen stitching away at garments that were destined to be donated to the less fortunate, while listening to one of her chaplains reading a suitably devotional text.

Although her own personal habits were on the abstemious side, Antoinette still knew what was owed to both her own rank and that of her husband, so the family were always magnificently dressed to emphasise their prestige and, more importantly, their royal lineage. The Lorraine colours of crimson and gold could be seen everywhere at their court, either painted on the ceilings, hinted at in the gold edging of a scarlet velvet curtain or, on occasion, worn by the family themselves as their own, more luxurious, brand of the livery worn by their servants. As a small girl, Marie would have worn miniature versions of her mother's clothes: a linen smock worn with petticoats and a kirtle and gown. For special occasions, she would have worn silks, velvets and brocades trimmed with fur, gold thread and seed pearls like the older women of her family, but her everyday wear would have been much more hardwearing in deference to her age. The iconic round French hood, later made famous by Anne Boleyn, would have been worn at the Guise court during Marie's childhood, usually over a linen coif, which in the 1520s might well have been a fashionable red rather than the more usual white.

The overall effect in the Guise household during the first quarter of the sixteenth century was one of lavish splendour; but it came at a price. As a younger son, albeit a generously landed one, Claude's income was never as large as he might have wished, although it seems extraordinarily huge to us today. In the early 1540s, after having various court honours heaped upon him and being elevated to a dukedom, his annual income was in the region of 65,000 livres, a substantial amount that would be roughly equivalent to just over £3 million today. However, thanks to his own generous nature, wealth of interests, the cost of his large household and the need to present a properly ostentatious appearance at court, Claude usually overspent by around 10,000 livres every year. Twenty years earlier, during Marie's childhood, finances were even tighter for the Guise family; to such an extent that Antoinette, as always the more sensible and thrifty of the two, had to step in on more than one occasion and metaphorically slap her husband's hand away from his purse and warn him to curb his open-handed ways.

Such admonitory behaviour may be considered surprising from a sixteenth-century wife, even one as well born and intelligent as Antoinette de Bourbon, but in actual fact, it is clear that Claude de Guise always considered his wife to be his absolute equal and partner both in their marriage and also when it came to running their household and organising their affairs. His absolute faith in Antoinette's judgement is borne out in 1520 when, rather than appoint a steward to administer his estates while he was absent at court or war, he made her his official proxy, giving her total authority to deal with his official business and accounts. Brought up by her mother, Marie de Luxembourg, to be the perfect chatelaine of a great estate, Antoinette took up her mantle with considerable aplomb, handling Claude's affairs with great efficiency and acumen and even continuing to act in the same advisory capacity for her sons, who naturally turned to her for help with their own domestic and business arrangements.

It's clear from her later marital history that the young Marie de Guise took the example of her parents' equal and deeply mutually respectful marriage very much to heart and would enter into matrimony herself in full expectation of being treated in the same way as her mother, as an honoured partner and valuable advisor. To Marie, unlike many of her peers, marriage was an equal partnership, with both parties pulling their weight in order to support the other and sharing the load of household and business concerns. As the sixteenth century progressed, educated, strong, astute women became increasingly common, especially in the latter half of the century when Elizabeth I was on the throne of England and Marie de Guise's contemporary Catherine de' Medici was effectively ruling France. It was Marie's early observations of her mother as something more than just a loyal helpmeet, but rather a capable and intelligent administrator in her own right, that would stand her in good stead when her own time came to govern a country.

Although the atmosphere at Joinville could be a little on the austere side thanks to Antoinette's extreme piety, it is clear that the Guise family, both parents and children, were a close-knit and affectionate bunch, who genuinely enjoyed each others company and took each others interests very much to heart. They behaved much as a close family does today with regular visits and exchanges of lively, loving letters when apart and, most crucially, a whole-hearted willingness to drop everything and come to each others assistance should it be required. To the Guises, with their rousing motto of '*Toutes pour une*' or 'One for all', family really was everything and Marie, as the eldest child, would certainly have been a central and important member of the clan while growing up.

Chapter 3

Dynastic Ambitions

Although Claude de Guise naturally preferred to be at Joinville with his wife and family, he was still forced by necessity and loyalty to his friend, King François, to be absent from home often to participate in the wars that ravaged Europe during the first quarter of the sixteenth century. Although primarily instigated by a dispute over the ownership of Naples and the duchy of Milan, these conflicts were inflamed by the posturing and ambitions of the personalities behind them; at the time of Marie's childhood, these were primarily King François, Henry VIII of England, King Ferdinand of Aragon, Archduke Charles of Habsburg and the Holy Roman Emperor. Bound together, often unwillingly as in the case of Henry VIII and Ferdinand of Aragon, by family ties, the tussling of these men dominated European politics as they made and broke treaties, formed alliances and backstabbed in their pursuit of more power and territories.

Usually, Claude's military exploits took place far away from home, but as the majority of the Lorraine family's lands were in northern France, close to the borders of the territory ruled by the Holy Roman Emperor, the war could sometimes come worryingly close to home for Antoinette and her children. This was certainly the case in the 1520s, after relations between France and the empire had completely broken down thanks, in the first instance, to the death of Ferdinand of Aragon in 1516, which had resulted in his grandson, Charles of Habsburg, inheriting vast territories in Spain; secondly, the death of Charles' other grandfather, the Emperor Maximilian, in 1519 left the position of Holy Roman Emperor once again open to election.

Although it was well known to be Maximilian's wish that his grandson would be selected as the next emperor by the seven electors – princes both of the blood and the church whose traditional duty it was to elect the new emperor – François was determined to seize the title for himself. Encouraged by the fact that, although the empire had been under Habsburg rule for as long as anyone could remember, it was not actually a hereditary title and could be contested by anyone. His mother's nickname for him had long been 'César' in tribute to his imperious ways as a child and then, perhaps less charmingly, as an adult, and here at last was an opportunity to become an emperor in truth. Besides personal glory, however, he was also motivated by a desire to nip Charles' territorial ambitions in the bud and prevent France from being almost completely encircled by her enemies, which would be the case with Spain, the Netherlands and the imperial territories in Germany, all under Habsburg control. He also suspected that as emperor, Charles would renew the hostilities over the Italian territory that François had fought so hard to seize for himself.

You understand, he wrote, *the reason which moves me to gain the empire, which is to prevent the said Catholic King from doing so. If he were to succeed, seeing the extent of his kingdoms and lordships, this could do me immeasurable harm; he would always be mistrustful and suspicious, and would doubtless throw me out of Italy.*

Winning the backing of the Pope, who also had concerns about the threatened Habsburg pre-eminence in Europe, François set about flattering and bribing the electors to look favourably on his suit; even promising one, the Margrave of Brandenburg, the hand in marriage of his sister-in-law, Princesse Renée, for his son in exchange for his vote. It was all in vain and the hostility of the German princes and people forced François to withdraw from the election in June 1519, which left Charles' way clear to an unanimous victory just two days later. Although François was obviously bitterly disappointed, he tried to put a brave face on things and, somewhat disingenuously, tried to assure the English ambassador, the undoubtedly sceptical Sir Thomas Boleyn, that he believed he ought to be thankful to God for having intervened and spared him the burden that becoming emperor would have entailed.

Behind the scenes however, François was already working to defend his territories from the Habsburg threat, which now loomed from Spain, the Netherlands and Germany. At the same time, he was doing everything within his power to prevent Charles from getting to Rome for his imperial coronation by the Pope with the crown of Charlemagne, which would make his position as emperor completely unassailable and beyond all doubt. Although this was undoubtedly motivated by petty annoyance that he had lost out to his younger rival, François was also keen to keep the new emperor and his troops out of Italy, fearing, quite rightly as it happened, that it would have calamitous repercussions with regard to his own position and territories there.

As one of his most capable and trusted military commanders, Claude de Guise was an essential part of François preparations for war against the empire, not least because he was required to defend his own native Champagne region in northern France against invasion and the opportunistic harryings of imperial troops. He was also sent further afield and, in 1521, could be found fighting for the French in Navarre as part of an invasion of Spain, where he managed to distinguish himself at the siege of the allegedly impregnable fortress town of Fuenterrabia, which was considered to be the key to north-western Spain.

He was there under the command of Admiral Bonnivet, who had been entrusted with the mission of securing Fuenterrabia for the French and gaining them precious access to Spain. However, the Admiral was thwarted in his plans by the heavy rain that had stricken the region and caused the river Bidassoa, which lay between his army and their goal, to swell to many times its usual size. He was also put off by the heavy artillery that the defending Spanish had drawn up on the opposite bank, a daunting spectacle that made crossing the river and seizing the town look doubly impossible. With his typical optimistic daring, however, Claude de Guise was not discouraged by either the vagaries of Spanish weather, nor the apparently invincible might of their enemy. Disobeying his commander's orders that the crossing should not be attempted under any circumstances, snatched up a pike and plunged into the water with the fearsome Black Band of *landsknechts* who he had commanded at Marignano following close behind; the Black Band having first superstitiously knelt to kiss the ground before entering the water, probably assuming that they were following their young leader to their deaths.

The river came up to their shoulders and the Spanish immediately opened fire so that cannonballs and arquebus shot scattered the water around them but, by some miracle, Claude and his troops made it to the opposite bank, only to find that the enemy had ignominiously fled, leaving them free to march on and take the town. It was a daring move and one that could easily have ended in disaster, but Claude had always lived a charmed life and once again his famous good luck brought not just a victory for France, but also fulsome praise for his bold heroism and sang froid in the face of danger. Admiral Bonnivet was, as might be expected, less than impressed by his subordinate's daring but had no choice other than to praise him in his despatches to the French court.

For all her commitment to her husband's welfare and career, Antoinette was no camp follower and had remained behind at Joinville to look after her children and oversee their household affairs during Claude's absence. She must have been delighted by the news of her husband's heroism though and gratified to receive a letter from King François' mother, Louise de Savoie, which said that 'she ought to consider herself the happiest princess in France, since she possessed the most valiant and most fortunate husband on earth.' A graceful tribute to the personal risk that Claude had taken, as well as his bravery. She must have been even more pleased when a pecuniary reward fell into their hands shortly afterwards in the form of revenues and profits from the salt granaries of Mayenne-la-Juhee and Ferte-Bernard, which reaped the Guise family an extra 24,000 livres a year. The first year was paid in advance and would have been a healthy boost to coffers depleted by King François' warmongering.

A year later, Claude was back in northern France, there to defend the region against English invasion led by his old nemesis, Charles Brandon, Duke of Suffolk, whom he had unhorsed at a joust during

31

celebrations for the marriage of Princess Mary Tudor and Louis XII. The English Princess had gone on to marry Brandon just six months later after her husband's premature death, but the rivalry between the two men continued nonetheless. Once again, however, Guise was the one to distinguish himself with his bravery and military cunning; by the end of the year, he was yet again being hailed as a national hero, much to the satisfaction of his wife and children. No doubt kept fully up to date with their father's victories and heroics, the Guise children must have been thrilled by tales of his courageous exploits and proud to have such a man as their father. The Guise boys would expect to follow in Claude's impressive footsteps one day, but did Marie also have wistful thoughts of future battlefield exploits? She must have known that Jeanne d'Arc, another maid of Lorraine, born not all that far away at Domrémy, had allegedly once worshipped in the chapel at Joinville. Her later interest in military matters and insistence on personally supervising her troops strongly suggests that Marie drew inspiration from Jeanne's example.

On at least one occasion, however, the war came to the foot of their battlements when an imperial army, led by the Duke of Furstemburg, ventured over the French border and advanced on Joinville. Alarmed by the close proximity of enemy troops, Antoinette moved her household to the more impregnable fortress at Neufchâteau, while her husband, who had just 400 men and was considerably outnumbered, called upon noblemen in the region to lend support in repelling the enemy. Determined not to allow the emperor one inch of French soil, and to discourage any further hostilities, Claude and his supporters ruthlessly razed the local countryside so that the imperial troops were unable to find provisions before harrying them into retreat, pursuing them back across the Meuse. Furstemburg attempted one last defiant stand beneath the walls of Neufchâteau, where Antoinette and her household were lodged, but was routed by Claude's troops. Confident of victory, the Comte suggested to his wife that she might like to witness this skirmish for herself, so the ladies of the Guise court mounted the top of a battlement and watched as the imperial troops were cut to pieces. Marie was not quite 8 years old at this time and was doubtless permitted to share in this spectacle, which offered an unprecedented glimpse of her father's much-vaunted military prowess.

However, Marie's life underwent a dramatic change shortly after the grisly events at Neufchâteau; she was sent to Pont-à-Mousson to be educated under the aegis of her formidable paternal grandmother, Philippa de Guelders, who resided there in the Poor Clare convent. Although most girls were educated at home during the early sixteenth century, it was also common for young women of Marie's elevated social class to be sent away to convents or other aristocratic households to be educated and prepared for a career at court and marriage. Young girls would be expected to learn the rudiments of household management as well as languages, dancing, horse riding and music. There would also be other less formal, but no less necessary, lessons in the more arcane arts of flirtation, etiquette, manners and dress – all designed to turn out elegant, refined and sophisticated French noblewomen.

Intelligent, intimidating and extremely cultured, Philippa de Guelders was the perfect choice. Although she had announced her intention of devoting her life to God once she retired to the convent, she still remained a person of great influence who regularly corresponded with her royal relatives, including King François himself. Even after taking the veil she insisted upon signing her letters with regal flourish as Philippa, Queen of Cyprus, a reminder that although she may have renounced the outside world, she had far from forgotten the dynastic ambitions of her family.

Unlike many other great ladies who retired to convents but intended to live out their days surrounded by all the luxuries and comforts to which they had been accustomed, making a desultory effort to join in with the religious activities of the nuns, Philippa had thrown herself into convent life. So great was her enthusiasm in fact, that she became famous for her piety and was even reputed to have had prophetic visions, most notably one that foretold the death of her son, François, in the battle of Pavia. On a more prosaic level, she was clearly keen to eschew all of the comforts of her previous life, preferring to sleep on a straw mattress on the floor like the other sisters rather than the opulent bed that her horrified son, the Cardinal de Lorraine, had sent to her after a tour of her austere living quarters in the convent.

During her time with the Poor Clares at Pont-à-Mousson, Marie was prepared for every aspect of court life by her grandmother, a veteran of the court of Louis XII and fully equipped to offer guidance to a young girl about to take her first steps into the decadent French court. However, thanks to their surroundings and Philippa's own devout lifestyle, Marie was also given a thorough spiritual education and while other girls in her position might have idled away their days in a whirl of flirtation, poetry, dancing and vanity, Marie helped the sisters with their daily duties in the kitchens, garden and laundry as well as sharing their religious observances. Although, unlike her counterpart Elizabeth I, she was never heard to boast that if she were turned out in her petticoat then she could make her living anywhere in Christendom, Marie was raised to be as resourceful and uncomplaining.

Although the convent was effectively cut off from the outside world, a quiet place where the hush of the sunlit cloisters was broken only by the occasional murmuring of the nuns and the tolling of the chapel bell calling them to prayers, it was not possible to keep that outside world at bay. While Marie was settling into her new life at Pont-à-Mousson, the royal house of Valois and their relations, the aristocratic Bourbons, had become embroiled in an undignified scandal which started as a private family squabble but spiralled so far out of control that it became a very public threat to the crown itself and the security of the whole nation. It began, quietly enough, with the death of Suzanne, Duchesse de Bourbon, the only daughter of the Duc de Bourbon and his formidable wife Anne de France. Suzanne had been married at a young age to her cousin, Charles de Bourbon, who was the heir to her father's duchy; brother (by marriage) of Marie's aunt Renée, and a distant relative of her mother Antoinette, as well as Constable of France. Handsome, charming and fabulously wealthy, the grieving widower became one of the most eligible bachelors in Europe and it soon became apparent that an equally eligible widow had him in her sights as a possible second husband.

Louise de Savoie, mother of François I and first cousin to both Charles and Suzanne de Bourbon, was still just 45 years old when Suzanne passed away, leaving all of her vast estates and fortune to her husband. Louise had always considered herself to be Suzanne's heir and was piqued to have been overlooked in her will. She delayed making a legal claim on the lands however, signalling instead her willingness to resolve the issue by marrying Charles herself. The fact that she had always had a liking for the dashing young Duke, who was fourteen years her junior, probably being as much a motivation as the vast wealth she stood to gain from the arrangement – while her son looked forward to eventually acquiring it all for himself in due course. There was always a chance that Louise might have another child of course, but it seemed unlikely and François was only too happy to encourage the scheme, regarding it as the best possible outcome to an difficult situation.

However, it soon became very apparent that Charles de Bourbon didn't share Louise's enthusiasm for the match and was keen to marry one of the sisters of the Holy Roman Emperor Charles V, François' greatest enemy and rival. His loyalty to François had always been questionable and his refusal to contemplate a match with Louise was regarded as not just personally insulting, but also confirmation that his interests no longer aligned with those of the ruling family. Humiliated, Louise took the Duke to court for the lands that she considered to be her due while her son pre-emptively swept in and seized them for himself, effectively forcing Charles' hand and resulting in him leaving France and throwing his lot in with the Emperor.

Although Marie's family were closely linked both by marriage and blood to the Bourbons, they made it clear that King François, the Valois King, had their complete and unequivocal loyalty. They may well have criticised the behaviour of both François and his mother behind closed doors, but in public at least, there could be no doubt that they stood behind him. They reaped rich rewards for their loyalty when François began to silence any rumblings of dissent within the nobility with the open-handed distribution of lands, titles and choice jobs. Naturally, Claude de Guise did very well out of this royal largesse and was promoted to the position of Governor of Champagne in May 1524 – a key role at a time when relations between France and the Emperor Charles, whose lands bordered Champagne, were steadily disintegrating and the threat of invasion became increasingly likely.

Claude was kept busy holding off the occasional harrying forays of the imperial troops and harboured ambitions of riding alongside François as he led his troops into Italy in the autumn of 1524, intending yet again to seize control of Milan. Claude had hoped to be entrusted with a position of command at the head of the French troops, but was dismayed to find himself left behind; he was entrusted with the defence of Champagne and a position on the Privy Council, which was headed up by Louise de Savoie during her son's absence in Italy. However, as Claude bade farewell to his younger brother, François, who had taken over as commander of the Black Band of *landsknechts*, the same regiment he had led into the field at Marignano, he could have had no idea that things were about to go disastrously wrong.

François' Italian campaign began well but took a sudden and catastrophic turn in the early hours of 24 February 1525; his army was decimated by imperial forces outside the town of Pavia with enormous casualties on the French side. Many of the nobles who had accompanied him were killed amidst the slaughter, while François himself was captured and taken to the fortress of Pizzighettone. Amongst the maimed corpses that scattered the field was that of Marie's uncle, François de Lorraine, Comte de Lambesc who had perished with most of his *landsknechts* during a heroic attempt to fight his way across the field to the King's side.

Barely a noble family in all France was untouched by the terrible events at Pavia and for months afterwards, the nation's churches and cathedrals were draped in black cloth and crammed with mourners attending memorial masses to pray; both for their dearly departed, and the imprisoned King. It would have been small consolation to Marie's family to learn that François had been buried in a tomb in the Augustinian Church in Pavia by order of his relative by marriage, the treacherous Duc de Bourbon, who had fought on the side of the Empire against the French. Alongside him lay his friend and brother in arms,

Richard de la Pole, Duke of Suffolk and the so called White Rose, who, prior to his untimely death fighting for the French at Pavia, had been the last member of the House of York to actively lay claim to the English throne. While an undoubted tragedy, the events at Pavia reveal just how complicated the game of political allegiance could be in sixteenth-century Europe, with expediency creating all manner of strange bedfellows and alliances – something that Marie de Guise would eventually discover for herself.

The defeat at Pavia was a serious and devastating blow to France, on a par with that dealt by Henry V at Agincourt. The decimation of the army and capture of the King left the nation weakened, demoralised and open to attack on all sides. While everyone was reeling from the terrible news from Italy, Claude de Guise was already thinking ahead to the potential repercussions and making urgent preparations for the defence of France's borders. Hampered by low morale and pitiful resources, Claude made ready to defend against the Emperor and his allies, in particular Henry VIII of England who wasted no time in assembling an army to invade northern France, declaring that 'Now is the time for the emperor and myself to devise means of getting full satisfaction from France. Not an hour is to be lost.' It was his intention that François, whose capture had proved him incapable of kingship, should be deprived of his kingdom, which would be carved up and divided between his enemies, with particularly choice morsels coming to England. Thanks to the Emperor Charles' lukewarm response, his grandiose plans came to nothing, but for the Lorraine family it was another reminder of the English King's opportunistic belligerence – a lesson that Marie would take with her into adulthood.

As Governor of Champagne, it was Claude's duty to oversee the defence of northern France, which he did with great aplomb. At the same time, he kept a wary eye on the activities of anti-clerical peasant bands who were targeting church property and bringing mayhem and destruction to Germany and were rampaging a little too close to the French border for comfort. When the violence finally spilled over the frontier in the spring of 1525, just a few months after the battle of

Pavia, Claude was swift to take action – not just to do his duty and defend his country, but also to defend the church that he had been raised to revere. He joined forces with his elder brother, Antoine, Duc de Lorraine, and together they raised an army to crush the peasant hordes that had seized the city of Saverne and looked set to make further inroads into northern France.

On their way to battle, the brothers called at Pont-à-Mousson to request a blessing from their mother, who was only too delighted to send them on their way with some encouraging words that demonstrate where Claude and his descendants inherited their bravado and undaunted spirit.

Do not recoil now that the occasion presents itself to die gloriously for Him, who with the infamy and opprobrium of the world upon him, died on the cross for you... Hurry yourselves... and against all who oppose you with arms strike, chop and cut. Do not fear to be cruel... heresy is of the nature of gangrene, it will spread over the whole country, if one does not confront it with fire and steel.

During his brief stay at the convent, it is likely that Claude also spent some time with his eldest daughter, Marie, who was just 9 years old and would no doubt have been impressed by the sight of her father, uncle and all their men in their armour. Although she would tread a rather more liberal path in later life, as a child, she worshipped her charismatic father and would have seen nothing wrong with his forthright and violently anti-protestant views.

The combined forces of the two Lorraine brothers had little difficulty decimating the untrained and poorly equipped peasant army, bringing an effective end to the threat they posed to Lorraine and boosting Claude's already impressive reputation as a defender of French soil. The campaign also displayed the Duc de Guise's softer side, as we are told that he encountered a small peasant girl while riding through a burnt-out village, the sole survivor of a massacre carried out by the peasant army. Moved by the child's plight, he rescued her from the ruins of her former home and sent her off to his wife, Antoinette, at Joinville to be raised in his own household.

Meanwhile at Pont-à-Mousson, Marie was still being prepared for her future life at court and as the chatelaine of her own noble household. Although she had taken the veil, Philippa of Guelders had not entirely renounced the outside world so news of her sons' escapades would have arrived at the convent regularly and been shared with her granddaughter. However, for the most part, life at the convent was a quiet one; devoted to prayer, learning, quiet reflection and domestic tasks. It's possible that her family were considering a religious life for Marie, probably as the honoured Abbess of her own convent, but events would soon place her on a very different path.

Chapter 4

Mademoiselle de Guise

King François was released from captivity in March 1526, his freedom coming at the price of that of his young sons, the 8-year-old Dauphin François and his younger brother Henri, Duke d'Orléans, who would be kept as hostages by the Emperor Charles for over four years while their father prevaricated over the humiliating terms of the Treaty of Madrid, which he had been forced to sign before his release and which held his sons to ransom. One of the terms had been an agreement that the widower French King would take the emperor's sister, Eleonore, the dowager Queen of Portugal, as his wife. Although they were formally betrothed before his release from captivity, both François and Charles dragged their heels over actually sealing the bargain until finally a rapprochement was reached in late 1529 with the signing of the Treaty of Cambrai, which modified the less palatable terms of the earlier treaty and enabled François to secure the return of his sons and also make good on his promise to marry Charles' sister. Luckily for Marie's family, he managed to step around Charles' demands that Claude de Guise, his brother-in-law the Duc de Vendôme, future son-in-law, the adolescent Duc de Longueville and several other high ranking French nobles, should be handed over as hostages in exchange for the princes.

The French court had been without a queen since the death of François' first wife, Claude de France, in July 1524. Although his mother Louise and sister Marguerite, who had recently married the King of Navarre, were prominent figures at his court, the lack of an actual queen greatly diminished the opportunities available for aristocratic young women who might otherwise have become ladies in waiting, or filled other royal household positions which now lay vacant. It is only natural, therefore, that the ambitious Lorraine family's thoughts turned towards Marie, who was now 14 years old and, by the standards of the day, ready for marriage and a great household of her own.

Her father's star had risen sharply in the aftermath of Pavia when he had proved himself once again as an able and loyal defender of his adopted country and a capable member of the royal council. One of King François' first actions after returning to France was to further ennoble Claude, raising him to the rank of Duc de Guise, which greatly enhanced his family's prestige and prospects at court even if, as he often had cause to lament, his finances did not quite match the distinction of his new rank. For Antoinette, preoccupied with child rearing (the couple had seven surviving children by the end of 1529 and would go on to have four more) and looking after their estate at Joinville, the expectation that she would now spend more time at court was something of a burden. For her eldest children, however, the family's new rank offered unprecedented opportunities and would bring them even closer to the royal circle.

Keen to capitalise on the changes in the royal household, the Duc de Lorraine secured permission from his brother and sister-in-law to remove Marie from the care of his mother at Pont-à-Mousson and move her to his own household at Nancy, a beautiful ducal palace built by his father René II. Marie was welcomed by her aunt, Renée de Bourbon, the sister of the disgraced Duc de Bourbon, who had died two years earlier while leading the imperial troops in the sack of Rome. Through her late mother, Clara Gonzaga, daughter of the Marquess of Mantua, Renée was related to most of the noble houses of Italy as well as France. She had been educated in the household of Anne de France, Duchesse de Bourbon along with such luminaries as her cousins Louise de Savoie, the mother of King François; her future sister-in-law, Suzanne de Bourbon, and Diane de Poitiers. By the time Marie arrived in Nancy, Renée had left the schoolroom far behind and was mother to three young children: François, who was betrothed to Anne of Cleves, Nicolas and Anna. Like most ladies of her rank, Renée had no objection to taking promising young ladies under her wing.

After the peace and quiet of Pont-à-Mousson, the bustling, magnificent Lorraine ducal court at Nancy must have taken some getting used to; however, Marie was an adaptable, cheerful girl who took things in her stride and quickly fitted in to her uncle and aunt's household. Although her family were, somewhat surprisingly, not able to secure a position in the new Queen of France's household for her, it's clear that King François was still keen to honour Marie and it seems likely that he placed her in the satellite household of his daughters, Madeleine and Marguerite, although no lists survive to confirm this. Whatever the case, she made the long journey from Nancy to Paris in the spring of 1531 to take part in the coronation of Queen Eleonore on 5 March. Her official entry into the capital city, was a splendid occasion worthy of an emperor's sister who was already Dowager Queen of Portugal and was rumoured to have brought with her a King's ransom worth of jewels; the magnificent spoils of the Portuguese conquest of Brazil.

Undaunted by the torrential rain that lashed against the stained glass windows, the entire court crammed into St Denis cathedral on the outskirts of Paris to witness the coronation of the new Queen of France. The ceremony was led by Marie's uncle, the Cardinal de Bourbon (the elder brother of her mother Antoinette), and her other uncle, Jean, Cardinal de Lorraine, stood to one side. The Lorraine family were well represented at the coronation with Marie, her mother, aunt Renée and maternal grandmother, Marie de Luxembourg, all in the congregation. Her father, and uncle Antoine, who had long ago been mooted as a prospective husband for Queen Eleonore when her brother was casting about for Lorraine support, had their places in the royal procession behind the Grand Chamberlain of France, the Duc de Longueville, who at 21 was just five years older than Marie.

Sadly, Eleonore's much anticipated official entry into her new capital was postponed thanks to the terrible weather, which made riding through the un-cobbled and winding medieval streets unpleasant at best and, at worst, downright perilous. This must have been a serious blow to the younger members of the party, which included Marie and her elder brother, the 12-year-old François, Comte d'Aumale, who was to act as page boy to Diane de Poitiers, said to be the most beautiful woman at court. Like his sister, François was welcomed to court to act as a companion to the royal children; in particular the Dauphin and his younger brother, Henri, who had returned to France after their captivity with Spanish manners and were, in their father's opinion, in need of reintegration back into the French court to which end he surrounded them with the promising young sons of his most favoured courtiers. His plan had limited success, however; for, although his sons became very close to François and his lively band of brothers, neither boy would ever quite shake off the emotional effects of their captivity and would remain, understandably, somewhat dour and lacking in the good humour and high spirits that their father liked to have about him.

Although the shocking weather deterred Antoinette – who was five months pregnant with her tenth baby – from taking part in the royal procession, her eldest daughter had no such qualms and eagerly donning her purple and ermine robes, took her place amongst the new Queen's entourage. Encrusted in jewels and dressed even more splendidly than her ladies, Queen Eleonore was greeted with wild acclaim by the notoriously fickle Parisians, who regarded her not just as their Queen, but also as a living symbol of what everyone hoped would be an ongoing peace between France and the rest of Europe and an end to such crushing humiliations as the defeat at Pavia. Her husband, whom she adored, was rather less enamoured and insisted upon watching the procession from a private balcony overlooking the Rue Saint Denis, where he scandalised the court by openly fondling his latest mistress, Anne de Pisseleu d'Heilly, whom he would create Duchesse d'Étampes in 1533.

The procession started at St Denis Gate, then passed through the streets of Paris, stopping at regular intervals to allow the new Queen to be serenaded by the different guilds, who also took turns to carry her cloth of gold canopy over her litter. The final stop was at Notre Dame bridge, where the glittering canopy was taken by four members of the goldsmith's guild, who carried it above her until they reached the Palais de la Cité, which comprised the Palais de Justice, Conciergerie and Sainte Chapelle. Here, the exhausted Queen

Eleonore was treated to a lavish banquet in the Grande Salle, where the royal family sat at the black marble table at the far end of the hall while the rest of the court ate at long tables. For Marie, this was a heady first taste of court life as she took her place at the table, escorted by her cousin François, the eldest son and heir of her uncle Antoine.

The good manners that her family had instilled into her from birth served Marie well when she began her career at the court of François I, one of the most pleasure seeking and magnificent courts in history. This was partly due to the King's insistence upon making women, normally relegated to the sidelines and back stairs of court life, an integral part of every ceremony. The focus of his own gallantry with his adored mother Louise and sister Marguerite, being the particular jewels in his bevy of ladies who were, also unusually, valued as much for their wit and intelligence as they were for their beauty. Carefully raised, well mannered and possessed of a combination of good looks, intelligence and humour, the young Marie de Guise was a welcome addition to the royal court, where it pleased the King to treat her as though she were a member of his own family.

Although many girls reared in a convent might have balked at the licentious goings on at King François' opulent court, Marie seems to have barely turned a hair. Naturally she did not participate in the more scandalous court entertainments, which involved prostitutes being provided for the male guests and open promiscuity on the part of courtiers of both sexes. Raised to have pride in both herself and her family name, Marie would have had no part in any of this, concentrating instead on enjoying the endless round of more sedate court activities – dressing up for masques, partnering her father's venerable old brothers-in-arms at balls, and smiling politely at the many court gallants who vied for her favours. Although the high minded and extremely pious Philippa of Guelders and Antoinette de Bourbon could be rather humourless and judgemental at times, there was nothing austere or self righteous about Marie, and she thoroughly enjoyed her time at the French court while remaining untainted by its more dissipated side.

Perhaps one of the most useful lessons that Marie had learned from her grandmother and the other nuns at Pont-à-Mousson was the ability to remain silent; a valuable skill to have at the royal court where intrigue and scheming abounded and everyone, even honourable men like her father, had to dissemble in order to hide their true feelings and side step potential vilification. For Marie the main issue was the constant envious whispering about her family's Germanic origins but she rose above it with her usual blend of tact, good nature and amiability. Marie became one of the most popular and sought-after young women at court, honoured not just for her wit and charm but also for her ability to get along with everyone and calmly navigate the stormy and dangerous waters of court life.

Like most royal courts of the period, that of François I was peripatetic and constantly on the move, meaning that France had two capitals: Paris and wherever the King happened to be living at the time, usually one of his châteaux in the Loire valley. While in Paris, Marie had a choice of family mansions to live in, including her uncle Jean's magnificent residence on the left bank of the city, the Hôtel de Cluny and the Lorraine Hôtel particulier on the Rue du Roi de Sicile in the Marais. She also had the option of residing with the other unmarried ladies of the court in the Hôtel de Tournelles, an enormous old royal palace which sprawled across over 20 acres in the Marais, close to what is now the Place des Vosges. Here she would have fallen under the charge of the formidable *gouvernante des filles*, an older lady whose unenviable job it was to supervise the flighty young maids of honour and deter any attempts upon their honour by the predatory gentlemen of the court.

Outside Paris, Marie would have spent a great deal of time at King François' favourite château, Amboise, where he had spent much of his childhood, nearby Blois, which was the traditional residence of the French royal children and the stately Saint-Germain-en-Laye close to Paris, which had beautiful gardens. There was also the palace of Fontainebleau to the south east of Paris, where the court would reside in the autumn to take full advantage of the hunting in the surrounding forest. Travelling between these different residences was an arduous and time consuming process, which involved transporting not just the royal family, their courtiers and servants, but also furnishings for the rooms, which were left empty between visits. King François, a notorious bookworm, even travelled with a crate of books which would be carefully unpacked at each château then packed up again at the end of the visit.

When Marie wasn't with the court, she was with her family at Joinville, where she enjoyed riding excursions and picnics, including one at nearby Roches in June 1532, where the family enjoyed a meal of trout pastries, strawberries, figs and cheese. Back at Joinville, her father was working on his plans for a beautiful grand pavilion, or *maison des plaisance*, close to the main château and surrounded by its own exquisite gardens, which could be used for the elaborate entertainments that were expected of a man of his influence. Work eventually began in 1533.

In October 1532, Claude was called away from his pleasant life at Joinville to join King François' sizeable male entourage for his much anticipated meeting with Henry VIII. The meeting had very nearly been cancelled when Henry made it known that he intended to bring his mistress, Anne Boleyn, who had spent her youth at the French court and acted as a maid of honour to King François' first wife, Claude. As the niece of Henry's estranged wife Catherine of Aragon, Queen Eleonore was understandably displeased by this turn of events and declared that she had no wish to meet either Henry or his lady love, causing Henry to retort that he had no great desire to meet her either. Perhaps he also remembered that (the then 6-year-old) Eleonore had been his father's choice of bride for him before he had repudiated their betrothal and taken his former sister-in-law Catherine as his bride, which had led to his current matrimonial predicament.

Diplomatic disaster was averted when the two sides agreed to go ahead with their meeting but without any ladies present, which must have been a blow to King François who loved to have the ladies of his court about him at all times. Anne Boleyn, to her great displeasure, was to be left behind in Calais while her royal lover rode on to Boulogne with an entirely male entourage to be entertained by the French for four days before accompanying them back to Calais, where they would return the hospitality with a series of banquets, tournaments and other manly entertainments. Although Marie was unable to attend, the Lorraine family were well represented by her brother, François, her father and her uncle, Jean, the Cardinal de Lorraine, who was King François' boon companion at all times and was even rumoured to have procured young women for his master.

We are not privy to Claude de Guise's feelings about coming face to face with his old enemy Henry VIII, whose ham-fisted attempt to seize northern France had preoccupied him in the wake of Pavia, but he must surely have taken a certain grim satisfaction in beating the English King in a game of tennis. He won £46 13s 4d (around £24,000 in today's currency so not a bad result) in the process. His brother, the wily Cardinal, who had said Mass for Henry upon his arrival in Boulogne, triumphed over him at both tennis and cards, and amassed even more money from the English monarch's privy purse. At Calais, they may have felt even more rewarded when Anne Boleyn and her ladies deliberately flouted the rule about no women being present at the meetings. Making an unexpected appearance at the evening, they danced masked before the gentlemen and took King François and the other French nobles as their partners before dramatically unmasking and revealing their true identities. Claude and his brother had probably encountered the young Mademoiselle Boleyn several times in the retinue of Queen Claude, but had almost certainly failed to notice her – the charming manners and exquisite dress sense that had rendered her extraordinary at the English court being par for the course in France.

Thwarted of this royal encounter in October 1532, Marie was to have more luck a year later when she accompanied the court to the balmy seaside port of Marseilles for the lavish wedding of King François' second son, Henri, Duc d'Orléans, and Pope Clement VII's beloved cousin, Catherine de' Medici. It was a splendid match for the King's second son as Catherine was not only well connected but also fabulously wealthy thanks to being the sole heiress of her young parents who had both died shortly after her birth, and the favourite cousin of the Pope. She was also a relative of Marie de Guise, as her

French mother, Madeleine de la Tour d'Auvergne, had a Bourbon mother and was the first cousin of Antoinette, Duchesse de Guise.

The royal wedding took place in the Église Saint-Ferréol les Augustins in Marseilles with the Pope himself presiding. The entire French court, no doubt gossiping about the recent birth of Henry VIII and Anne Boleyn's daughter, Elizabeth, were in attendance to watch tiny 14-year-old Catherine, who was wearing high-heeled shoes in an attempt to make herself look taller and more graceful, walk down the aisle in a golden brocade gown, encrusted in pearls and precious stones and trimmed with ermine and purple velvet. Her bridegroom was no less opulently garbed, but all eyes were really upon her new father-in-law King François, who wore white satin embroidered all over with gold fleurs-de-lys, and a cloth-of-gold cloak covered with a dazzling array of gems. After the young couple had exchanged their vows, everyone went off to a banquet hosted by Pope Clement, followed by a masked ball. The proceedings rapidly descended into an orgy after the nervous new Duchesse d'Orléans had been whisked away to her marital bed by Queen Eleonore and a group of French ladies in waiting, which may well have included Marie as she was one of the bride's few female relatives present at the ceremony.

By this time, Marie was less than a month shy of her eighteenth birthday and at an age when most girls of her rank were already married and preoccupied with the business of producing an heir for their husband. That she was not even betrothed by this stage is a little surprising when one considers the rank and prestige of her family. But then again, the Lorraine family were unusually close knit even by sixteenth-century standards and Claude and Antoinette were not the sort of parents likely to force one of their children into a match that they did not want.

That she would have had several contenders for her hand cannot be doubted – very few gentlemen at François I's court would have passed up an opportunity to align themselves with the Guise family, whose power and influence grew with each passing year and looked set to continue into the next generation. However, when a match finally occurred, it was with someone that she had almost certainly known all of her life and was prestigious enough to make even the most ambitious and exacting parents happy.

Louis d'Orléans, Duc de Longueville and Comte de Dunois, was five years older than Marie and was the current head of a cadet branch of the royal Orléans family that had started with Jean d'Orléans, better known as the Bastard d'Orléans; the illegitimate son of Charles V's younger son, Louis. Fully acknowledged by his father, and treated with honour and affection by his royal relatives, Jean amassed a fortune that formed the basis for the enormous wealth and huge tracts of land, supplemented by shrewd marriages, enjoyed by the Longueville family in the early sixteenth century. Marie, however, was probably more interested in the important and heroic role he had played in the campaigns of the Lorraine heroine Jeanne d'Arc, with whom he had lifted the siege of Orléans and then driven the English out of northern France; a feat that would have earned the respect of Claude de Guise's favourite daughter.

Very little is known about Louis d'Orléans-Longueville nowadays, giving the probably erroneous impression of a nebulous, colourless young man, completely eclipsed by his debonair relatives and lively young wife. He was his parents' second son, his father being the famously charming Duc de Longueville who had been taken prisoner by the English at the battle of Spurs. While languishing in the Tower of London, he distracted himself by taking one of Catherine of Aragon's ladies in waiting as a mistress, while his mother was the only child and heiress of the Margrave of Hachberg Sausenberg. Their elder son, Claude, was rather more of a chip off the dashing Orléans family block but he was killed at the age of just 16 during the siege of Pavia in autumn 1524. His younger brother inherited the title, extensive lands in northern France, several châteaux and the important court function of Grand Chamberlain of France, a position that was traditionally held by the senior member of the Orléans-Longueville family. By all accounts, he handled himself with aplomb at important ceremonies such as the coronation of Queen Eleonore. However, the impression still remains of a quiet young man who kept himself apart from the more scurrilous activities at court. Certainly, he never features in lists of King François' boon companions, and the only light that shines upon him is that of Marie's obvious affection and the happiness that she felt in their marriage. With this we must be content and draw our own conclusions about the sort of man that Louis d'Orléans-Longueville was.

The betrothal became official on the feast day of Pentecost in May 1534, when the marriage articles were signed at Joinville in the presence of the young couple and their families. It was agreed that Marie would be augmenting the already vast fortune of her future husband's family with a dowry of 80,000 livres, supplemented with an extra 40,000 livres from King François, who was very fond of Marie and wished to show his approval of this match. It's also possible that he had noted the fact that her father's expenses, as a relatively novice Duke and head of an increasingly numerous family (by this stage, Claude and Antoinette had nine surviving children to provide for), far outstripped his income and this was his tactful way of ensuring that Marie at least would make a good marriage. In return, Louis settled the beautiful Loire valley château of Châteaudun upon his betrothed, along with all of its lands.

This much anticipated wedding took place in the royal chapel of the old Louvre palace on the 4 August 1534, with all of the royal family, Lorraine clan and court in attendance to witness the marriage of the Duc de Guise's daughter and one of the highest ranking noblemen in France. Sadly, no one present thought to describe the ceremony or outfits worn by the main participants, but it's likely that Marie wore her long auburn hair loose about her shoulders as befitted a bride, perhaps with a ducal coronet on her head, and was dressed in the most costly and sumptuous fabrics that money could buy – cloth of gold, silver lace, crimson velvet and the ermine trimmings that denoted her new rank as Duchesse de Longueville and wife of the Lord Chamberlain of France. The wedding celebrations went on for over a fortnight; with banquets, jousts and other entertainments hosted by King François and the Guises, who were naturally keen to show off just how much their family had risen in prestige and wealth and give their eldest child a proud and proper send off.

Marie's new life as Duchesse de Longueville was the culmination of many years of careful preparation, which had readied her for the daunting task of running her own great household. In this, she also had the examples of her mother and grandmothers to guide her, and she took particular pleasure in emulating their concern for the poor and needy. Whereas some great ladies performed these duties with a certain distaste, preferring to let their stewards deal with supplicants and charity cases, Marie took a genuine interest in the wellbeing of others and would frequently be seen sallying forth on her estates to visit the elderly, frail and disadvantaged. Like her industrious mother, who had raised her daughters in the firm belief that the devil makes work for idle hands, Marie liked to be kept busy and to take a more hands-on approach to her charity work and would sit with her ladies, sewing clothes for the poor on her estates.

Other beneficiaries of her open-handed generosity included orphans, the unsupported elderly, promising students who would not otherwise be able to afford schooling and young girls who needed a dowry in order to be able to marry. Her charity work was not unusual in a period when the nobility were expected to take an interest in the wellbeing of their social inferiors, but it's unlikely that many great ladies performed their duties as cheerfully or with as much genuine concern and interest as Marie did. The cheerful good humour, compassion and tactful good sense made her popular as a demoiselle at King François' court and just as loved by her own people. If she had lived a few centuries later, she would probably have made an excellent nurse or a brisk, but kindly, ward sister.

As Duchesse de Longueville, Marie was now châtelaine of her husband's estates, which included magnificent mansions in Amiens and Rouen and the lovely châteaux of Beaugency and Châteaudun, which was poised on a cliff face overlooking the Loire and was to become an especially favourite country retreat for the healthy young Duchesse, whose enthusiasm for riding, hunting and other outdoor pursuits had not diminished. The couple's summer progress between their estates was on a more modest scale than that enjoyed by the royal household, which involved the labours of several hundred people and a huge cavalcade of litters, horses and covered wagons bearing all of the royal furniture, wardrobe and household goods. Nonetheless, it was still quite an elaborate enterprise, attended by dozens of servants and requiring a ceremonial welcome to each of the towns which lay within their demesne, where an enchanted Marie would be greeted with gifts, speeches, tableaux and flowers gathered by the local children.

For most of the time, however, the new Duc and Duchesse resided at court just as they had always done and were very popular members of the royal circle, although Louis was never quite rakish enough to figure amongst the King's most favoured companions who would join him in drinking and womanising, while Marie's already blemish free reputation remained as spotless as ever. They were always present at grand royal occasions though, with Marie generally to be found with the King's sister, Marguerite, Queen of Navarre, his daughters Madeleine and Marguerite, and his daughter-in-law, Catherine, Duchesse d'Orléans. The Duchesse's star had rather fallen since the death of her cousin, Pope Clement in September 1534, the non-appearance of the vast dowry that had been promised upon her marriage, and the fact that she had not yet managed to conceive a child, hampered no doubt by the fact that her young husband clearly preferred the rather more mature charms of the recently widowed Diane de Poitiers.

Marie had no such worries on this score and quickly became pregnant with her first child, news that would have occasioned great joy within her close family as this was to be Claude and Antoinette's first grandchild. The mother-to-be retired from court to Amiens to prepare for the birth and, on the 30 October 1535, gave birth to a son, who was named François for the King.

Chapter 5

The Auld Alliance

For several centuries, ever since John Balliol and Philippe IV of France had signed a treaty to form a league against Edward I of England in 1295, a cordial understanding known as 'The Auld Alliance' had existed between France and Scotland. It was based less on tepid affection than a need to form a cohesive front against England, their mutual neighbour and antagonist, very much a case of 'my enemy's enemy is my friend'. Successive treaties had reinforced the bond between the two nations, particularly during the Hundred Years War, but it had been allowed to slide by the start of the sixteenth century when James IV of Scotland married the English princess Margaret Tudor, daughter of Henry VII, and looked set to maintain a more cordial relationship with his former enemies. Naturally, James IV's death at Flodden eleven years later, while fighting against the army of his brother-in-law Henry VIII, put paid to this rather lukewarm friendship. When his half English son, James V, succeeded him to the throne, who knew where Scotland's loyalties would lie if relations between France and England broke down again.

In the event, there was no love lost between James V and his uncle Henry VIII and, on 26 August 1517, the young King of Scotland renewed the Auld Alliance by signing the Treaty of Rouen, which promised Scottish aid to France in return for reciprocal assistance, and also a match between James and one of King François' daughters. The French princesses were in great demand as putative brides on the never-ending merry-go-round of broken engagements that went on between European royal houses, so it seemed unlikely that this match would ever take place and the Scottish looked elsewhere for a bride for their young King, considering both Catherine de Medici and Princess Christina of Denmark as possible candidates. France still remained their first choice though and, in 1534, negotiations began again for a match between James and one of the French princesses, preferably the eldest, Madeleine.

Madeleine was of sickly disposition though and had already contracted the tuberculosis that would eventually kill her. Unwilling to send her off to the inclement climate of Scotland, King François suggested a match with either one of the Duc de Guise's younger daughters, or Marie de Bourbon, daughter of the Duc de Vendôme and first cousin of Marie de Guise, instead, promising a huge dowry of 200,000 livres and an annual income of 15,000 livres, to sweeten the disappointment. James, who no doubt felt that this was something of a step down when he had been angling for an actual princess, dragged his heels over the match but sent his herald, James Aickenhead, to France to inspect Mademoiselle de Bourbon and report back on her suitability. Obviously reassured by Aickenhead's missives, James decided to go ahead and, in March 1536, the marriage contract was authorised by King François, who then sent the Order of St Michel off to the bridegroom-to-be in Scotland, a signal honour that underlined his approval of both the match and the Scottish King.

James's uncle, Henry VIII, was rather less pleased with developments though and had no desire to see his nephew cement his alliance with France with a marriage. In this, he was motivated as much by personal jealousy as by diplomatic concerns – his own marriage with Anne Boleyn was going rapidly downhill (and would end in her execution in May of that year) and he was painfully aware of the fact that, as the father of one daughter who had been declared illegitimate and another whose legitimacy was questioned and mocked by the rest of Europe, he had nothing to bring to the table himself. James was young, handsome, healthy and charming in a way that recalled to mind both his father, James IV, and his Plantagenet great-grandfather, Edward IV of England; crucially, he was also free to marry whomever he pleased. He represented everything that the ageing Henry VIII no longer was, and he hated him for it. That James, as son of his elder sister, Margaret, also happened to be his heir until he managed to produce a son of his own just added insult to the injury.

Appraised of his nephew's interest in Princesse Madeleine, Henry had done everything in his power to put a stop to the match. In the end, he extracted a promise from King François that he would not allow a match between James and one of his daughters; he found the projected match with Mademoiselle de Bourbon just as displeasing. It's hardly surprising, therefore, that James decided to employ subterfuge when he left Scotland in September 1536 (an earlier attempt in July had been thwarted by poor weather conditions) to travel to France. He announced that he was visiting his northern islands before changing course to sail along the east coast of England; his ruse designed to prevent interception by his uncle's ships.

Upon his arrival in France, James headed straight for St Quentin in Picardy, intending to inspect Mademoiselle de Bourbon for himself. In a bold move that recalls the romantic courtly japes of his uncle Henry VIII, he decided to do so in disguise, swapping clothes with his purse master. His plan was thwarted by Marie de Bourbon, who was no fool and recognised him immediately from portrait sent to her some months earlier. Although King François' sister, Marguerite, had been dismissive of Marie de Bourbon's charms when discussing the match with the English Ambassador, a Clouet drawing of the young woman shows a round face, pleasant features and a certain frank, honesty about the eyes. James, however, was less than impressed by what he saw and made it clear that there was to be no marriage between them before making his way on to Paris where he hoped to meet with King François and persuade him to break his promise to Henry VIII.

At the time of his arrival in the French capital, James V was just 24 and had been King of Scotland since he was 17 months old. Although outwardly cheerful, cultured and likeable, the early loss of his father, a restricted childhood, a series of regents and then the attempt by his step-father, the Earl of Angus, to seize power by keeping the adolescent James as a virtual prisoner for over three years, had all left their mark on him. Inwardly, he was troubled, untrusting, neurotic, insensitive and, increasingly, prone to bouts of melancholy.

Unfortunately, King François was away hunting on his Loire estates when James arrived in Paris in October 1536. Undaunted by this, the King of Scotland settled down to enjoy his first visit to the French capital, which must have been quite an eye opening experience to a young man who had never been outside his own realm. Like his father James IV, the King was predisposed to be a Francophile and enjoyed himself enormously in the same way that young men visiting Paris for the first time have always done – spending lavish amounts on new clothes and furnishings for his palaces back in Scotland; enjoying the wine; taking in the sights; gambling and perhaps indulging in a few discreet sexual liaisons. He took especial delight in going out on the town in disguise, touchingly unaware that everyone he encountered knew exactly what he was and upped their prices accordingly; tales of the Scottish King's open-handed largesse and taste for luxury having spread through the city.

In the end though, even the delights of Paris began to pall and James, keen to resolve the matter of his marriage once and for all, headed off to the Loire Valley in pursuit of King François, eventually catching up with him near Lyon. He was welcomed like a long-lost son and, perhaps a little reluctantly, introduced to the French princesses, 16-year-old Madeleine and her 13-year-old sister, Marguerite. King François was still unwilling to let James claim the hand of Madeleine, believing her to be far too delicate for the notoriously inclement Scottish climate. He had, in fact, been making plans with Claude de Guise to marry her to his eldest son François, Comte d'Aumale – a match that would have kept her close by him at the French court. However, James gave every appearance of being smitten by the pretty and delicate young Madeleine; while she, for her part, was infatuated with the handsome Scotsman and declared to her father that she would rather be a Queen than a mere Duchesse, which would be her fate should she marry François de Guise.

James was also able to reassure his prospective father-in-law that the climate and living conditions in Scotland were nowhere near as inhospitable and uncivilised as was widely believed. True, they had some way to go before they reached the exquisite sophistication of the

French court, but the Scottish royal palaces had been modelled on French châteaux and he enjoyed a comfortable and luxurious lifestyle at his own court. The only remaining barrier, it seemed, was the promise that King François had made to Henry VIII that he would not allow James to marry one of his daughters. The mischievous French King had never been backward when it came to defying the wishes and pricking the pomposity of his English rival however, so whatever objections King Henry might have were shrugged off and arrangements for the marriage went ahead, the contract being signed at Blois on 26 November.

The betrothal of James and Madeleine was a serious blow to the Guise family who had hoped to see the King of Scotland married to Antoinette's niece, Marie de Bourbon, and the princess settled with the heir to the duchy, François. They hid their disappointment well however, and even offered the use of the Cardinal de Lorraine's opulent Parisian residence, the Hôtel de Cluny, to the Scottish King when he returned to the capital on the last day of 1536. He was King François' future son-in-law and most honoured guest and was accorded a royal entry to the city with a magnificent procession through the streets in tribute to his new position as a member of the French royal family.

The wedding ceremony took place the next morning, New Year's Day 1537, on a raised platform outside the cathedral of Notre Dame where, in the presence of the royal family, members of nobility and English ambassadors and in front of a huge crowd of ordinary Parisians, the young couple were married. After the ceremony, they solemnly trooped into the gloomy splendour of the cathedral to hear a nuptial mass, while largesse was distributed to the cheering crowds outside. The Duc and Duchesse de Longueville were present at the wedding and had doubtless already made the acquaintance of the Scottish King during his sojourn with the French court although there is no reason to think that James and Marie made an especial impression on each other at this point. Any attempts at conversation would have been stilted as James was not yet proficient in the French language and Marie's Scots English was non-existent. The English ambassador,

Stephen Gardiner, was particularly amused by the Scottish King's lack of ability in the French language and commented that, 'His wife shall temper him well, for she can speak, and if she spake as little as he, the house should be very quiet.'

The royal wedding was followed by a feast in the Bishop of Paris' palace and then another lavish banquet later in the great hall of the Palais of Justice, where the royal family were seated at the famous black marble top table; no expense was spared to put on a good show for the gathered guests. Another English ambassador, Sir John Wallop, would later write about the magnificence of James's entry into the city, the wedding and the following festivities; he commented on the fabulously rich apparel worn by the French court ladies, including the Duchesse de Guise and her daughter, the Duchesse de Longueville, and concluded that *'the King of Scots never saw such a sight.'* Afterwards, flushed with good wine and success, King James, led the dancing with his new brothers-in-law and the Cardinal de Lorraine. The celebration went on until the early hours of the morning, by which time, of course, the bridal couple had been ceremoniously packed off to bed to consummate their marriage.

The thwarted Henry VIII at least had the grace to know when he had been beaten and even managed to send a letter of congratulation to his errant nephew, writing that:

Having certain knowledge from those parties of your determination and conclusion for marriage with the daughter of our dearest brother and perpetual ally the French king, our office, our proximity of blood and our friendship towards you have moved us to congratulate with you in the same and to desire Almighty God to send you that issue and fruit thereof that may be to your satisfaction and to the weal, utility and comfort of your realm.

The wedding festivities went on for over a fortnight, with King François spending a fortune entertaining the entourage of Scottish nobles who had loyally travelled over to attend the wedding. There were all the usual banquets, tournaments, balls, masques, parties and fireworks displays over the city as well a naval battle conducted in a specially flooded makeshift arena. Whatever apprehension Madeleine's family and friends may have felt about likelihood of her surviving the harsh Scottish climate was forgotten, or at least carefully concealed, in what seemed to be wholehearted delight in the match that she had made.

The young couple remained in France until the end of spring, enjoying time with Madeleine's family and touring the châteaux of the Loire where James fell in love, just as his father had done, with French architecture and style and vowed to replicate them as much as possible once they returned to Scotland. His marriage to Madeleine had made him a rich man, her 225,000 livres dowry amounting to around £16 million in modern currency while her doting father, determined that she should live in lavish style in her new kingdom, also undertook to provide her with an annual income of 30,000 livres a year. The couple had more than enough income to renovate the Scottish royal palaces in the French style and fill them with treasures.

King James and Queen Madeleine left France in May 1537, enduring a stormy and difficult four-day crossing before finally landing at Leith on 19 May. The exhausted and ailing young Queen was whisked off to Holyrood Palace, the most luxurious of the royal residences, where it was hoped that she would soon make a full recovery from the rigours of her journey. Sadly it was not to be, and it soon became apparent to her accompanying French household, the royal physicians, and her anguished new husband, that the already frail Madeleine was fading away. She died on the morning of Saturday 7 July, just seven weeks after her arrival in Scotland.

Back in France, Marie was naturally deeply saddened to learn of the death of her childhood friend, Princesse Madeleine, but was also preoccupied with her own problems. Around the time of the royal wedding, she had discovered that she was pregnant again. Following the departure of the Scottish royal couple, Marie retired to her favourite residence Châteaudun with her young son, François, to await the birth of her second child. Her husband stayed on at court then set off on the annual summer tour of his extensive property in Picardy and Normandy. He wrote to her from the Château de Peronne at Pentecost, which fell on 23 May in 1537 and was special to the couple as the anniversary of the day they had become officially betrothed. The Duc explained that he had written in haste to inform his pregnant wife that he was:

> *anxious to let you know that I have had a headache for the past five or six days. Today, however, the doctors have diagnosed my illness as chicken pox. The rash is well out now and they assure me that I am almost better, for which I am very glad. I shall say no more, praying God to give you always what you desire. From Peronne, this day of Pentecost, your good husband and friend, Louis.*

Believing himself recovered, Louis de Longueville continued on to Rouen where he collapsed and died, presumably of the same illness, on 9 June. His widow, just 21 years old and heavily pregnant, was devastated by his death. Practical as always, however, she consoled herself with the reflection that she had been fortunate to enjoy so much personal happiness in her marriage. Concerned that the sudden bereavement could have a detrimental effect on Marie's pregnancy, the Duchesse de Guise hurried to Châteaudun to support her through the first months of widowhood and was at her side when her son, named Louis for his father, was born on 4 August.

Distressed by the untimely death of her husband, Marie announced her wish to retire from court in order to devote herself to the upbringing of her young sons. The eldest, François, had succeeded his father as Duc de Longueville and Lord Chamberlain of France at the age of not quite 2 years old. There was also the matter of the vast Longueville estates to consider and although Marie would naturally entrust their running to stewards and officers, she was still keen to personally oversee her sons' inheritance just as her mother would have done under the same circumstances. Honoured widows were very much an accepted part of French society and with three younger sisters, all of whom were said to be extraordinarily pretty, she had every reason to suppose that there would be no great call for her to remarry any time soon.

Her fate was sealed, however, when King James sent his advisor, David Beaton, to his erstwhile father-in-law, King François, to discreetly request another French bride in order to seal the terms of the Treaty of Rouen. It must have been a difficult request for the young King of Scotland to make, but it's unlikely that the pragmatic and wily François thought any less of him for it, nor thought that James's haste to find another wife was a slight upon the memory of his daughter. Nonetheless, he was unwilling to give his sole remaining daughter Marguerite to James and offered instead a solution in the recently widowed and extremely comely Duchesse de Longueville, whom James would recall meeting at his recent nuptials in Paris and who had proven her fertility by producing two sons.

No doubt feeling rather pleased with himself for coming up with such a neat solution, François wrote to both James and Marie appraising them of his decision. James did indeed remember the tall and strikingly lovely Madame de Longueville. Her ruddy cheeked, glowing health and vitality had been such a contrast to the pallid and fragile sickliness of the consumptive Madeleine and James reacted with enthusiasm to the plan. Marie, however, was rather less impressed; much to the disappointment of King François who had expected her to be delighted by the prospect of becoming Queen of Scotland. The Guise family had always been ambitious, he reasoned, and surely they would leap at the opportunity to add a crown to their ever-increasing hoard of honours.

To his surprise, Marie's parents would also prove to be unexpectedly resistant to King François' plans for their eldest daughter. As we have seen, they may have been ambitious, but they were not likely to take advantage of Marie's loyalty and attachment to her family in order to pressurise her into accepting a match that was not to her liking. In their opinion, King James's overtures had come indecently soon after the death of Marie's husband. She should have been allowed more time to properly mourn Louis' passing before being pressed to think of another marriage. There was also the fact that Scotland was so far away to consider; both Marie's parents were fond enough of her to regard her departure from France with much dismay, not to mention the fact that the match would involve either Marie taking her sons away with her to Scotland or, much more likely, being forced to leave them behind in France. It's also possible that the Guises had been less than impressed by the character of their prospective son-in-law when they had met him during the celebrations for his marriage to Princesse Madeleine. He was charming, yes, and rather good looking, but he could also be conceited, brusque, thoughtless and moody; none of which were personality traits likely to appeal to Claude and Antoinette or, more crucially, their daughter, whose personality was quite the opposite.

Frustrated and annoyed by the Guise family's unexpected lack of compliance, King François summoned Claude to his presence in order to demand the acquiescence of his daughter and the reluctant Duke was forced to comply. Worried that he stood in real danger of losing the King's favour, Claude had to pretend that he could think of nothing he would like more than to see his beloved daughter separated from her children and packed off to Scotland. However, without Marie's consent – which she staunchly refused to give – there was nothing that anyone could do to bring the match to a conclusion. Matters had reached a stalemate in October 1537 when the shocking news arrived from England that Queen Jane Seymour had died in childbed and there was yet another high ranking widower on the prowl in Europe.

Madame de Longueville was first mentioned as a prospective bride for the widowed King Henry mere days after Queen Jane's death in a secret letter sent by Thomas Cromwell to Stephen Gardiner and Lord William Howard, who were both on diplomatic missions in Paris.

And forasmuch as, though his Majesty is not anything disposed to marry again, albeit his Highness, God be thanked, taketh this chance as a man that by reason with force overcometh his affection may take such an extreme adventure, yet, as sundry of his Grace's Council here have thought it meet for us to be most humble suitors to his Majesty to consider the state of his realm, and to enter eftsoons into another matrimony in place for his Highness' satisfaction convenient, so his tender zeal to his subjects hath already so much overcome his Grace's said disposition and framed his mind both to be indifferent to the thing and to the election of any person from any part that with deliberation shall be thought meet for him, that, as we live in hope that his Grace will again couple himself to our comforts, so considering what personages in Christendom be meet for him, amongst the rest there be two in France that may be thought on. The one is the French King's daughter, which, as it is said, is not the meetest. The other is Madame de Longueville, whom they say the King of Scots doth desire. Of whose conditions and qualities in every point his Majesty desireth you both, with all your dexterity and good means to inquire; and likewise in what point and terms the said King of Scots standeth towards either of them: which his Highness is so desirous to know (his Grace's desire therein to be, nevertheless, in anywise kept secret to yourselves) that his pleasure is that you, my lord William, shall not return till you may learn both how the King of Scots standeth in his suit, and what the condition and qualities of both persons be.

The results of Gardiner and Howard's discreet enquiries were enough to convince King Henry that Marie was precisely what he was looking for – tall, healthy, fertile, good looking and good natured as well. The fact that she came with an enormous dowry and was already being keenly pursued by his nephew only served to make her all the more attractive and, in early November, he could not resist bringing the subject up with Monsieur de Castillon, the French Ambassador, suggesting that he might be amenable to a match with either Marie, her cousin Mademoiselle de Bourbon or Princesse Marguerite, King Francois' sole remaining daughter. Castillon immediately hastened to appraise the astonished, and rather amused, King of France, who had no doubt at all that King Henry's well-known dislike of his recalcitrant nephew was his prime motivator in this unexpected proposal. Castillon received the rather dampening reply that François thought the English treated women in the same way as they treated horses – trotting them out to see which one went best and he was rather offended that his own daughter, a princess of the royal blood, had been tactlessly included in the line up.

Perhaps encouraged by Castillon's carefully polite non-committal, Henry impatiently ordered his Lord Privy Seal, Thomas Cromwell, to enter the fray and rather more formally suggest a match with either Marie, her cousin or Princesse Marguerite. François was again irritated by the cavalier treatment of his daughter's name but nonetheless managed to craft a carefully measured response, informing Henry that he would *'think it a great honour if the King take a wife in his realm, and there is no lady who is not at his commandment except Madame de Longueville, whose marriage with the King of Scots has been arranged.'*

Henry was not put off by this though because he had heard that Marie had not yet given her consent to the match and, a month later, the unfortunate Castillon was forced to write to his master, King François that:

...he is so amorous of Madame de Longueville that he cannot refrain from coming back upon it. I assured him that the marriage between the king of Scots and her had been already sworn before my first letters; but that no lady in France would be denied him. He replied that he could not believe, even though her father M. de Guise had sworn and promised with M. d'Albrot [David Beaton, Abbot of Arbroath], that Madame de Longueville had consented to it; for when I said to him, "Would you marry another man's wife?" he said he knew well that she had not spoken, and asked me to write to you, if matters were not so far advanced that they could not be broken off, to deliver her to him, and he would do twice as much for you as the king of Scots would.

Castillon then informed King François that:

I asked who caused him to be more inclined to her than to others, and he said Wallop was so loud in her praises that nothing could exceed them. Moreover, he said that he was big in person and had need of a big wife, that your daughter was too young for him, and as to Madame de Vendosme [Marie's cousin, Mademoiselle de Bourbon], *he would not take the king of Scots' leavings. Could not keep him off the subject.*

One can imagine how stressful and awkward this interview must have been for the unfortunate Castillon, forced to remain diplomatically impassive in the face of Henry VIII's blustering, and then straight faced when he made his unflattering remark about Marie's physique. Naturally, it was this comment that would do the rounds at the merciless French court, eventually reaching the ears of Marie herself, who was still ensconced at Châteaudun with her children. 'I may be big in person,' she is said to have observed with her usual wry humour, 'but my neck is small.'

However, when Cromwell sent a trusted agent, Sir Peter Mewtes on a secret mission to Marie at Châteaudun, she proved quite willing to let the English know that although her father had assured King François that the Scottish match met with her approval, she herself had not yet given her consent, demurely adding that she was 'ready to obey Francis in everything, but she never specially promised to marry the king of Scotland, and Francis might grant her to Henry.' All of which rather implies that she was not as adverse to the prospect of marrying the King of England as had been generally supposed even if, as she rightly pointed out, the final decision must always rest with King François. For his part, King François was not averse to this new twist in the tale, agreeing with Castillon that this 'pretty comedy' could easily be turned to his own advantage if he was of a mind to use the Longueville marriage as bait to lure the enamoured Henry to agree to other diplomatic demands.

Unfortunately, while her marital prospects were the subject of much diplomatic discussion, another tragedy had struck the young widow when her baby son Louis, who had been born after the death of his father, died suddenly at the age of just 4 months old on 7 December. His body was interred beside his father's in the crypt of the Sainte Chapelle of Châteaudun.

Chapter 6

A Farewell to France

Even in the sixteenth century, the first day of a new calendar year was a time for reflection and a stock take of the year that had just gone by. For Marie de Guise this would have been especially poignant at the start of January 1538 as she cast her mind back to the wedding of King James and Princesse Madeleine on New Year's Day 1537, which she had attended with her husband at her side, newly pregnant and glowing with happiness. Now Madeleine, Louis and her child were dead and she faced an uncertain future as Queen of either England or Scotland.

At the end of January, Sir Francis Bryan was sent to France to discuss the matter with King François, who had been warned of his imminent arrival by Castillon, who also delivered some advice about the most tactful way of letting the English King down.

Unless it is intended to keep him in suspense, M. d'Albrot [David Beaton, the Scottish King's agent in the matter] *should be made to speak a little sharply pointing out that the King of England is wrong to attempt to get the wife of the king of Scots, who would hazard his kingdom rather than suffer such a wrong.*

François swiftly replied to his beleaguered ambassador with an assurance that:

…as to the Duchess of Longueville, if Henry speaks again of it, [you] *shall say her marriage is quite concluded with the King of Scots, and to break it now would neither be honourable nor reasonable, and the king of France would not lose such a friend as the King of Scots, whom he looks upon as his own son.*

Keen to get things moving, King François had already prepared the contract for a marriage between Marie and the King of Scotland, offering James a dowry of 150,000 livres, most of which was to be raised from the revenue and lands settled on Marie by her first husband as a jointure intended to support her in proper style if he predeceased her. Her agent, Monsieur de Puiguillon, who had been despatched from Châteaudun in order to act for her during this delicate negotiation, was scandalised by these unusual terms. It was not the custom to fund a widow's second marriage with the jointure from her first, because this revenue was payable to her only during her lifetime and would naturally revert back to the estate upon her death. It was also unthinkable that Longueville lands, eventually intended to form part of her son's inheritance, should pass into the hands of the Scottish crown. The rest of the dowry, some 30,000 livres, was to be provided by King François himself, who no doubt thought that he was being generous under the circumstances, especially as her own family were dragging their heels over contributing anything, perhaps because they secretly preferred the much grander and more advantageous English match.

He must have been astounded when Claude and Antoinette, always keen to protect the interests of their children, expressed their displeasure at the terms of the contract. They let it be known that it was absolutely unacceptable that Marie's Longueville inheritance should be diverted into the hands of the Scottish King when it was intended for her own use during her lifetime before reverting back to her son. On 28 January, Antoinette, obviously agitated by the situation, wrote to her daughter at Châteaudun to appraise her of the situation and let her know that she was:

...much afraid things will not be done so much for your advantage as I wished. I am surprised at the talk of making up once more that which has once been given to you, and the wrong done to your son in taking from him that which has already fallen to him. I wonder wise men can propose such things, which they have no power to do, and I should never advise you to grant this. I think also you have no mind to do so.

68

She advised her daughter to approach King François herself, but to be careful not to irritate him and make matters worse, adding that François' sister, the Queen of Navarre, was also planning to speak on her behalf.

Unconvinced by this activity, and unable to believe that the French could possibly prefer a match with Scotland over one with England, Cromwell once again despatched Sir Peter Mewtes to Châteaudun at the start of February for another conference with Marie. Mewtes was given strict instructions to inform Marie that:

> *...he is sent ... to intimate that albeit at his late being with her she said she was free from all contract of marriage, and thereupon the lord Privy Seal proposed to have made some overture for her marriage with the King, yet as the King of Scots has since urged his suit therein, and her own father has come down for the conclusion of the same, and the King of Scots intends secretly to repair thither for the solemnisation of the same, I [Cromwell] am perplexed how to proceed, and have sent the said [Mewtes] to know whether to break the matter to the King according to her former words. If she is still free from any consent of marriage, and seems to have any inclination to this, he shall say that if her father or any of her friends would make any indifferent overture to the King, and so show their good wills, it would give me sufficient ground so to work as I trust should be to her honour and comfort.*

In other words, Cromwell was hopeful that Marie's own lack of agreement with the Scottish match meant that she was actually more in favour of one with England and, if that was indeed the case, he was willing to do the necessary donkey work to bring it about.

He then added that if Marie showed signs of complaisance, then Mewtes was to endeavour to acquire a portrait of her for his master, who had heard much of her beauty but never actually beheld it for himself. Sadly, we do not know what Marie's response was to Cromwell's overtures, but the fact that he despatched another agent,

Philip Hoby, to Châteaudun later in the same month with instructions to observe Marie and her younger sister, Louise, together and bring back a double portrait of the two so that he could show it to Henry, would suggest that she had not been displeased by his advances. She may also have been less than pleased to learn that the frustrated Henry was already widening his net and that Hoby had instructions to ride on to her uncle, the Duc de Lorraine, at Nancy, and acquire a portrait of his daughter, her cousin, Anna, as well. Any young woman would be flattered to have not one, but two kings jostling for her hand in marriage, but it all becomes rather less impressive if they have their eye on other young ladies as well.

In England, King Henry was still summoning the unfortunate Castillon to his presence to ask questions about Marie and ramble on at length about how much he longed to make her his wife. On one occasion he lost his temper and expressed his surprise that King François was so keen to marry her to his enemy King James and, if it wasn't for the current good relations between England and France, he would be suspicious of François' motivation in trying to curry favour with the King of Scotland. Feeling rather put on the spot, Castillon replied that his master had no wish to upset King James, whom he regarded like a son and, furthermore, the match had been arranged between Marie's father and David Beaton before the death of Queen Jane and before Henry had expressed an interest in taking a French wife. Henry then huffily suggested that he believed the lady herself was unwilling to marry his nephew and that 'marriages should be free', before going on to petulantly list other matches he was considering, including one with another beautiful young widow, Christina, Duchess of Milan. He made it plain that if France didn't want to provide him with a new queen, then there were plenty of other options available to him, not all of which might be entirely to François' liking.

By the end of March, the Duc de Guise had given in to the inevitable and agreed to raid his coffers in order to pay 80,000 livres towards Marie's dowry while King François, in recognition of the high status of the match, equalled this with 70,000 livres from his own purse. This meant that there was no need to draw upon the income from the Longueville jointure lands, which would still be for Marie's own personal use and would return to her son after her death. He also bestowed upon Marie the jewels that had once belonged to his daughter, Madeleine. In exchange, James agreed to bestow Marie with a further jointure of Scottish lands, which would provide her with a projected income of around 15,000 livres a year should he predecease her. They included the earldom of Strathearn with Stirling Castle, the earldom of Fife with Falkland Castle, the earldom of Orkney, the lordship of Galloway with Threave Castle, the lordship of Ardmannach, the earldom of Ross with Dingwall Castle and the lordship of the Isles. These were some of the traditional dower lands of the Scottish Queens previously held by James's mother, Margaret Tudor, before he felt compelled to remove them from her control in the aftermath of her divorce from the Earl of Angus.

Monsieur de Puiguillon and the Guises had done their best for Marie and the result was a marriage contract that firmly protected her interests and those of her son, the Duc de Longueville. In the event of James dying before her, it was agreed that she would retain her jointure income, keep all of her own possessions and that a third of her dowry would be returned to her if there were any surviving children of the marriage, and half if they had not been thus blessed. She would also be free to either remain in Scotland or return to France, where she could live out the rest of her days more than adequately supported by the jointure provided by her dower lands in both Scotland and France. In short, in the event of her husband's death, Marie would become a very rich woman.

The marriage contract was formally signed at Lyon in April and preparations for the wedding began immediately. It was to be a more low key affair than Marie and James's previous nuptials, in part because Marie had not yet come out of mourning for her first husband, but also because her groom had decided that one ostentatious Parisian wedding was quite enough. He declined to return to France for the ceremony, nominating the Lord High Admiral of Scotland, Lord Maxwell, as a proxy to act in his stead and, in a move that ought to have signalled what kind of husband he was likely to be, sent a diamond wedding ring to his affianced that was significantly smaller than the one he had so happily bestowed upon Madeleine just over a year earlier.

The wedding took place in the lovely Sainte Chapelle at Châteaudun on 9 May in front of Marie's family and friends, who had gathered together to support her. Pale but dignified, she walked down the aisle, past the spot where her first husband and baby son had been laid to rest, to say her vows and receive her diamond ring and a chaste kiss from Lord Maxwell. Afterwards they walked out through a guard of honour provided by King François, who did not attend but wished to contribute a touch of flamboyance to what would otherwise have been a simple ceremony.

The rest of the month was spent preparing for departure and saying goodbye to her family, who were all genuinely distressed to see her go. As she had gloomily predicted, her 2-year-old son's high rank as Duc de Longueville and Lord Chamberlain of France meant that she was unable to take him with her to Scotland. Her parents, who adored the little boy, were only too ready to welcome him into their household and undertake the administration of his vast estates, but it was still a terrible wrench for Marie to leave him behind when, only a few months earlier, she had envisioned living in retirement at Châteaudun and devoting her life to his care. Luckily, the little Duc was still too young to understand what was happening and was probably thrilled to be moving with his household to Joinville where he would be raised alongside his mother's numerous younger siblings; the youngest of whom, René, was almost a year younger than his nephew.

When news of Marie's marriage reached England, Henry made a great show of hiding his annoyance at being thwarted by his nephew and losing the hand of a lady he had persuaded himself would make the perfect Queen of England. He summoned Castillon immediately and bemoaned the fact that, despite his overtures of friendship and his wish to reinforce the relationship between their two nations by taking a French wife, King François still plainly preferred the Scottish King to him. Castillon reminded Henry that Marie had been promised to James before the death of Queen Jane, then added that François felt so bad about the whole situation that he would give Henry the choice of anyone else in his kingdom that his eye might fall upon. 'That's all very well,' Henry replied, 'but Madame de Longueville was of so gentle a race that is not often found.' Castillon pointed out that she had a younger sister who was said to be exceedingly beautiful and 'as graceful, clever and well fitted to please and obey him as any other'. He then chanced his arm with a risqué joke, nudging Henry and whispering that as 'Mademoiselle de Guise was a virgin, he would also have the advantage of moulding her to his measure.' To his relief, the often extraordinarily prim Henry found this amusing and gave him a friendly punch on the shoulder before sending him on his way.

The next morning, he was surprised to get a visit from Mr Russell, a gentleman of the King's Chamber, member of the Privy Council and Comptroller of his household. After rambling on at length about King Henry's great love of King François, he asked if it really was too late to arrange a match with Marie de Longueville, and once again the long suffering Castillon was forced to explain that Madame la Duchesse had been promised to King James before his uncle became a widower. 'Then,' Russell exclaimed, 'has she no sister or near relation or is there no one in France suitable?' Castillon patiently replied that France was teeming with honourable and lovely ladies, whereupon Russell returned to the subject of Marie's younger sister, Louise, asking if she was beautiful. 'She is the very counterpart of Madame de Longueville,' Castillon gallantly responded. 'I have not seen her for quite some time but I can assure you that she is esteemed above any other lady in the kingdom.'

Before departing, Russell suggested that Castillon should find a way for his master to offer King Henry the hand of Mademoiselle de Guise instead. The French Ambassador was left in no doubt that the whole awkward conversation had been orchestrated by Henry as a discreet means of signalling his interest in Louise de Guise without alerting Emperor Charles, with whom he was also in discussions about finding a suitable bride. By engineering this rather ridiculous courtly masquerade, Henry could plausibly deny any knowledge of the matter if word of it ever reached Charles' ears.

Back at Châteaudun, Marie could delay no longer and, with her large entourage of family, friends and servants, she set off on the long journey to Rouen, a place of painful memories as it was there that her first husband had succumbed to his illness. With no time to dwell on the past, she put on a brave face and did her best to make the most of those last precious days with the people she loved best, in particular her son, whom she feared she would never see again. It had been arranged that her father and sister, Louise, the new object of Henry VIII's attentions, would be accompanying her to Scotland so that she would not be entirely without family support at the beginning of her new life. At the start of June, after one last tearful and anguished leave-taking of the rest of her family, they set out for Le Havre where three fine galleys, the *Salamander*, the *Moriset* and the *Mary Willoughby* (named for Maria de Salinas, Lady Willoughby, before it was captured from the English in 1536); the same galleys that had taken James and Madeleine to Scotland over a year earlier, awaited them.

Sailing with Marie was a large entourage of servants and household members, which included her jester, Ferat; laundress, Jeanne Pasquiere; ladies in waiting, Mahout d'Essartz, Mlle de Curel, Renée d'Antigay, Mlle de la Touche; physician, Maître Michel Vial; embroiderers, Henri le Meine and Jacques Herpon; patissier (a very important job in any aristocratic French household), Ambroise Bontel; maids of honour, Jeanne de la Rainville, Jeanne Pieddeser and Françoise de la Touche and chaplain, Messire Jean Guillet, as well as a host of cooks, bakers, gardeners, gentlewomen of the bedchamber and other household staff. Everyone necessary, in fact, to ensure that her life in Scotland was every bit as comfortable and stress free as the life she was leaving in France. With so many members of her French household, it would almost be as though she had never left the country of her birth; she would still be surrounded by French chatter, French songs and French jokes all day long as she rested in rooms furnished in the French style and filled with treasures that she had brought with her from home.

As Marie and her retinue boarded their ships on the morning of 10 June 1538, exactly a year and a day after the death of her first husband, there was an unseemly tussle on the harbour side between Beaton and Lord Maxwell. Beaton had attempted to board the same ship as the new Queen only to be forcibly prevented by Maxwell, which ended with both men coming to blows. From what we know of Marie de Guise, it is likely that the spectacle of the Lord High Admiral of Scotland, struggling with the Bishop of Arbroath in front of a crowd of catcalling courtiers and sailors, would have amused her enormously and may have been a welcome distraction from her trepidation as she stood on the deck of the ship that was to transport her to her new life. As they sailed away from Le Havre, it is tempting to imagine Marie leaning against the rail of her ship's stern, gazing mournfully at her last glimpse of France as it slipped from view, just as her daughter, Mary, would do almost twenty-three years later. However, Marie was not by nature or upbringing as sentimental as her daughter would prove to be: and it is far more likely that she briskly took charge of her rooms below deck, or enjoyed a conversation with the captain and her companions, than allow herself to wallow in melancholy thoughts.

That's not to say that she did not privately suffer pangs of regret and unhappiness when she thought of her little boy, but it was not in her nature to make a public display of her feelings and she knew that as Queen of Scotland, everything she did or said would be endlessly scrutinised, dissected and discussed. Luckily for Marie, she turned out to be an excellent sailor and bloomed with health and energy while the rest of her party, most notably her father, were wracked with nausea and sickness during the six-day journey to Scotland. As she sat in her cabin, playing cards, reading or quietly strumming a lute to drown out the sound of retching and wailing, it must have been a small consolation to her that, perhaps, returning to France one day might not be quite so arduous after all. This was no help to her ailing, beleaguered father who would have to make the return journey whether he wanted to or not.

Although Marie and her party were due to land at St Andrews, where James impatiently awaited her arrival, unfavourable sailing conditions forced them to land at Balcomie beach further down the coast. Realising that it might be some time before news of their arrival reached King James, Marie and her entourage disembarked and hastened to take shelter in Balcomie Castle, which was hurriedly made ready for its unexpected visitor. It was Trinity Sunday and the church bells were ringing as Marie rode at the head of a bedraggled procession through the castle gates, craning her head to make the most of her first glimpse of Scotland, which must have seemed gloomy and uninspiring on that overcast and windswept day. The French had heard that Scotland was bleak and miserably cold, and nothing they had seen so far served to contradict this, although the people seemed hospitable enough.

Informed of his bride's arrival, James rode over from St Andrews the next morning to greet her, bringing much of his court with him, all dressed in their finest clothes and desperately eager to see Marie for themselves. For his part, James had not set eyes on his new Queen for just over year and was doubtless relieved to see that the events of the past year, followed by a notoriously difficult sea voyage, had done nothing to harm her good looks and amiable personality. Quite the reverse in fact – the fresh sea air seemed to have agreed with Marie and she looked the picture of pink cheeked, rude and robust health as she stood beside her new husband (who was noticeably a few inches shorter than her), to receive the congratulations and compliments of his highest-ranking courtiers. To everyone who had met the sickly Queen Madeleine, the obvious health and florid vitality of the new Queen must have come as a relief; an excellent augur for the success of this second attempt at a French marriage, which would naturally be judged more on its production of heirs than its personal felicity.

Marie had not been in Scotland long enough to be able to tell one person from another, but a few of her husband's most significant nobles would have been brought to her attention, the 22-year-old James Hamilton, Earl of Arran, among them. James was head of the Hamilton family and, thanks to his direct descent from James II and his wife, Mary of Guelders (which made him a cousin of both James and Marie), the next in line to the throne should King James die without legitimate issue. He seemed pleasant enough and was certainly much easier to get along with than his argumentative and ambitious rival, Matthew Stewart, Earl of Lennox, who also claimed descent from James II. Lennox believed his claim to the throne was better, claiming that Arran was illegitimate and therefore had no right to succeed as King of Scotland. Lennox had left Scotland for France six years earlier and it's more than likely that Marie had encountered him several times at King François' court where he was regarded with great favour and had even been presented with French citizenship in recognition of his service in the French army. He had not seen fit to return to Scotland for his own King's marriage however, which was probably a relief to Arran and everyone else he had fallen out with before his departure.

Once the introductions had been completed, the royal couple mounted their horses and rode together back to St Andrews, where the streets were thronged with courtiers and townsfolk, all keen to catch their first glimpse of the new Queen as she approached the New Abbey Gate of the city, where a charming and welcoming tableau, prepared for the occasion by Sir David Lindsay, awaited her. Marie and her entourage clapped their hands with delight as an enormous cloud descended from the top of the gate as if from heaven before opening to reveal a lovely young lady dressed as an angel who ceremoniously proceeded to present Marie with the keys of Scotland before delivering a speech of welcome, assuring the new Queen that 'all the hearts of Scotland were opened to the receiving of Her Grace.'

After several more lengthy Latin speeches extolling Marie's virtues as the very model of womanhood and exhorting her to 'serve her God, obey her husband and keep her body clean according to God's will and commandment', the procession continued on its way through winding streets, lined with cheering crowds. Marie did not yet know very much of the Scots language (an often impenetrable version of the English spoken across the border with its own lively idiom and dialects), so the blessings and compliments being shouted at her would have made very little sense – there was no mistaking the atmosphere of excited delight, however, or the genuine smiles on the faces of her new subjects as she rode past.

She spent the night before her wedding at the cathedral's splendid new guesthouse, known as the New Inns or *Novum Hospitium,* where honoured visitors to the city were housed and magnificently entertained. Whereas the impromptu accommodation at Balcomie had been basic in its nature, Marie and her entourage could have no complaints about their freshly decorated rooms in St Andrews, which had been prepared especially for her and were furnished in the French style that had won the King's heart during his visit.

The next morning, 18 June 1538, Marie, her sister, Louise, and her other ladies left the New Inns and went on foot to the nearby cathedral, a ruin nowadays but once the largest and most impressive church built in Scotland; it dominated the town with its enormous central tower and six turrets. The cathedral was bursting with people as Marie slowly made her way up the aisle to the altar where James was waiting for her. Their second wedding had all the pomp and magnificence lacking in the first, but it's possible that Marie felt that the smaller, more low-key affair had been more meaningful because it had taken place in a spot that she loved, and which was full of memories.

The presence of her father, sister and French companions must have been a great comfort, but she must have scanned the faces of the rest of the congregation as she went past, wondering who would prove to be a friend and who would be a foe.

After the ceremony, the bridal couple led their guests to the old Guest House of the cathedral where they sat down to a splendid banquet and entertainments that went on late into the night. The sophisticated French entourage had been unsure what to expect when they made the journey to Scotland for the wedding, but were able to report back that the celebrations had been both novel and magnificent. The wedding festivities continued for the next two weeks with the usual balls, banquets, mock battles and jousts to entertain the Scottish court, their French visitors and the population of St Andrews, who were keen to participate. We are told that noblemen travelled up from England for the opportunity to joust against that celebrated master of the tiltyard, Claude de Guise, and his daughters applauded delightedly as he took them on. Interspersed with all the fun and frivolity, there were visits to the colleges of St Andrews university, where she met some of the students, and trips to local churches, hospitals and other venerable institutions, much like the courtesy visits made by modern royalty today. With her usual charm, good sense and genuine interest in people, Marie won hearts wherever she went; pleasing and impressing everyone with her kindness, unfailing friendliness and gracious manner as well as the intelligence of her questions and responses.

Before her departure for Scotland, Marie had been warned that she would find her new home a 'barbarous country, destitute and void of all commodity'. Instead, she was delighted to find that, although lacking the polish and wealth of her native France, it was nowhere near as primitive as she had been led to believe. In fact it was just as civilised, bustling and pleasant as any other nation in Europe. She was particularly taken with the attractiveness of the people, informing her husband that 'she never saw so many fair personages of men and women and also young babes and children.'

Never a great or diligent letter writer, a tendency she seems to have inherited from her father and one that she would need to overcome now that she lived so far from her family, Marie managed to send some letters to her mother after her father and sister set out on their return journey. Sadly her missives have not survived, but it's clear from her mother's affectionate and relieved response that she had been full of praise for Scotland and her new husband.

> *I must tell you what joy your letters have brought your father and me ... I assure you that we took great pleasure in learning of the health of the King and yourself and of the honest welcome and the honour which greeted your arrival. We and you have good cause to thank God that you are so well settled.*

Chapter 7

Queen of Scots

With celebrations at St Andrews at an end, it was time for the newly married couple to make their way by easy stages to the capital city, Edinburgh, where Marie would make another triumphant formal entry. The Fife countryside is especially beautiful in the summer and must have given Marie pleasure as she cantered at the King's side with a falcon on her wrist, as was the custom during long rides. She would set it loose to hunt for small birds and other prey in the skies above as she rode.

They stopped first to dine at Cupar Castle, before carrying on to Falkland Palace, which was one of the royal properties settled on Marie as part of her marriage contract. Falkland had started life as a small castle before being confiscated by James II, who presented it to his wife, Mary of Guelders, the aunt of Marie's grandmother, Philippa. Thanks to its sheltered position and beautiful views, it had become a favourite country retreat of the Stewart Kings and was particularly loved by James's father, who had started extensive renovations at around the time of his marriage to Margaret Tudor in 1503. Unfortunately, his ambitious plans for the building had never been realised due to his premature death in battle in 1513.

His son was also extremely fond of Falkland and earmarked a significant amount from Marie's dowry to be used in further renovations, turning the palace into a building site for the next few years. Falkland was extended and remodelled in the style of the charming domestic châteaux that James had admired during his visit to the Loire Valley.

Marie and James spent four days at Falkland in the summer of

1538, hunting deer and going for long rides with their hawks in the surrounding countryside, before feasting and dancing until the early hours. Like his new wife, James enjoyed outdoor pursuits and was even planning to have a tennis court installed in the grounds, inspired by the ones at the French palaces. Marie took a close interest in James's plans for Falkland and liked to personally supervise the workmen when she was in residence, going out every day to check their work and suggest improvements. Whereas many high ranking women of the period would have seen it as below their dignity to take such a close interest in building work, Marie regarded it as part of her duty as both Queen and chatelaine of James's residences to ensure that they were as comfortable and aesthetically pleasing as possible.

After leaving Falkland, the royal party continued on to another one of Marie's jointure properties – the imposing Stirling Castle, which dominated the landscape for miles around from its position on a huge volcanic crag overlooking the River Forth. It commanded wonderful views that took in rolling countryside, great forests and craggy mountains, which would be snow tipped and wreathed with mist in the winter. There had been a royal fortress at Stirling since the twelfth century thanks to its crucial strategic position, which meant it controlled the crossing of the River Forth. Although its primary concern was defensive, successive monarchs had done their best to transform the inner buildings at Stirling Castle into a comfortable and even luxurious home. The impressive size and location of the fortress made it an ideal royal residence – a reminder of the might and power of the Scottish monarchy, challenged many times by their English neighbours, but never overthrown.

James IV had done a great deal to improve the castle at the start of the sixteenth century. A splendid group of buildings had been constructed in the Inner Close, including a sumptuous great hall, royal chapel, great kitchens and suite of lodgings for himself, his Queen and their family. He fully grasped Stirling's potential not just as a powerful fortress, but also as a royal residence. As at Falkland, he introduced an elegant French touch to the castle's domestic buildings, designed to reflect the new magnificence and sophistication of the Stewart

Kings. His ambitions had been interrupted by Flodden in 1513 and the subsequent long minority of his successor, but now his son was full of plans to continue improvements at the castle.

Riding up the narrow, rocky approach to the main gate, Marie could hardly have failed to be impressed by the grandeur of the enormous castle, with its turreted fore work defences, which had been installed by her husband's father, and incredible views in every direction. It might even have reminded her of her family home at Joinville, which was similarly elevated on a rock above a river. The similarity ended there, however; for while orchards, beautiful gardens and miles of vineyards surrounded Joinville, Stirling was surrounded by wild beauty that could be bleak, even in the height of summer.

The court spent a few days at Stirling that July, enjoying the same round of hunting, feasts and court entertainments that they had done at Falkland, although on an altogether more magnificent scale. James IV's splendid great hall, completed in 1503 and the largest secular space of its type in Scotland at the time, was the focus of court life in the castle. It would have been used for meals, masques and other evening entertainments, all presided over by King James and Queen Marie from their seats on a wide dais at the far end of the hall.

James's plans for Stirling were ambitious and involved building a spectacular new palace heavily influenced by those he had stayed in during his trip to France. It would prove to be a huge and expensive undertaking, but he knew he could rely on the support of his wife, who was just as keen to introduce some sophistication to the royal residences and, by doing so, increase Scotland's international prestige. The new royal palace was to be built around an inner courtyard known as the 'Lion's Den' and would enjoy sumptuous, modern furnishings and decoration in the royal apartments. Outside, there would be an impressive array of embellishments such as emblematic sculptures, crenellation and statues depicting characters from mythology and the Bible. In addition, there was a fanciful statue of James himself, sporting an formidably long beard, which makes him look more like a Biblical prophet than a handsome young King.

After a few days, it was time to take their leave of Stirling and press on towards Edinburgh, making a third stop along the way so that James could show his wife the Palace of Linlithgow, where he had been born twenty-six years earlier. Of all the palaces, it was perhaps Linlithgow that most captured Marie's heart. She was heard to declare to her husband that it was as fine as any French châteaux – possibly nothing more than a tactful compliment but quite likely to be true. Although it is hard to perceive much loveliness in the austere and forbidding edifice of Linlithgow as it looks today, it was considered a beautiful spot in the sixteenth century and was, perhaps, the most palatial of the various Stewart residences.

Standing on a hill overlooking a picturesque loch, Linlithgow was the Stewart family's chief pleasure palace and the interiors were decorated to reflect the sophisticated and expensive tastes of James's parents. The Queen's apartments, which had been arranged for Margaret Tudor at the time of her marriage and then renovated by her son in readiness for his own Queen, were particularly lovely and would have pleased Marie very much as she looked out across the loch from the oriel window of her bedchamber.

The slow progress around Scotland provided Marie and her husband with a prolonged honeymoon; a halcyon start to what everyone hoped would be a successful and fertile marriage. She had seen the Scottish countryside at its very best as sunlight warmed the rough stone of the buildings, purple heather covered the hillsides and soft mists hung above the lochs. She had expected a brutal wilderness but instead fell in love, if not with the husband who was already revealing himself to be moody, difficult and insensitive, then with the country itself and its people, who took her to their hearts in return. She was genuinely captivated by the castles and impressed by the tasteful splendour of their interiors; so different to the barbaric, unpleasant and shabby conditions that she had been warned to expect. Although they were still perhaps a little scuffed around the edges, this wouldn't put off someone as energetic and purposeful as Marie de Guise who was looking forward to making her mark on the royal residences and adding some French sophistication to the Scottish court. She had been reared to embrace hard work and to regard every challenge as a new opportunity. The daunting task of bringing the Scottish royal court up to French standards was one she thoroughly relished and one that would keep her busily occupied over the next few years.

Marie de Guise made her official entry into Edinburgh on 20 July 1538 after spending the previous night in Dunfermline as a guest of the abbot. Before her arrival, the city's officials ordered that the procession route should be cleared of all 'filth and refuse' (both human and animal) and that beggars and vagrants should be moved on so that they did not 'offend' the Queen's eyes. The city was generally spruced up for her arrival with a fresh coat of paint applied to the famous Mercat Cross by St Giles' Church on the Royal Mile and grandstands built at various stops along her route in readiness for the pageants, orations and tableaux due to be staged as she proceeded through the city. That fact that most of the plays, costumes, props, poems and speeches had been thriftily recycled from the official entry that had been planned, but hurriedly cancelled, for Queen Madeleine was tactfully left unmentioned. In that case, the official entry had been planned as a prelude to the young Queen's (also cancelled) coronation in Holyrood Abbey, but as Marie was of a lower social rank than her predecessor, there was to be no coronation until she had proved her worth as a Queen and produced an heir.

Not that Marie seems to have minded this slight as she rode beneath a cloth of gold pall through the streets of her new capital. Preceded by royal heralds, musicians and a great procession of nobles and clergy, the Queen was escorted by her ladies in waiting and the King's guards, in their scarlet and yellow livery. No contemporary account of Marie's state entrance has survived, but its likely that it followed the same pattern as the one enjoyed by her mother-in-law, Queen Margaret, which had included being met at the West Port gate by Greyfriars monks bearing relics, which she would have been invited to kiss before being presented with the city keys by a group of young women dressed as angels. Other tableaux had involved the holy marriage of the Virgin Mary and Joseph, the four virtues trampling on vices, and a short play about the judgement of Paris; all of which had included complimentary asides about the virtues of the new Queen and her husband.

Marie's procession took her down the Royal Mile to the Palace of Holyroodhouse, which was to be her residence in the capital. Once again she was delighted by the acclamation of the crowds that had gathered to see her pass, their enthusiasm no doubt increased by the free red wine that flowed all day from a large fountain by St Giles' Church. Although no contemporary accounts have survived, the few chroniclers are in agreement that Marie's reception in Edinburgh was a 'great triumph'; a day she would recall with pleasure for the rest of her life.

Holyroodhouse Palace had been the chief residence to the Stewart Kings for well over a century, ever since they'd decamped from the exposed and chilly but impressive Edinburgh Castle high up on its volcanic rock. They settled instead in the comfortable royal lodgings of the more sheltered and salubrious surroundings of Holyrood Abbey, nestled in beautiful grounds beneath the slopes of Arthur's Seat. As ever, it was James IV, King James's mercurial and much lamented father, who had decided in 1502 that the abbey lodgings were not nearly magnificent enough to house his new Tudor bride, and embarked on a project to build an entirely new palace next to the abbey.

His son continued the project, expanding and embellishing the palace, adding a large rectangular tower to the corner, which would house the new royal apartments he was planning for himself and his future wife. When he had begun building work, that wife was to be either Princesse Madeleine or Mademoiselle de Bourbon, and so he had naturally drawn on French influences to soften the traditional Scottish style of the edifice. It was at Holyrood that the unfortunate Madeleine had died after seven weeks of near isolation in her rooms as she struggled to recover from the rigours of her difficult passage from France; she had been buried with great ceremony in a prominent position in the abbey. The King had ordered that a *castrum doloris* (a small temporary construction devoted to mourning an individual) should be constructed by her tomb to hold 210 large candles, and many other smaller candles, which were kept permanently lit in her memory for two years. There was also an annual Mass said for her soul on the anniversary of her death, for which the abbey bell tolled and the walls were draped in black mourning cloth along with Madeleine's arms and emblems.

Marie had been friends with Madeleine and bore her no ill will, but it must have been strange nonetheless to find herself married to her friend's widower and inhabiting the same rooms in which she had passed away just over a year earlier. No expense had been spared in making her apartments in James's new tower as comfortable as possible but they were still filled with the ornaments and decorations brought from France by her predecessor. Most of Madeleine's clothes would have been distributed amongst her ladies, but it's likely that the most luxurious items, including her furs and jewels, would have been kept back for the next wife – in much the same way as Henry VIII's parade of wives inherited each other's jewels and dresses. This might seem odd, and even quite callous, to our modern sensibilities but court garments, particularly those worn by royalty, were extraordinarily costly and it made financial sense to pass them on rather than hide them away in trunks never to be seen again.

The court remained at Holyrood for the rest of the year, giving Marie a chance to feel properly at home. She also took the opportunity to get acquainted with her mother-in-law, Queen Margaret, the elder sister of Henry VIII. Like her siblings, Henry and Mary, Margaret Tudor owed much more to her tall, charming and charismatic Plantagenet ancestors (as exemplified by her maternal grandfather Edward IV), than she did to her thin lipped, cautious and rather humourless Tudor forefathers. The result was that she had weathered more than her fair share of drama and scandal during her forty-eight years. Margaret's position was an uncomfortable one thanks to the two disastrous marriages after the death of James IV, which had gradually estranged her from both her son, who loathed her first husband, and her brother, who had taken somewhat hypocritical objection to her chaotic personal life. They had also resulted in her son claiming back some of her valuable jointure lands and caused her own fortune to dwindle, meaning she was no longer able to maintain a separate household and was dependent upon the favour of her male relatives.

Like her brother, Margaret was capable of extraordinary charm but could also be temperamental, egotistical, petulant and self pitying – all unhelpful qualities in a mother-in-law. It would have been all too easy for Marie, the confident product of several generations of strong, intelligent and capable women, to dismiss Margaret as so many others had done. Instead, Marie treated her with marked kindness and respect and seems not to have condemned her, publicly at least, for the sad shambles that she had made of her life. However, future events would show that although she did not appear to condemn, she certainly seems to have learned a lesson from Margaret's hard example of how a widowed Queen of Scotland, with the custody of an infant monarch, ought to conduct herself in such an unashamedly patriarchal society.

For her part, Margaret was extremely curious to meet this young woman, still not quite 23 years old, who had very nearly been her sister-in-law rather than her daughter-in-law. Whatever she had expected, she was as impressed as everyone else was by Marie who, with her pale skin, unusual height and red hair, could almost be of Tudor blood herself. When James sent a letter to his uncle requesting safe passage for members of Marie's French entourage who were returning home via England, his mother took the opportunity to enclose a rather sad little letter to her brother at the same time.

Thinks it very long since she heard from him. The King, her son, is in good health, and the Queen, his wife, and great love between them. Great honour is done to her now she is come into the realm. It is well seen that she has good friends. Hopes she will prove a wise princess. She conducts herself very honourably towards Margaret, and asked what news she had from Henry. I said but short sen I heard from you. Begs now that there is another princess here Henry will let it be seen that he is a kind and loving brother to his only sister. His silence looks as if he cared not how she was treated. Edinburgh, 31 July.

Marie's life in Scotland was enlivened by a regular flow of letters from her family. She would always be an indifferent correspondent, perhaps because she was the sort of energetic, busy person who hated being confined to a desk for more than a few minutes. Luckily, her mother was quite the reverse and kept up a chatty and informative stream of letters that fully appraised her daughter of events back home in France; from a seemingly endless series of family illnesses, to general gossip and chatter, to the more mundane details of issues pertaining to the Longueville lands, which her father had taken over in her absence. There was also an exchange of letters about the miners who had been sent over from France to take a look at the reserves of gold and precious metals in Scottish soil; Marie believed it would boost the country's precarious economy if it could be properly mined.

More touchingly, Duchesse Antoinette never fails to give an update about the progress of Marie's son, François, assuring her in August 1538 that:

> *Our grandson is as well as can be; you never saw him so en bon point. His grandfather has managed him well, and the two were so friendly that they could only separate with tears. He enjoyed himself so much with him that he has lost part of his naughtiness.*

There were also assurances that the boy had not forgotten his mother or previous life at Châteaudun, and talked of them both constantly.

Of more international interest was Henry VIII's continued interest in Marie's sister, Louise, encouraged by a striking portrait of her and reports that she was even lovelier than her elder sister. His interest further piqued by reports of 'a Scotchman has come hither who has said he wonders at the king of Scots taking a widow rather than a young girl her sister, the most beautiful creature that ever he saw.' However, his suggestion that Louise should be brought to Calais with her cousins, Mademoiselle de Bourbon and Mademoiselle de Lorraine, so that Henry could inspect them for himself and choose the most suitable bride was greeted with shocked derision by the French court; particularly King François who soundly condemned Henry's wish to treat such noble ladies like 'hackneys'. Marie's parents seem to have regarded Henry's interest in their second daughter with the same reserve as they had treated his ardent pursuit of her elder sister.

Although this swift transference of his affections from one sister to another might strike modern readers as crass, no one in the sixteenth century would have regarded this as worthy of censure. His desire to see the ladies paraded in their finery at Calais so he could choose the prettiest, like some grotesque caricature of Paris of Troy with his golden apple, was quite a different matter though.

If Marie felt any pique about the situation (and it would be entirely human to do so), she hid it well as she threw herself into her new life with her usual energy and drive. Tormented by homesickness and a longing to be back in France with her son and family, she distracted herself by keeping busy. She had retained plenty of French people about her and could have hidden away in an entirely French enclave if she had so desired, but that was not at all Marie's style and she quickly began to add Scottish courtiers and servants to her household, enlisting them to teach her Scottish dances, customs and, most importantly, their language. James's French was still extremely sketchy and for the first few months of their marriage, the couple could only communicate in a rudimentary way – not an unusual situation for a royal marriage of that period, but an unsatisfactory one if they were to make a successful life together.

Naturally, Marie directed a lot of her energy into trying to forge a strong relationship with her husband. There is reason to suspect that her first marriage had been based on a sincere affection if not actual love, and after experiencing this level of felicity in the past, it's natural that she should seek to emulate it in her second marriage. The fact that she was far away from home and felt that James was the natural person to turn to for support may also have made her eager to engage his affections. It shouldn't have been a difficult matter to achieve – at 22 she was, if not beautiful, then certainly extremely attractive in a style that was admired during that period. At 24 years old, James had inherited the good looks of his two attractive parents, and already had a reputation as something of a philanderer with numerous former mistresses and illegitimate children to his name. It is, therefore, fair to assume that they enjoyed an enthusiastic physical relationship, even if a deeper emotional bond failed to materialise.

Certainly, as 1538 drew to a close, Marie gave every sign of being pleased with the husband that had been provided for her, even if she was still longing to be reunited with her family. Her grasp of the Scottish language was improving all the time, which improved relations with her husband, his family and the court. Although the relationship between Scotland and France was as amicable as always, there were the usual petty tensions in the royal household between the King's old retainers, many of whom had known and attended him since he was a toddler, and the French ladies and gentlemen who had accompanied Marie and remained in her service.

One of the main issues came from the fact that the court had been overseen by a bachelor King for almost a quarter of a century and, without a Queen to form her own household and preside over court ceremonials, the court had taken on a rather masculine atmosphere with virtually all the top jobs going to men. The King had also surrounded himself with a gang of favoured cronies, such as Oliver Sinclair of Pitcairns, the Earl of Huntly and Lord Somerville, who could be relied upon to enter into his favoured pastimes of womanising, drinking and raising hell on the streets of Edinburgh.

When Marie had arrived on the scene, few women were to be seen at the Scottish court. This must have immediately felt strange in comparison to the sophisticated French court, where women were encouraged to fully participate in court life rather than simply support their husbands or provide sexual favours. The masculine tone of James's court must have come as a culture shock to the new Queen of Scots, but it was a challenge that she was fully able to meet; Marie was keen to make her new court as cosmopolitan, refined and polished as that of France.

The presence of a pretty Queen, dressed in elegant French clothes, presiding over every banquet and court entertainment did much to temper the wilder excesses of the gentlemen; while the sight of her ladies in waiting, many of whom were now drawn from noble Scottish families, certainly lightened the mood and made it more decorous.

Marie was keen to foster good feeling between the Scottish nobility and her own French attendants, taking the view that they should all do their best to get along despite the language barrier and differences in customs. She proved to be exceedingly successful and there were romances between ardent, rugged Scotsmen and the Queen's elegantly dressed French ladies, some of which even resulted in marriage, such as that between Marie Pierres and the widowed Lord Seton. On the whole though, the sense of mutual suspicion never quite disappeared, even though both sides tacitly agreed to get on as best they could.

Marie made great efforts to get along not just with her husband's often difficult mother, but also with his friends and, more contentiously, his various illegitimate children who had been born before her arrival in Scotland. James had had several mistresses, mostly of noble birth, during his bachelor years and had fathered numerous children with them – at least nine in total. It was said that his stepfather, Lord Angus, had introduced the young King to the dubious joys of womanising when he was just an adolescent, in the hope that this dissipated lifestyle would prevent him being interested in politics, leaving the field clear for Angus himself to take control.

Although the young James had raised little objection to this ploy and seems to have enjoyed himself excessively, he still made a point of acknowledging and providing for the children that resulted from these liaisons. He welcomed them to court, providing them with excellent educations and eventually arranging good marriages or careers in the church. Most of the King's children were boys and away at school so had very little contact with Marie and her household, but she did treat them with kindness when they were around, buying them little treats and making sure they were well fed and entertained. The one exception was the King's only daughter, Lady Jean Stewart, the product of his liaison with Elizabeth Bethune. Jean was just 5 years old when Marie arrived in Scotland and seems to have captured the young Queen's heart because she was moved into Marie's household, where she was treated with affection and honour.

Like most other European courts, that of James V was peripatetic, although on a much less lavish scale than those of his nearest rivals Henry VIII and François I. Still, the transportation of several hundred people is always going to be an impressive spectacle and require a superhuman effort at a time when most roads were unpaved; the winters could be harsh and the main means of transportation were horses, carts, litters and boats. When James and Marie moved on to Linlithgow after spending their first Christmas together at Holyroodhouse, they did so accompanied by a cavalcade of courtiers and servants while their possessions were all carefully transported on twenty-four carts drawn by fifteen mules. The royal palaces lay mostly empty when the court were not in residence so beds, tapestries, plate, carpets, favourite paintings, books, clothes and bedding would all be taken along for the ride and carefully unpacked on arrival and arranged by a team of maids and stewards.

Marie was still young enough to find the whole process exciting rather than exhausting and enjoyed opportunities to see more of the wild Scottish countryside, so different to the soft, rolling meadows of France. Then as now, the Scottish were a complicated people – fearsome in battle, fascinated by science, nostalgic about the past and fond of a good party. An odd but compelling mixture of romantic and pragmatic, best experienced during gatherings on winter nights when they openly wept while singing sad old songs about battles and women lost and won.

Banquets at the Scottish court went on for hours and were noisy, chaotic events. On their dais at the top end of the hall, the royal couple would be served the most choice foods first before sending it on to their favoured courtiers, who would be seated at the temporary trestle tables that accompanied the court on its travels. Food served to the Scottish court was hearty and filling as suited the cold, wet climate and active lives of the royal family and courtiers. Fish was popular, as was venison, spit roasted pork, pigeon, hare and rabbit pie, oatcakes and spiced mince pies; all of which were washed down with the usual ale, wine, whisky and beer.

King James had inherited a virtually empty treasury thanks to his father's various expensive interests and the disastrous war with England. The already uncomfortable situation had then been made even worse for the infant King by the avarice of his stepfather and regent, Lord Angus, and the extravagance of his mother. However, his two advantageous marriages had considerably enriched him, enabling him to live in some style at court and complete the building work begun by his parents. He loved to wear rich, flamboyant clothes in colours that showed off his auburn colouring and also encouraged Marie to dress in gowns designed and made for her by the Parisian tailors that had accompanied her from France. Glittering with jewels and dressed in lustrous crimson and purple velvets, silks and brocades, trimmed with fine lace, gold, sables and ermine, she must have looked an impressive sight as she strode about the court. Her personal income meant that she was able to live in very fine style and also able to invest in small improvements to the palaces. She had relatives and friends in France send over paintings, ornaments, furnishings and other luxuries like fine wines, rich cloth, jewellery, spices and dried fruit that made her surroundings a little more elegant.

She also took a close interest in James's building projects, which were intended to enlarge existing royal palaces, making them even more impressive. Her mother sent over half a dozen French masons to work on them while another old friend, Mademoiselle de Tern, was asked to send over cuttings of various fruit trees so that she could grow French hybrids of plums and pears in the royal gardens. The older courtiers may well have grumbled about the ever-increasing French influence on the royal palaces, but to James it was a symbol of his country's proud position as an increasingly cosmopolitan and powerful state ruled by a true Renaissance King; to Marie it was simply a reminder of a home she might never see again.

Chapter 8

The Baby Princes

In the summer of 1539, Marie discovered she was pregnant. Just over a year had passed since her marriage to James and arrival in Scotland, and her influence was already apparent everywhere; from the refined furnishings of the palaces to the delicately spiced and flavoured French cuisine being served at the royal table. There was a definite French influence to the way that the courtiers were beginning to dress as well, with the court ladies in particular wearing elegant, and often ruinously expensive, ensembles modelled on the clothes that the Queen and her French ladies wore. Even the King was not immune to his wife's influence and his accounts show that he ordered French style clothes, including an elegant black velvet jacket in the latest mode, and even a French saddle for his horse.

After leaving Linlithgow, the court had moved on to Falkland before heading to Stirling to observe the traditional Easter festivities in the castle, which involved feasting, entertainments and a celebratory Mass in the chapel royal. As always, summer was spent in St Andrews, where they could enjoy the fresh sea air, and Falkland, where the King and his gentlemen spent their days hunting. It was possibly while they were at Falkland that Marie first suspected that she was expecting another child, which would have been confirmed by her French physician, Maître Michel Vial, before she informed her husband and family of the happy news.

Although Marie had already given birth to two children and came from a family that was notable for its fertility, she had been deeply anxious about her prospects of bearing a child for her new husband. She was well aware that a great deal depended upon her producing an

94

heir to the Scottish throne and keeping it from the hands of James's relatives, the Earls of Arran and Angus, who would come to blows, and perhaps even go to war, in order to secure what each man saw as his birthright. Marie also had a sneaking feeling, underlined by the inferior wedding ring and lack of a coronation, that her husband didn't really view her as a suitable wife and wanted to prove her worth by providing him with a healthy son. After the initial honeymoon period, their relationship had settled into one of friendly formality, which was not entirely displeasing but still cooler than Marie would have liked.

Naturally Marie's mother, Antoinette, entered into her hopes and fears, but her letters are tactfully free of admonishments about her daughter's slowness to conceive. Instead, she continued to keep Marie up to date with how little François was doing at Joinville. In October 1538, she writes that he had been ill with vomiting and a fever but had recovered and that 'it has done him good, for he was too full and he is as well as ever, eats with good appetite, and sleeps ten or twelve hours. He is fat and round and very pretty.' In March of the following year, she wrote that 'his face is so round and nice that it is a pleasure to look at him. His grandfather adores him and he chatters beautifully.'

She also sent sketches of the little boy and two portraits, keen that his mother should see for herself just how well he looked.

In June 1539, her mother wrote to let her know that her aunt, Renée, Duchesse de Lorraine and sister of the disgraced Duc de Bourbon, had died after a short illness which was a 'great loss to all the house', and goes into a great deal of detail about the Duchesse's final moments. In the same letter she adds a postscript about visiting her mother-in-law, Philippa at Pont-à-Mousson, and lets Marie know that she is well and has sent a letter with a priest travelling to Scotland. The letter that Marie's uncle Antoine wrote to her at the same time goes into rather less detail than that of her mother, saying only that 'he has had the misfortune to lose his wife, who died the day after Pentecost. She made a devout and Christian end. Which will end his letter but for his assurance that he is at the King's service and at hers.'

Other family letters concerned Antoinette's attempts to secure the services of miners for her daughter; updates about the activities of her father; complaints about Marie's former mother-in-law (who seems to have been a deeply unpleasant woman) and the ever-pressing matter of Louise's marriage. The match with Henry VIII had come to nothing when he decided to marry an obscure German princess, Anne of Cleves, instead. Anne had previously been betrothed to Marie's cousin, François, Marquis de Pont Mousson, the eldest son and heir of her uncle Antoine; in fact this prior agreement was used to break the marriage a few years later, although by then François had already married another one of Henry VIII's putative brides, Christina of Denmark, dowager Duchess of Milan.

While on their summer progress in August 1539, Marie and James went to the Isle of May in the Firth of Forth to pray at the shrine of St Adrian, who was believed to show particular favour to women who were struggling to conceive. It was a little early for such measures, but Marie certainly seems to have felt disproportionally worried about the lack of a child, not to mention the fact that she still desperately missed her son. It must have been a tremendous joy to her when she was able to inform her husband and mother that she had conceived and was expecting a baby in the summer of the following year.

As soon as the pregnancy was confirmed, arrangements went ahead for Marie's delayed coronation, which was scheduled to take place at Holyrood Abbey on 22 February 1540. Marie would already be well advanced in pregnancy by the time it took place, but this was considered all the better as it would provide visual proof of her fecundity and worthiness to be Queen; perhaps James was inspired by the splendid coronation of his uncle's second wife, Anne Boleyn, which had taken place in May 1533, when she was obviously pregnant with her daughter. This display had caused a scandal throughout Europe but that had not troubled Henry, who was only too pleased to have his virility on public show.

Preparations for the coronation began in October when Marie was probably only two months pregnant. Keen to enhance the increasing prestige of the Scottish monarchy with an impressive display of royal magnificence, James ordered a new gold crown decorated with pearls and precious stones, and a gilded silver sceptre with a raised hand at

Marie de Guise and James V. *Blair Castle/Duke of Atholl*

Claude de Guise.
*Royal Collection
Trust/Her Majesty
Queen Elizabeth II*

Antoinette de Guise. *Royal Collection Trust/Her Majesty Queen Elizabeth II*

Renée de Bourbon, Duchesse de Lorraine. *Royal Collection Trust/Her Majesty Queen Elizabeth II*

François I of France, after Joos van Cleve, c1530. *Royal Collection Trust/Her Majesty Queen Elizabeth II*

Henry VIII, after Hans Holbein the Younger, c1538. *Royal Collection Trust/Her Majesty Queen Elizabeth II*

Margaret Tudor, Daniel Mytens, c1620. *Royal Collection Trust/Her Majesty Queen Elizabeth II*

James V of Scotland, unknown artist, c1540. *Royal Collection Trust/Her Majesty Queen Elizabeth II*

Linlithgow Palace.
Melanie Clegg

Probable location of
the Queen's
bedchamber in
Linlithgow Palace.
Melanie Clegg

Falkland Palace. *Royal Collection Trust/Her Majesty Queen Elizabeth II*

Falkland Palace. *Melanie Clegg*

Stirling Castle, William Leighton Leitch. *Royal Collection Trust/Her Majesty Queen Elizabeth II*

Details of the sculptures at Stirling Castle. *Melanie Clegg*

Stirling Castle Queen's bedchamber. *Melanie Clegg*

Marie de Guise's Stirling Castle head. *Melanie Clegg*

Stirling Castle Queen's bedchamber. *Melanie Clegg*

Holyroodhouse Palace. *Melanie Clegg*

The Queen's Tower, Holyroodhouse Palace. *Melanie Clegg*

View of Holyroodhouse Palace in the 17th Century. *Royal Collection Trust/Her Majesty Queen Elizabeth II*

Interior of Holyrood Abbey. *Royal Collection Trust/Her*

Holyrood Abbey. *Melanie Clegg*

Henri II of France, studio of François Clouet, 1559. *Royal Collection Trust/Her Majesty Queen Elizabeth II*

Catherine de Medici. *Royal Collection Trust/Her Majesty Queen Elizabeth II*

François de Lorraine, Duc de Guise, after Léonard Limosin. *Royal Collection Trust/Her Majesty Queen Elizabeth II*

Charles de Lorraine, Cardinal de Lorraine, unknown artist. *Royal Collection Trust/Her Majesty Queen Elizabeth II*

Francois II of France. *Royal Collection Trust/Her Majesty Queen Elizabeth II*

Mary Queen of Scots, François Clouet, c1558. *Royal Collection Trust/Her Majesty Queen Elizabeth II*

Edward VI, attributed to William Scrots, c1546. *Royal Collection Trust/Her Majesty Queen Elizabeth II*

Countess of Lennox, unknown artist, c1572. *Royal Collection Trust/Her Majesty Queen Elizabeth II*

Mary I, after Anthonis Mor van Dashorst, c1550. *Royal Collection Trust/Her Majesty Queen Elizabeth II*

Philip II of Spain, after Anthonis Mor van Dashorst, 1554. *Royal Collection Trust/Her Majesty Queen Elizabeth II*

Elizabeth I, Nicholas Hilliard, c.1560. *Royal Collection Trust/Her Majesty Queen Elizabeth I.*

The Death of Henri II of France, German School, c1559. *Royal Collection Trust/He Majesty Queen Elizabeth II*

Mary Queen of Scots in mourning, François Clouet, 1560. *Royal Collection Trust/Her Majesty Queen Elizabeth II*

Marie de Guise, unknown artist, 17th century copy of an original painting. *Royal Collection Trust/Her Majesty Queen Elizabeth II*

Edinburgh Castle. *Melanie Clegg*

St Margaret's Chapel, Edinburgh Castle. *Melanie Clegg*

the end in the French style for his wife. His own crown was remodelled and embellished with twenty-three precious stones, including an enormous amethyst and three beautiful garnets. His own coronation had taken place when he was just 17 months old and had been a hurried, miserable affair carried out in the chapel royal of Stirling Castle amidst the chaos and uncertainty following his father's death at Flodden. The fact that he couldn't remember it didn't make him any less a King, but it's likely that James regarded Marie's coronation as an opportunity to compensate for the un-ceremoniousness of his own crowning and reinforce his authority upon his nobles, his people and the other crowned heads of Europe.

The couple spent their second Christmas together at Linlithgow Palace before returning to Edinburgh to ready themselves for the coronation celebrations. The city buzzed with excitement that winter as it began to fill with people, including several hundred nobles and their wives and children, who had been invited by the King to attend his wife's crowning. As with any public royal event, there were also thousands of less exalted spectators, who crammed themselves into the city in the weeks preceding the coronation. At Holyrood Abbey, preparations were also well underway as tiered stands were erected inside to accommodate the guests, which included the most well-born ladies in the kingdom, all of whom had been summoned by letter to come to Edinburgh in order to attend the Queen on her special day.

Sadly, no contemporary description of Marie's coronation has survived but we know from the records that she was a dazzling sight in a robe of purple velvet, lined with ten ells of white corded taffeta. The records inform us that James also ordered a new robe for himself, made of thirty-eight ells of purple velvet and lined with forty dozen ermine skins. He also ordered a turquoise ring and a gold belt set with a sapphire – although the latter may have been for Marie's benefit rather than his own. It's clear that the royal couple, a pair of tall, attractive redheads must have looked impressive as they walked together down the aisle of Holyrood Abbey where Cardinal Beaton (the Bishop of Arbroath had been promoted to Cardinal in December 1538), was waiting to perform the crowning and then celebrate Mass before the royal couple and their court returned to the state apartments for a banquet and entertainments.

A week after the coronation, Sir Ralph Sadler, favourite protegé of Thomas Cromwell and a trusted envoy of Henry VIII, arrived in Edinburgh to seek an audience with King James and deliver some letters from his uncle. He brought a gift of six geldings but although their meeting after morning prayers in the chapel seemed amicable enough, tensions were clearly simmering beneath the surface as James 'gently embraced' Sadler and welcomed him to his court. Although the visit appeared little more than a courtesy from one monarch to another, Sadler had been ordered to seek an audience with James in order to arrange a formal meeting between the two Kings and persuade the Catholic Scottish King to throw in his lot with his uncle and put an end to his support of the Papacy. Although he knew that his nephew's coffers had been enriched by his two French marriages, Henry was well aware just how expensive his lifestyle was and that he was keen to make himself wealthier still. By promoting the potential bounty to be gained from breaking with Rome and suppressing the religious orders, he hoped to gain James's support and win him away from France.

Sadler was also keen to get a glimpse of Queen Marie, perhaps to give his master a first-hand report of her appearance and demeanour. Thwarted on the first day because Marie was too ill with morning sickness to leave her apartments, he had better luck the following morning when he went to the royal chapel and found Marie listening to a sermon in French without her husband at her side. When Sadler got the opportunity to speak to her, he offered the compliments of his master, King Henry, for which she very prettily thanked him, offering in return to do all that she could to strengthen the precarious amity between her husband and his uncle. Unfortunately, Sadler's meeting with her husband later that day did not go quite so well and there were even more annoyances later when he had an audience with the Dowager Queen Margaret. Realising that he had come empty handed, Margaret immediately began to bend his ear about the fact that her brother never bothered to write to her. She was certain that this perceived lack of influence, with either her brother or her son, was one of the reasons why she was treated with disdain at the Scottish court, although she was forced to admit that the latter at least 'was never better inclined to amity, and that she was well treated and much made of by the new Queen.'

The court moved to Stirling in the spring, which must have been a welcome change of scenery for Marie as she prepared for the birth of her third child. She had grown to love Stirling and was more than happy to recover from the ordeal of the coronation there with her ladies beside her. Mindful of the precious burden that she carried, she spent most of her time either tending her small garden within the walls of Stirling, or indoors in her luxuriously appointed chambers with her ladies and mother-in-law, Margaret, where they busied themselves sewing a trousseau for the coming baby, ordering gold and white silk threads for the purpose. Like a lot of expectant mothers, Marie thoroughly enjoyed these last few months before the birth of her baby, making the most of the peace and calm as she looked forward to meeting her child for the first time.

Perhaps thinking that he was surplus to requirements in the softly feminine enclave that Marie had created for herself, James arranged to visit the Western Isles after escorting Marie and her household to Saint Andrews where she was to have her lying in. As was traditional, the Queen of Scotland was ceremoniously sequestered in her rooms to await the birth of her child, with only women in attendance to entertain and support her. The expectant mother's chambers were kept dimly lit while thick carpets, tapestries and curtains effectively blocked out light and sound from the outside world, creating a womb like atmosphere. Marie was provided with two great beds for her lying in, one of which was hung with yellow damask trimmed with gold, while the other had curtains of white damask. Beside the bed there waited a beautifully carved cradle, created by a French carpenter, André Manson, and prepared with the white and gold layette that Marie and her ladies had been working on throughout the pregnancy.

It came of something of a surprise when Marie went into labour towards the end of May, either because she had got her dates wrong or perhaps because the baby arrived a few weeks early. Either way,

James was just about to leave Dumbarton on the west coast when a royal messenger, Andrew Michelson, arrived with the news that his wife had been unexpectedly taken to bed and given birth to a 'fair and lusty' son on 22 May. James immediately leapt from his ship and rode back to St Andrews, promising the exhausted Michelson a whole new suit of clothes in thanks for his endeavours in the 'bringing of tidings to the King's Grace of the nativity of My Lord Prince'.

Propped up against lace edged pillows in her great bed and dressed in a flowered purple-damask robe, Marie presented her husband with his first legitimate son and heir. The baby was to be called James like his father and was christened four days after his birth on Wednesday, 26 May in St Andrews cathedral, also receiving the title Duke of Rothesay. In keeping with tradition, the ceremony took place at night with torches lighting the way as the court went in procession to the altar where Cardinal Beaton, the Archbishop of Dunbar, and Queen Margaret were waiting to act as godparents. It was not customary for mothers to be present at the christening as they were often still confined to bed as part of their lying in. They were also absolved from attending any religious rituals until they had been officially 'churched' forty days after childbirth, at which point they could resume their devotions and attend services again.

Childbirth was a perilous experience in the sixteenth century and maternal post-natal death was a tragedy that had touched almost everyone in one way or another, killing thousands of women a year irrespective of social standing, marital status, income or age. As the tragic death of Queen Jane Seymour in October 1533 had proved, even queens were not immune. Marie would have been carefully watched in those first dangerous days after giving birth although, as everyone knew, fevers could strike new mothers with alarming swiftness, coming as if out of nowhere and apparently resistant to any forms of treatment. Marie was strikingly robust however, and it's likely that she recovered swiftly from the arduous process of labour, probably even beginning to chafe at the restrictions placed upon her. She liked to be kept busy and lying in bed for days on end was almost certainly not her idea of a good time.

Both of the proud new parents must have taken satisfaction from the task of writing letters announcing the new arrival to their fellow monarchs, with particular care being taken over the missives sent south to François I and Henry VIII. The English King was currently embroiled in trying to rid himself of his latest Queen, Anne of Cleves, and was almost certainly in no mood to hear about his nephew's success in siring a legitimate male heir from a wife who he himself had pursued. While Henry might have received the news badly, François was absolutely delighted by the successful outcome of a match that he had engineered. He ordered the Constable of France, Anne de Montmorency, to write a letter of congratulations on his behalf as soon as the news arrived, informing Marie that the King of France was 'as pleased to hear of her having a handsome son and that she is doing well, as he would have been if she were indeed his own daughter'.

As might be expected, Duchesse Antoinette was also thrilled and wrote a letter of congratulations to her daughter, telling her that she was desperate for news of Marie, her husband and her new baby. Meanwhile, Marie's uncle, the Cardinal de Lorraine, positively crows in his own letter of congratulation, telling his niece that he:

cannot express the satisfaction of himself and all her house at the news that she has had a handsome son. The King has been quite as much pleased at it as if he himself had had one and is sending the King, her husband, three Spanish horses and a racing steed.

A fine gift indeed and one hopes that Marie received something equally as fine in recompense for the sacrifices she had made to make her family and King François so happy.

For Marie, the birth of her son consolidated her position as Queen of Scotland while at the same time drawing her husband closer to her side. Her new position as mother of the heir to a throne increased her own family's prestige, both at the French court and also throughout Europe; a happy bonus that gave her great pleasure. She would always miss her eldest son and long for the French countryside, but at least she had the satisfaction of knowing she had done her duty to her family which, given the Lorraine family motto of 'Toutes pour une', was no small matter.

The Guise family don't appear to have been particularly perturbed by Henry VIII's failure to marry another one of their daughters and, on 30 November 1540, Antoinette wrote to inform her eldest daughter that the Duke of Aarschot had requested Louise's hand for his eldest son, the Prince de Chimay. The match was a good one and met with everyone's approval as the prospective bridegroom was allegedly 'aged about 20, handsome and honest'. Even better, his lands lay near Guise, which meant that Louise would be able to remain close to her family after her marriage, which took place on 20 February 1541.

In the same letter, Antoinette expresses her anxiety over the 'pretty little prince' James, who had fallen ill for some days after his nurse's milk had suddenly failed and he was switched to another wet nurse. Antoinette, with her long experience of childrearing, reassured her daughter that this was not an unusual occurrence, before rather ruefully adding – in the manner of all grandmothers who are afraid that their concern might be misconstrued as interference – that she 'could not refrain from writing to express her anxiety as I feel so much affection for this little creature whom I have never seen.' She adjures Marie to make sure she is getting plenty of rest for she has heard a rumour, and one wonders where from, that she is expecting another child.

As it turned out, Antoinette's maternal radar turned out to be correct because at the beginning of Autumn, a mere four months after the birth of the little Duke of Rothesay, Marie began to suspect that she was once again pregnant. At the time she was at Falkland, where she had accompanied her husband for the court's traditional hunting party after first visiting Glamis Castle and Dundee in the south. Their son already had his own separate establishment in St Andrews where he was cared for by his own large household, which included his own almoner, keeper of silver vessels, *patissiere*, laundress, tailor and nursemaids. Although it must have been a wrench for Marie to leave him behind at St Andrews, both parents kept up a close communication with the prince's Master of the Household and were kept informed of everything that happened while they were apart.

The new sense of accord between Marie and her husband became strained that autumn when James, always prone to paranoia, suddenly turned against one of his oldest friends, Sir James Hamilton of Finnart, ordering his arrest on a nebulous charge of plotting against the King. No one at court, least of all the Queen, knew what Hamilton was supposed to have done, although the court was rife with rumour, and truly shocked when the unfortunate Hamilton was summarily sentenced to death and executed. What Marie thought of this turn of affairs is not known, but she must have felt unease at her husband's neurotic changeability which, it was whispered, was not all that dissimilar to that of his uncle: Henry. However secure Marie must have felt after the birth of her son and her quick second conception, the sudden fall from grace of Sir James Hamilton must have worried everyone who entered into James's personal orbit. His latest bout of depression only seemed to increase afterwards as, wracked with guilt, he woke up screaming from terrible nightmares in which his former friend came back to kill him.

Luckily for Marie, it was decided that she should remain at Falkland Palace for the next few months, enjoying the tranquillity and fresh country air while her husband and the rest of the court travelled between the other palaces. The couple were reunited in December when Marie travelled to Stirling Castle for the court's Christmas festivities. Renovations were still going on to transform the royal apartments at Stirling with a large team of masons and other craftsmen working hard to make the old castle worthy of a modern, Renaissance royal family. When completed, the statues and emblems on the castle façade were painted in bright colours, creating a cheerful aspect that reflected the magnificence of the interior. Work had also begun on the so called 'Stirling Heads', a series of wooden roundels, carved and painted in the Italian style, probably under the aegis of André Manson and destined for the ceiling of the King's Inner Hall. They featured portraits of James and Marie as well as notable figures from their court and elsewhere, including Henry VIII, Queen Margaret and even the sad little Queen Madeleine, whose almost forgotten visage was destined to gaze down at her former husband as he sat on his gilded throne below.

At the start of 1541, Marie was back at Falkland again with her household, to await the birth of her baby. Building work was still in progress and she busied herself overseeing the renovations, her input giving the palace a hefty dash of French sophistication. In February her younger sister, Louise, married the Prince de Chimay, and Marie must have felt a pang of sadness that she could not be present at the ceremony and had to rely on her mother's account of the nuptials instead. The grand occasion had been graced by the presence of their cousin, Anna, who was now Princess of Orange, as well as the Queen of Hungary and dowager Duchess of Milan. Louise herself took pen to paper shortly after her marriage, writing to let her sister know that she was delighted with her husband and that 'you ought ... to be well pleased with your sister's happiness.' If she regretted the failure of Henry VIII's attempt to make her Queen of England then she gave no sign, although it is tempting to imagine that she, the Princess of Orange and Duchess of Milan, all of them putative brides of the English King who had been painted and appraised for his delectation, had much to talk about when they got together at the wedding.

In April, Marie was back at Stirling Castle again to await the birth of her fourth baby. Blooming with health and a veteran of three successful labours, there was no reason to suppose that anything would go wrong and so the castle bustled with excitement when news spread that the Queen had gone into labour. Her fourth child, another boy, was born later that day, a triumphant salvo from a great cannon on the castle ramparts announced his birth. The Scottish King had another male heir, the succession was secure and the country safe from threat of future civil war between rival claimants.

The new baby prince was christened in the chapel royal of Stirling Castle when he was three days old, given the name Robert and the title of Duke of Albany. The sky above Stirling Castle exploded with fireworks as the court celebrated the birth of another Scottish prince while, closeted away in her splendid apartments, Queen Marie watched over his beautifully carved cradle and thanked God for the good fortune that he had showered upon her. Her joy and relief were destined to be short lived. Just over a week after the baby's birth, on 21 April, a messenger arrived at Stirling to inform the royal couple that their eldest son, Prince James, was gravely ill.

Marie had not yet been churched and was still sequestered in her apartments so it was her husband who immediately set out to ride the 52 miles that lay between Stirling and St Andrews where Prince James's household was still based. He was too late – the baby prince, who was just a month shy of his first birthday, died before he arrived.

The distraught King was weeping at his son's bedside when a messenger arrived from Stirling to inform him that his younger boy, Prince Robert was also mortally ill and the Queen was frantic with worry. Appalled by this terrible and almost unbelievably cruel turn of events, James left St Andrews at once and rode back to Stirling, arriving back at the castle just in time to see his younger son, who was eight days old, pass away. In less than twenty-four hours, James and Marie had gone from being the proud parents of two thriving male heirs, to mourning the loss of their sons and the future stability they had represented. As Marie, dressed in heavy mourning and pale with misery, watched the tiny black coffin of her youngest son being carried down to the chapel, she must have wondered what terrible blow lay in store for her next and what this turn of events would mean for her already precarious relationship with her husband.

Chapter 9

Solway Moss

The baby princes were buried together in Holyrood Abbey in a small, discreet ceremony that had none of the austere magnificence or pomp of most royal funerals. There were no crowds of mourners, no processions through the streets, no effigies and no purchasing of any new mourning clothes for the royal couple and their court. It seems likely that Marie and James were so genuinely distraught that they could not face a grand public parade of their grief and so kept things as low key and private as they could.

Queen Margaret was on hand at Stirling to offer her sympathy and do her best to comfort her grieving son and daughter-in-law. Although her relationship with James was strained, she got on well with Marie and was genuinely distressed by her sadness, writing to her brother, Henry VIII, on 12 May that there 'has been great displeasure for the death of the Prince and his brother, both with the King and Queen; and the writer is ever with them to comfort them, so that she has no leisure to write of her own matters.' She felt no need to add that the young couple's distress was increased by rumours at court that their little boys had been poisoned, probably by either the Earl of Arran or the Earl of Lennox. In a period when paranoia about poisoning was rife, any sudden or potentially suspicious high-profile death would immediately give rise to whispers of foul play so it's not surprising that the deaths of two healthy young princes within such a short period of time would give rise to gossip and conjecture.

Marie seems to have had doubts about the cause of her sons' deaths, probably inflamed by court gossip and James's naturally suspicious nature, which had fixated on some anomaly in the post mortem appearance of Prince Robert. News of the princes' deaths did not reach France until June, whereupon Marie's mother immediately sent letters of condolence to both grieving parents. Her letter to James is calm but sad, informing him that she has learnt from Marie's letter that 'God has taken back to Himself the children He gave you. As you have borne it with resignation, I have hopes that He will soon give you others.' She repeats this sentiment in her letter to her daughter, adding that as both she and James are still so young, there is every chance that they will have other children. She then addresses Marie's concerns about poisoning, gently assuring her that no one could have wished the boys harm and that it was her belief that a superfluity of wet-nurses and over feeding had led to the death of Prince James, while his younger brother, like so many babies at the time, was evidently not intended by God to linger in this world.

Inspired by the calm and collected way that her husband appeared to be bearing their loss, Marie resolved to follow his lead and put a brave face on her troubles, reminding herself that there was no reason to suppose that she would not conceive again. It was undeniably difficult time for her though and, despite the optimism of her family that she would have more children, she must have found herself wondering if in fact God intended her to be a mother. True, her eldest son, François, was still alive and well but he was far away in France, being raised alongside her siblings by her parents, which wasn't at all the same as having him close beside her and under her own care. For a warm-hearted, caring woman like Marie de Guise who had grown up expecting to be matriarch of a fine family like her mother and grandmother before her, this must have been a terrible disappointment and one that it would not be easy to overcome.

A tragic loss such as that endured by Marie and her husband in the spring of 1541 would be a make-or-break situation for even the strongest of relationships, as the couple is either brought closer together or pushed further apart by their grief. Although relations between them had always been amicable enough and they were initially bonded by their mutual loss, the underlying tensions that lay beneath Marie and James's marriage quickly placed a wedge between them and made them more distant than ever. Marie had always struggled with James's black moods and jealous nature while he, despite his love of all things French, did not always appreciate her animated, some might say flirtatious, manner with the male denizens of the court. The light morals of the ladies of the French court were famous throughout Europe and, although Marie had remained apart from the seamier side of King François' circle and never given her husband any real cause to question her loyalty to him, still he found himself turning against her. Even English spies were reporting to Henry VIII that James had no appetite for war as he was so preoccupied with his 'jealousy over the Queen'.

Towards the end of 1541, there was talk of James travelling down to York to meet with his uncle, Henry VIII, who was touring the north of his country with his new wife, Catherine Howard. Tensions had been rising between England and Scotland for quite some time thanks to James's refusal to turn his back on the Papacy and his strong bonds with King François, who in turn let it be known that he regarded the Scottish King as 'another son', while James referred to him as his 'father' – an attitude unlikely to foster good feeling with his uncle Henry. In the event of hostilities breaking out between France and England once more, it seemed certain that James, even though he was half Tudor himself, would side with the French rather than his own uncle and might even be tempted to invade the north of the country while the King and his troops were occupied elsewhere. Strangely, the two Kings had never actually met, and perhaps in an attempt to impress the bonds of family loyalty upon his recalcitrant nephew, Henry invited him to York in September.

James, deeply mistrustful at the best of times, was naturally sceptical about his uncle's motives for asking him to venture on to English soil. Although Henry promised him safe conduct through his northern territory, James still did not trust him and even suspected that he might be kidnapped or worse. He also received word that King François had, unsurprisingly, reacted with alarm when he heard about the proposed meeting and had pressed Cardinal Beaton, currently on mission to France, for reassurance that this summit was not actually going to take place. He need not have worried – James had no intention of going to York, realising that such an endeavour would not benefit either himself or his country, and might even be to the detriment of his precious alliance with France. He acted with caution though, keen to avoid outright offence by showing his hand too soon, and politely evaded the attempts of Henry's envoy, Sir Ralph Sadler, to discover his intentions.

When September rolled around, James remained in residence at Falkland Palace with Marie and a small group of favoured courtiers and gave no sign that he was planning an imminent trip to England. Meanwhile, his uncle lingered in York for several weeks, clearly expecting his arrival while his courtiers placed bets on whether or not the Scottish King would turn up. Those in the know were of the opinion that he would not, but without any official word either way, no one knew what to expect. By the end of the month it was obvious, even to Henry, that James wasn't going to make an appearance and he vented his rage and humiliation upon his courtiers; furious that his nephew had snubbed him so publicly and deeply offended that he had not even bothered to let him know. James, enjoying himself hunting at Falkland Palace, was completely oblivious that his actions and careless treatment of his uncle had effectively marked a definite turning point in relations between the two nations.

A few weeks later, James received word that his mother, Margaret, was gravely ill after suffering a stroke at her residence, Methven Castle, a few days earlier. He immediately left Falkland Palace to be at her side but, yet again, he was too late and she died before his arrival. Although James put on a good show of being the dutiful mourning son, he made the true contempt that he felt for his mother clear by ignoring her final deathbed wishes that he forgive her second husband, Lord Angus, and give her few remaining jewels to her daughter, his step sister, Lady Margaret Douglas, who was living at their uncle Henry's court. He could hardly be seen to stint when it came to his mother's funeral however, most of which he had to pay for himself as she had left a legacy of just 2,500 marks, a pitiful amount for a Princess of England and former Queen of Scotland to leave. The entire court was summoned to attend Margaret's state funeral at the charterhouse of Perth and the royal couple remained in mourning for several months afterwards, even celebrating Christmas with unusual solemnity, while their chambers and the chapel royal were hung with black drapes.

The death of Queen Margaret, of whom Marie had been sincerely fond, did nothing to heal the rift that was steadily growing between her son and his wife. Like many depressed people, James had a tendency to push away the people closest to him. He wallowed in self-pity and attempted to assuage his bleakness and self-doubt with drink and hedonism, which of course made matters much worse. Although he seems to have remained faithful to Marie for a number of years, he once again took up some aspects of his old bachelor lifestyle in the wake of the Princes' deaths, seeking out other women for casual encounters and even, it was rumoured, setting up a mistress again. He was not especially discreet about this and naturally it didn't take too long before word of his misdeeds reached the ears of his wife, who was naturally hurt and chagrined by his lack of respect for her feelings. It was to be expected, of course, that a virile young King in the prime of life should have mistresses, and Marie would have been counselled by her mother to expect this and turn a blind eye, as she had done, to any peccadilloes that might well occur. However, gentlemen were expected to be discreet about such things to spare their wives' feelings and it would have seemed like an unpardonable insult to Marie to have her husband's infidelity paraded before her.

There is evidence of the discord between husband and wife in a small collection of letters sent by James V to Marie, which are undated but might well have been written during this difficult year. In the first he complains that he is 'surprised by your letter, seeing as I have been so ill for the last three days. I beg you to consider me a man of my word and one who will never fail you. The rest of my reply, I shall give you in person.' The next, which may well have been sent to Perth while James was winding up his dead mother's affairs, is even more worrying as, after sarcastically thanking her for the letter 'which it has pleased you to write to me', James goes on to say that:

...those who have told you that I mean to go away have falsely lied, because I have no other thought but of being with you on Sunday. As for my mother's things, I will not forget, begging you not to be so thundering until you know the truth. Praying you to be of good cheer until my return, which will be on Sunday, and praying Our Lord to give you a good and long life.

It's impossible to say now what had upset Marie so much that she wrote to her husband to berate him, but it's clear that someone had been mischievously causing trouble between the couple, perhaps telling Marie that her husband was away with other women.

Rumours of some dissent between the couple even seem to have reached France because Duchesse Antoinette wrote to her daughter in November to say that she was relieved to hear from Mademoiselle de Curel, one of Marie's ladies in waiting who had recently returned from Scotland, that both Marie and her husband were in good health and that 'all is going better with you than we thought'. She went on to explain that she and her husband had been worried about their daughter because of disquieting rumours and that Duc Claude had been on the brink of travelling to Scotland himself to make sure all was well with her; a great sacrifice considering the fact that he was an exceedingly poor sailor. Of course Antoinette could have been referring to Marie's health, which had been unusually but understandably poor since the death of the princes that spring, but it is more likely that the gossips of French court had been whispering that the handsome young King and Queen of Scotland were experiencing some marital issues.

For the time being though, whatever Mademoiselle de Curel had to say about the couple seems to have reassured Antoinette and she was even able to imbue a cheerful note into the correspondence, asking Marie to pass on her thanks to James for the gift of a fine diamond, which she would 'treasure always for his sake' and teasing that the accompanying portrait sent with it had made her long to see him again for he was 'in truth such a handsome prince'. He was so good looking, she joked, that she herself might make her daughter jealous by falling in love with him.

As always there was a reassuring update about the health of the little Duc François, now 6 years old and, according to his doting grandmother, 'the best of children, big and healthy and should live to be a joy to his mother'. She apologised to Marie in November for not being able to find an artist to paint his portrait so she could see for herself how handsome he was, but it must have been enough for her to know that he, alone of all her children, was alive and well, albeit far away in France. It was at around this time that he started to send her his own letters, a bittersweet pleasure one imagines for his mother, who treasured each one alongside the final letter of his father, which remained amongst her personal papers until her death. In one, a barely legible scrawl typical of a child, he chides his mother for not writing enough and making him sad, before informing her that his grandfather has given him a horn to take hunting while his grandmother brings him black bread and cordial when he is in bed at night. In another, he tells her about a impromptu picnic in the gardens of Joinville, where he picked strawberries for his grandfather, whose pet, he assures her, he is.

Although outwardly cheerful and full of requests for horses and sweet anecdotes about family life at Joinville, where he is the doted-upon-pet of his grandparents and aunts and uncles, the letters still make for sad reading, redolent as they are of his longing to be reunited with his mother. In one he informs her that he has no desire to go to Scotland but very much wants to see Marie, while in another he tells her that when he is big enough, he will pay her a visit. Of James, the step father whom he had never met and who had effectively taken his mother away from him, he has very little to say other than a few polite courtesies.

Despite all of this, the couple were well aware of their duty so were delighted and relieved when they discovered, in the spring of 1542, that Marie was expecting another child. The Guise family were perhaps the most thrilled of all by the news, reassured that Marie's marriage had recovered from its earlier difficulties and that her position as Queen of Scotland was not in any imminent danger. The recent sad fates of Henry VIII's wives had served as a stark reminder of what could happen to women who did not fulfil their primary obligation of providing an heir and, although James was at loggerheads with his uncle, there were enough similarities between the two men to fill Marie's family with foreboding about how he would react should she provoke his displeasure in some way.

The pregnancy seems to have been an unusually difficult one, as evidenced by the large sum of £20 being paid to Marie's surgeon, Anthony Bassett, in July for 'his labours done by him to the Queen's Grace'. Perhaps this was the first hint that this baby was not going to be another boy. She seems to have sailed through her other pregnancies in excellent health, whereas this latest one provoked enough concern for Marie to go on more than one pilgrimage; to Peebles in July and then Musselburgh, and also to write up a memorandum of pilgrimages and offerings that should be made by her mother in the event of her death. It may also be that the terrible events of the previous year had left Marie feeling downhearted, pessimistic and frightened for the future as well as worried that disaster might strike again. Certainly her husband had become convinced that he was in some way cursed – an unhelpful attitude that may have transferred itself to his pregnant wife, leaving her feeling anxious and afraid.

The ever-increasing tensions between James and his uncle only served to make matters worse as the diplomatic relationship between them broke down to the extent that war began to look worryingly inevitable. James's very public snub of Henry the previous autumn and the death shortly afterwards of his mother, the one living link between them, had hastened the decline and caused Henry's antipathy towards his nephew to blossom into full-on loathing. His hatred was no doubt exacerbated by the personal humiliation he felt after the revelations about Catherine Howard's infidelity, which had resulted in her execution in February 1542. In short, Henry was in no mood to be trifled with by the younger members of his family and took a very dim view of his nephew's reluctance to toe the line. In an attempt to assert his authority, he made secret enquiries about the existence of documents which would prove that the Kings of England had overlordship of those of Scotland and required them to do homage in

113

exchange for their lands. This turned out to be a fruitless quest, but Henry's belief that James held Scotland at his sufferance did not entirely abate and influenced his future dealings with his nephew.

The state papers make for sobering reading as tit-for-tat discussions about border raids, skirmishes and prisoners taken by both sides gradually become increasingly acrimonious. In late September, Henry confided in the Imperial ambassador Chapuys that he did not believe there was much risk of outright war breaking out with Scotland and he was still hopeful that his nephew would come down to London before the end of the year to discuss their issues. What he didn't tell the ambassador is that he was considering having James kidnapped and taken to England by force if he did not come of his own free will. For his part, James appeared willing enough to meet with his uncle, but asked that the meeting be delayed until after Marie had given birth.

Marie was kept up-to-date with the situation by her husband and Cardinal Beaton and felt deeply anxious about the ever-growing threat from across the border. King François had offered to assist them in any way he could, but he and his troops were hundreds of miles away and would never get there in time if Henry decided to invade. She also had more personal troubles to contend with when the news arrived of the death of her sister, Louise, Princesse de Chimay, on 18 October, after just over eighteen months of marriage. This, the first loss of an adult sibling (two younger brothers had died in infancy) was a terrible blow to Marie and she immediately ordered that the entire court should show respect by going into mourning, adding a sombre note to the already careworn and cheerless Scottish court. In addition, her husband was preparing to mount a raid across the English border in retaliation for one that he had managed to defeat at Kelso. He was forced to cancel his plans, however, because many of his lords were less than keen to take arms against the English though, almost certainly because a number of them were in receipt of pensions from Henry VIII. James's inability to retaliate was yet another blow to his fragile confidence and made him even more mistrustful than ever.

At the start of November, Henry's plans for an invasion of Scotland gathered pace as he mustered men and gave orders to his Warden of the North, the Duke of Norfolk, who had been tasked with repulsing Scottish border raids. In his declaration of war, which claimed to contain 'the just causes and considerations of this present war with the Scots and also the true and right title that the King's most royal majesty has to the sovereignty of Scotland', Henry sets forth the argument that his hand had been forced by his nephew who had provoked hostilities despite his own gentle treatment and protection of him while at the same time asserting his own overlordship of the lands north of the border. According to the accompanying consultation, Henry intended to take 18,000 foot soldiers and 6,000 cavalry across the border and as far as Fife in order to claim territory, establish garrisons and while

> the possessors of these counties are to be allured by privy practices and open proclamation, and by the terror of the preparations now to be made at Berwick, to yield to the King as their sovereign. However if the King, out of pity for his nephew, will satisfy himself ... to chastise the Scots and force them to convenient conditions of peace, the great provisions are not needed, but only garrisons required.

Understandably antagonised by his uncle's high handed declarations, offended by his egregious assertions that his nephew had only himself to blame for his current predicament and worried about the threat of invasion, James decided to ignore his concerns about the loyalty of his lords and take the initiative. On 21 November he marched from Edinburgh to the border, where he intended to cross the Solway Firth and lead his forces into England on a surprise raid in an area where he knew that English troops would be easily outnumbered by his own army of 17,000 men, led by Lord Maxwell and Sir Oliver Sinclair. Unfortunately, his surprise was ruined when word of the approaching Scottish army reached Carlisle and Sir Thomas Wharton immediately mustered 3,000 men to meet the threat. The two armies clashed on a miserable bog known as Solway Moss and despite their superior size, the Scots found themselves completely routed.

James himself did not take part in the rout, probably mindful of the fate of his father at Flodden and the pleas of Marie that he should not risk his life when the succession wasn't completely assured. Instead he watched from a nearby hill as his beleaguered troops were perilously trapped between a bog and the River Esk before surrendering to the English in order to save themselves. Lord Maxwell and Oliver Sinclair were among the twenty-three high ranking nobles who gave themselves up and were taken as hostages to London, where Henry VIII intended to put them to good use in his policy of extracting obedience from his nephew, who had retreated to Edinburgh to lick his wounds and consider his next move.

The defeat at Solway Moss was humiliating but certainly not a disaster on a par with Flodden in 1513. Nonetheless, James felt the defeat and subsequent capture of some of his closest associates most keenly, and inevitably fell into a deep depression, blaming everyone but himself for this latest. As Christmas was approaching, he was eventually persuaded to leave Edinburgh and travel north to Falkland Castle where his remaining friends hoped the usual revelries of the season would cheer him out of his torpor of self-pity.

Marie had been safely installed at Linlithgow Palace, which had been formally returned to James's hands after the death of his mother, throughout autumn and intended to have her child there as she was already close to term and the wintry weather conditions prohibited movement elsewhere. She had been kept informed about her husband's plans to lead a raid into England, the disaster of Solway Moss and his subsequent unhappiness and must have been apprehensive when his heralds arrived to inform her that he intended to pay her a visit on his way to Falkland.

Marie was shocked by James's appearance; usually so handsome and careful about his dress, he arrived unshaven, raw eyed and raddled with misery and exhaustion. Distraught, he ranted at length about crushing his enemies, amongst whom he counted not just his uncle and the English, but also his own lords, whom he suspected of turning against him. Marie tried in vain to console him, but his misery was absolute.

By the time James arrived at Falkland Palace on 6 December, his ranting had become almost incoherent. He was feverish, vomiting and delirious and it soon became obvious that he had contracted typhoid, or possibly even cholera, during his time with the troops and that in his miserable mental state he might not be able to combat it. A messenger was sent through the snow to Linlithgow to inform Marie of her husband's illness but she was unable to go to him because her labour began just a few hours later, possibly prematurely, a dangerous scenario for both mother and child at this time. It is not known for certain where the Queen's apartments at Linlithgow Palace were located, but it's likely that they were either in the now-vanished north range, which collapsed in 1607, or rooms on the second floor above those we know were inhabited by the King in the nort-west corner of the palace. Either way, Marie would have been surrounded by luxury as she laboured in the very same room where her husband had been born thirty years earlier.

As usual, no men were admitted to the Queen's chamber while she was in labour and the women would have moved silently around the room, perhaps removing their shoes so that no untoward sounds interrupted the all-important business of birthing a new heir to the Scottish throne. It was common to use holy relics to assuage the suffering of labouring women and it's likely that Marie had several to choose from, either from her husband's collection or sent to her from France. The relics would have been placed beneath her pillow or pressed into her hands by her ladies when the pains became overwhelming although, as this was Marie's fifth baby, it's likely that the labour was mercifully swift.

The sad events of the previous year, devastating events at Solway Moss, the threat of English invasion and the pitiful state of the King, who was now known to be desperately ill, gave Marie's fifth labour a great deal of extra significance. A male would naturally be the preference and as Marie had already given birth to four boys (and James had fathered at least eight in his time) there may well have been an expectation that she would produce one more. Unfortunately for anyone who had wagered good money on this outcome to what had become a national predicament, the baby who came howling and bewildered into the world on 7 December 1542 was not the longed-for boy, but a girl.

As Marie hugged her first daughter close to her breast and watched her ladies prepare her caudle, a warm drink of beer or wine mixed with sugar, spices and eggs, which was traditionally shared by new mothers and their helpers immediately after childbirth, she must have wondered what fate had in store for them both. The bulletins from Falkland Palace were not promising and should the King not recover from his illness then this small scrap, who may well have been born before her time, was all that stood between Scotland and civil war. It was a terrifying thought and as Marie and her ladies bent their heads to pray for the new soul that had come amongst them, she must also have added a silent prayer for her husband and his continued survival.

Sadly, her prayers were not to be answered. James's illness continued to give grave concern to his physicians and companions, although he seems to have been coherent enough to receive the news that his wife had given birth to a healthy daughter. It's not likely that, in his weakened and barely lucid state, James uttered the famous words, 'It came with a lass and it will go with a lass,' referring to the fact that the Stewart dynasty had seized the throne thanks to Marjorie Bruce, but he might as well have done because the news from Linlithgow certainly didn't bring joy to the dying King.

James V died just before midnight on 14 December in his chamber at Falkland Palace. He briefly returned to lucidity just before passing away and managed to smile and kiss his hand to his companions before closing his eyes and breathing his last. Another messenger was dispatched through the snow to Linlithgow Palace where Marie was still closeted in her rooms, recovering from childbirth. Marie was once again a widow and, furthermore, her 6-day-old daughter was now Queen of Scotland with all the attendant troubles that the title brought with it.

Chapter 10

The Little Queen

The unexpected death of James V and infancy of his heir made the disaster at Solway Moss pale into insignificance as his widowed Queen, Cardinal Beaton and the court came to terms with what looked set to be a very uncertain and unstable future. Already those with long memories were harkening back to the dark days when James V had succeeded his father at the age of 17 months old, and the long period of conflict and instability that had followed as the lords battled over who would control the young King and his domains. Although Queen Margaret had initially managed to exert some control over her son as his Regent, her position was dependent on her remaining a widow. By marrying the deeply unpopular Earl of Angus she had lost custody of her young sons and alienated much of the nobility, forcing her to flee temporarily back to England.

Marie, however, was made of very different stuff to her erstwhile mother-in-law and, furthermore, had the benefit of wise council from her family and a strong will, both of which Margaret had lacked. Although she might have been romantic, as many young people are, in her youth at the French court, Marie had long since adopted a much more pragmatic and considered approach to life and was unlikely to let her heart rule her head, especially not when it came to the important matter of asserting her daughter's rights. She had been very fond of her mother-in-law when she was alive but was not likely to follow the same destructive path.

At the age of just 27, it was quite possible that Marie might want to marry again one day but for now, all of her considerable energy and talent were focussed on her daughter to the exclusion of everything else. The child was baptised Mary in the church of St Michael at Linlithgow, carried there by her faithful nurse, Janet Sinclair while her mother remained behind in her chambers. After she had been anointed, the baby Queen was wrapped in fine white taffeta then confirmed at the high altar, as was the usual practice with royal infants, before being taken back to her mother.

Henry VIII had been kept belatedly informed about events in Scotland and had been delighted to hear that the new Queen was apparently 'a very weak child' and therefore evidently considered highly unlikely to survive. However, Lord Lisle in a letter to Henry notes that the baby Mary was said to be 'alive and good looking' before adding that he wished that 'she and her nurse were in my lord Prince's house'. Meanwhile, Chapuys confided in his correspondent, the Queen of Hungary, that 'news had come that the king of Scotland, soon after learning the defeat of his men, from grief, regret, and rage, fell ill and died within a few days, and his daughter and the Queen, his wife, were also very ill and despaired of by the physicians.' He added that the Scottish prisoners currently housed in the Tower of London had been brought to court, where they were gently treated but would be

> *expected to do some good office for the King; and will have the better opportunity if (as some pretend) the Daughter, who was born much before her time, still lives; for, on pretext of marrying her to the Prince here, they could put that realm into the King's hands by suborning some of the four governors whom the King of Scotland is said to have left her.*

For the infant Queen of Scots to marry the heir to the English throne would be a very tidy solution to the messy relationship that had existed between the two neighbouring nations for several centuries with the additional benefit of drawing Scotland away from the influence of both the Papacy and the French. To this end, Henry invited his noble Scottish hostages to enjoy some of the sumptuous Christmas festivities at Hampton Court Palace, before beguiling them with promises of future wealth and influence, to agree to the terms of the secret article he had drawn up regarding his plans for Scotland and its Queen. They were informed that they were free to return home to Scotland if they agreed to do everything in their power to promote and support a match between Queen Mary and the Prince of Wales, uniting the nations of Scotland and England. Furthermore, they would do their best to deliver Mary into Henry's hands to be raised at the English court and if she should die prematurely then they would support Henry's claim to seize Scotland for himself.

Meanwhile, at Falkland Palace, James V's body lay in state in the chapel royal before being solemnly transferred to Holyrood Abbey for an ostentatious state burial on Monday, 8 January. An effigy of the dead King, dressed in full royal regalia and robes, was paraded through the streets with his coffin so that the populace could mourn his passing before he was interred beside his beloved Madeleine and his two dead sons in an elaborate tomb surmounted by a carved and gilded lion. Although James had spent his adult life battling with the emotional scars left by his disordered and difficult childhood, he had been a popular King, appreciated for his good looks, generosity and innovative vision both for the Scottish crown and the people it governed. Despite the odds being stacked against him, he had proved to be a fair and enlightened politician and ruler who governed his people with honesty and consideration. He had also shown himself to be a gifted administrator who, despite inheriting coffers parlously denuded by his father's artistic and martial ambitions, and then following a rather lavish lifestyle himself, still managed to leave behind a rather handsome fortune – a feat that his two nearest peers, Henry VIII and François I, were both unable to emulate, despite the fact that both had incomes and resources considerably larger than his. History has not been kind to James V, but certainly as far as his widow was concerned – although he had not been an entirely satisfactory husband on a personal level, his skills as a monarch and a statesman would be sadly missed.

Chaotic and short lived though her brief period of regency had been, Margaret Tudor had enjoyed one very important advantage over

Marie de Guise in that her husband had left behind a signed will and testament that clearly stated his intention that she should act as Regent in the event of his death during their son's minority. Unfortunately, James had left behind no such instructions and as it was widely believed that even if he had, he had had no intention of leaving power in the hands of his Queen, it looked certain that Lord Arran, who was next in line to the throne, would be asked to act as Regent during her daughter's minority. There was also a vague plan of betrothing the little Queen of Scotland to Arran's eldest son, thus neutralising the threat of her being whisked away to England.

Whatever her private feelings may have been, Marie seemed to react meekly enough to the decisions that were being made about her daughter's future but Cardinal Beaton, who had been her husband's closest advisor, was furious about the elevation of Arran because questions surrounding the validity of his parents' marriage meant his legitimacy did not stand up to scrutiny. He claimed that he had in his possession a genuine will and testament of the dead King, which had been signed in his presence and named the Lords of Moray, Argyll and Huntly as well as Beaton himself as James's own choice to assume the reins of power until Mary was old enough to govern for herself. Arran was naturally furious about this challenge and had to be prevented from drawing his sword upon the Cardinal when the will was presented at a council meeting. The fact that Marie was in favour of Beaton's claim, knowing him to be favourable to a continuation of the French alliance whereas Arran's allegiances were rather more fluid and debatable, was another blow to the ambitious Earl, who was determined to seize power. Nonetheless, it was Arran who won this particular war when he was officially made Regent of Scotland in January 1543, with the disappointed Cardinal Beaton being offered the consolation prize of Chancellor.

During all this, Marie remained at Linlithgow with her new baby and her household, which had swelled considerably since the death of her husband. James's considerable household was disbanded and his servants immediately petitioned his widow, who paid generous wages and was known to be a good mistress to her staff, to hire them instead.

Royal protocol had dictated that she was not present at her husband's funeral so she mourned him privately at Linlithgow, ordering several yards of black cloth to make mourning clothes for herself and her household.

Despite being denied the role of Regent, Marie did at least have the consolation that her daughter had been left in her care. For now at least. Her unenviable position as a foreigner, new widow and mother of a newborn baby made her pitiable even to English eyes, with even Lord Lisle being moved to pity by her plight and suggesting to his master, Henry, that it would be ungallant indeed to attack her at such a time. Arran, however, thirsty for power and jealous of the one advantage that she held over him – possession of the actual Queen herself, was quick to capitalise upon her apparently helpless and isolated position. He placed spies in her household and intercepted her correspondence with her anxious family in France, leaving both sides in the dark about how affairs were progressing – an especially cruel strategy when rumours were floating around Europe that Marie and her daughter had both died too.

Nonetheless, a letter from her uncle, Cardinal Lorraine, managed to get past Arran's clutches and Marie must have been reassured to hear that he was 'grieved, with all her kinsmen and friends, at what has befallen her and her kingdom'. Even more pleasing was his assertion that 'the King is very sorry and determined to help her as far as possible, for she is as much beloved as princess ever was.'

To Marie, isolated and feeling very alone in her black-hung rooms at Linlithgow, this timely reminder that she had not been forgotten in France must have been a relief. She would have been even more pleased had she known that her father was so concerned about events in Scotland that he was preparing to come to her assistance – an alarming prospect for both Henry VIII and Arran, as Guise was not a man to be trifled with and there was a real danger that he might decide to take his daughter and the little Queen back to France with him.

Alarmed by the threat of French interference, Henry dispatched George Douglas, the brother of Lord Angus who had been exiled with him to England by James V, back to Scotland to negotiate with Arran, hoping that the prospect of the Duc de Guise's arrival to save the day might make him amenable to throwing his lot in with the English instead. Douglas was instructed to press home the benefits of a match between Queen Mary and the Prince of Wales and do his best to persuade Arran that the little Queen would be better off in England. Arran was unexpectedly amenable enough to the idea of marrying Mary off to Prince Edward, but he turned out to be resistant to the prospect of sending her south of the border, not least because he did not have possession of her person. She remained at Linlithgow with her mother.

Although Arran did his best to isolate Marie from events at court and his negotiations with Henry VIII, he was not entirely successful and she still managed to keep herself up-to-date with matters. She had fully recovered from childbirth and all her old energy had returned, which meant that she felt able to put up a fight if matters came to it. For now, however, she decided to keep her head down and play her cards close to her chest, determined not to lose another child to the ambitions of others and well aware that the stakes in this particular game were high. Although she maintained a façade of smiling composure when dealing with Arran, whom she considered a vainglorious, conceited and stupid man, she was at the same time conducting secret meetings with his arch rival, Cardinal Beaton, who was still committed to upholding the Scottish alliance with France and was against the projected English marriage for the baby Queen. Unfortunately, Beaton had been as dismayed as anyone that James V's heir was a girl, and had made no secret of his support for another rival claimant, the Earl of Lennox, who was still living at the court of King François. Marie decided to overlook this issue because, at that time, he was the best chance she had of keeping her daughter out of the clutches of Henry VIII.

Aware that any public protest to the English alliance would bring all manner of trouble down upon her head and possibly even precipitate the removal of her daughter, Marie decided to play for time by pretending to regard the scheme with great favour. It must have been a struggle not to react with horror to suggestions that, due to the extreme youth of her baby daughter, it might be a good idea for the alliance to be immediately cemented with a match between herself and Henry VIII. Little did anyone know that behind her usual smiling complaisance, Marie and Cardinal Beaton had joined forces to write to the Earl of Lennox in France, offering him both the Governorship of Scotland and also Marie's hand in marriage if he would agree to return to Scotland and mount a coup to oust Arran from power. While they were waiting for Lennox's response to this offer, Marie travelled to Edinburgh to take up residence in Holyroodhouse Palace, leaving her daughter behind at Linlithgow. She had caught wind of Sir George Douglas's attempts to sway Arran to the English cause and decided that it might benefit her more if she was on the spot and able to keep a close eye on matters. However, as she had no official position on the council, she was not able to keep as close an eye on Arran and his cronies as she would have liked and was unable to intervene when one of the council meetings was interrupted by the arrest of Cardinal Beaton on the orders of Lord Arran.

Alarmed by this, and terrified that Beaton had been spirited away to England, Marie immediately returned to Linlithgow, only to find herself more isolated than ever. Arran, deeply suspicious of her motivation and determined to find some grounds to wrest her daughter away from her, stepped up his campaign to cut her off from the support of her family and neutralise the small amount of power that she had remaining to her. The fine stone walls of Linlithgow Palace began to feel like a prison and the more Marie started to feel she was being held captive by Arran, the more aware she became that Linlithgow was not equipped to keep her enemies out and that she and her daughter were in a vulnerable position while they remained there.

She was alarmed to hear that certain noblemen, including the reckless and untrustworthy Lord Bothwell, had been threatening to take the initiative and kidnap the baby Queen before delivering her to England themselves. Worse still was the ever-present suspicion that Arran might have her daughter murdered in order to seize the crown for himself. After all, as she knew only too well, infants died all the time, and with rumours flying all over Europe that her daughter was ailing, no one would bat an eyelash should she suddenly be stricken by a fatal 'illness'.

Stirling Castle, majestic and impenetrable on its volcanic rock, was the obvious choice for a new residence and had the bonus of being, along with Falkland Palace, one of Marie's dower lands provided for her accommodation in the event of her husband's death and therefore not falling, like Holyroodhouse and Edinburgh Castle, into the clutches of Arran. Although Arran was initially happy for Marie to move her household to Stirling, he was persuaded by the Douglas brothers (Lord Angus, James V's hated former step father had now returned to Scotland as well) that no good could come of this, so he ordered her to remain at Linlithgow, making her feel even more of a prisoner than ever. The news that her father was said to be preparing an enormous army to take control of Scotland and his granddaughter, its Queen, caused widespread panic in Edinburgh and elsewhere. Although Marie protested that she knew nothing about her family's plans because her mail was clearly being intercepted, she still found herself being held in increasingly close confinement with all her movements closely monitored.

One small consolation were the letters of an anonymous correspondent who secretly wrote to keep her informed about events in Edinburgh using a curious phonetic spelling that suggests that they were French, and possibly in the pay of her family. In one such missive, they apologised for their terrible handwriting before saying that Marie 'ought to have very secret intelligence of your enemies' intentions for ... what can they say of Scotsmen but that they are false and greedy.' In particular, the mysterious letter writer warns Marie to beware of Lord Huntly, whom she believed to be on her side, and Lord Bothwell, whom she already knew to be unpredictable and untrustworthy. The letter writer offers to show her what they have been secretly discussing with England before begging her to destroy his letter 'and all the writings that I intend to send, otherwise I can do you no good.'

It was in her apartments at Linlithgow that Marie received Sir Ralph Sadler once again after he was sent up to Scotland to ascertain precisely what was happening and settle the fate of the Scottish Queen once and for all. Sir Ralph had endured various unsatisfactory interviews with Arran and other Scottish lords before travelling out to Linlithgow to meet with Marie de Guise, whom he had met once before, shortly after her coronation. Not believing that the Dowager Queen could be as much in favour of the English alliance as she professed to be, and warned by Arran that she was duplicitous, not to be trusted and at all times loyal to France and its interests, Sadler was surprised to find himself taken in by her protestations of delight that her daughter was to be married to the Prince of Wales. She had, she told him, come to Scotland with the sole intention of doing as much good as possible to her adopted nation and she was proud to have given birth to the Princess who would bring an end to so many centuries of warfare and bloodshed. She told the admiring Sadler that 'she thought it God's work for the union of these realms that, where before she has had none but sons, it is now her chance to bring forth a daughter.'

Dressed in a black velvet gown that accentuated her pale complexion and auburn hair, Marie completely captivated Sadler during the hours they spent together; beguiling him not just with her good looks and charm, but also her keen intelligence. The golden age of European Queens had not yet arrived and, thanks to the disastrous regency of Margaret Tudor and recent scandals involving Henry VIII's wives, there was no respect in the 1540s, amongst Englishmen at least, for women's ability to rule and govern. Despite Sadler appreciating Marie's wit and erudition, it is unlikely that he saw her as a viable contender in the struggle for power. Not yet anyway. Cleverly, Marie herself made no attempt to promote her own claim to take power, but concentrated her efforts instead on undermining Arran, gently suggesting to Sadler that the Earl was untrustworthy, greedy and concerned only for himself and his own interests. After all, she said, it was well known in Scotland that Arran was determined to marry her daughter – if she survived – to his own son and was stringing the English along in the hope they would either deliver Mary into his own hands, or else that Henry would die before the match was completed.

The rumours about Queen Mary's poor health and unlikeliness to survive must have started somewhere, Marie reminded Sadler, and where else could they have begun but with Arran, the man who stood to benefit most from the death of the infant Queen of Scotland? Sadler couldn't deny that Arran had told him that the baby was puny and ailing, so Marie insisted upon taking him to her daughter's nursery, where the child was stripped and displayed to him so that he could see for himself what a fine and healthy specimen she was. 'It is as goodly a child as I have seen of her age, and as like to live, with the grace of God,' Sadler reported back to his master Henry. Clearly very different to the pathetic little scrap described by Arran, whom he now began to suspect of sinister motives towards the little Queen. Sadler began to feel sympathetic towards Marie, who seemed so candid and honest in her dealings with him and who, even Henry agreed, appeared to be entirely 'frank' and trustworthy.

Perhaps he would have felt differently had he known that the pretty and charming Marie was skilfully working behind the scenes to draw her supporters together to engineer the release of Cardinal Beaton, while all the time waiting for news that the Earl of Lennox, who had been ordered by King François to go to Scotland in the place of the Duc de Guise, had landed safely on Scottish soil. Arran had denied all knowledge of any plans to marry his own son to Queen Mary, and angrily informed Sadler that Marie was determined to sow discord between him and King Henry, stating that she was 'both subtle and wily, so she hath a vengeful mind and wit to work her purpose.' His assessment of her character seemed to be justified when news arrived not long afterwards that Lennox had landed at Dumbarton with a small army, and was making no secret of his intention of liberating Marie and seizing control of power. That she had masterminded some sort of coup was further suggested when Cardinal Beaton was liberated a few days later, thanks to the connivance of two of her known supporters, Lord Seton and Lord Huntly.

The arrival of Lennox, Arran's most hated rival and a man devoted to the continuation of the French alliance with Scotland, was a stroke of good fortune for Marie, who was beginning to feel increasingly beleaguered and anxious about the future. He was still young and not bad looking, and once she had turned the full beam of her charm upon him during their first meeting at Linlithgow, he was like putty in her hands. He determined to do whatever it took to end the control that Arran exerted over Marie and her daughter.

It didn't take him long to openly clash with Arran when they met in Edinburgh with the unfortunate result that Arran, whose already lukewarm enthusiasm for the English alliance was swiftly beginning to wane in the face of Henry VIII's incessant demands and determination to meddle, felt increasingly pushed towards the English as a result of Lennox's support for an alliance with the French. He was also suspicious of Lennox's intentions with regard to the infant Queen, and Sadler reported to Henry that Arran was hoping to seize Mary and transfer her to Edinburgh Castle before Lennox and Beaton could join forces and get hold of her first. The plan would fail to come to fruition to the great relief of Marie who, at this point, was in daily expectation of being separated against her will from her daughter.

On 1 July, the two Treaties of Greenwich were completed. Their terms agreed that there should be a peace between England and Scotland for the lifetimes of Henry VIII and his great niece Queen Mary and that, once the little Queen reached the age of 11, she would take up residence in England and marry the Prince of Wales thus uniting the two nations. If the marriage turned out to be childless, then she would be free to return home to Scotland, which would remain independent and governed by Lord Arran in her stead. The treaties were a triumph for Arran, whose authority was being upheld by King Henry, and Marie, who saw it as riddled with loop holes and easy to ignore, but were much less popular elsewhere once word got out because no one believed that Henry would allow Scotland to function independently once he had his hands on its Queen. The Scottish were never overly fond of their English neighbours at the best of times, but now anti-English sentiment became rife and even poor Ralph Sadler found himself being attacked on the streets of Edinburgh; the populace were emboldened by reports that the Earl of Lennox and Cardinal Beaton were said to be gathering troops together. While inside Edinburgh Castle, Arran was dismayed to receive the intelligence that a French fleet had supposedly been spotted off the Scottish coast.

Terrified that all of this movement presaged some sort of coup with the aim of whisking Marie de Guise and her daughter away to the safety of France, Arran quickly mobilised his men and marched to Linlithgow, where he surrounded the palace with enough manpower and artillery to see off an attack. Trapped inside, Marie wrote to Cardinal Beaton, Lennox and their coterie who had gathered at Stirling to plan their next move. The news that Arran had effectively imprisoned the Dowager Queen and her daughter was all the incentive they needed to finally show their hand. Their planned assault on Linlithgow went sadly awry when, thanks to a lack of artillery, they were forced to withdraw to the nearby countryside to consider their position while Marie remained trapped inside the palace. Luckily for Lennox and Beaton, Arran had no wish to force the issue with a battle, and the stand off ended peaceably enough with a series of meeting between envoys of both sides where they hammered out an agreement that Arran should rule with a council or else be made to resign; that the hated Douglas brothers should be made to leave Scotland again, and that the little Queen should be allowed to move to Stirling Castle where she would have four Scottish custodians appointed for her welfare.

For Marie, the most immediate benefit of all this wrangling was that the defence of Linlithgow was immediately lifted and she was free to travel to Stirling. The appointment of Lords Livingston, Erskine, Graham and Lindsay as custodians of her daughter was irksome, but with her increased confidence, she felt sure that she would able to handle them as successfully as she had manipulated Sadler, Lennox and others to do her bidding. By nature open and honest, Marie was not a naturally duplicitous woman, but she had lived at the French and Scottish courts for long enough to learn when to keep her mouth shut, when to smile, when to remain impassive, when to dissemble and when to tell the truth. Distasteful though it may have been to hide her true thoughts, she smiled at men she hated and lied when necessary; there was nothing she would not have done to secure her daughter's future. The terms of her marriage contract had stipulated that she should be able to return to France in the event of her husband's death, but although she must have longed for the familiar landscape and faces of home, there was never any doubt in Marie's mind that she would remain in Scotland for as long as she was needed there.

On 26 July, Marie and her daughter left Linlithgow Palace and made the short journey to Stirling Castle, escorted by the entirely besotted Earl of Lennox, who still believed that Marie would marry him once her mourning was at an end. Marie had been quietly dispatching her furnishings and goods to Stirling for quite a few months, optimistically preparing it for the day that she was finally liberated from her enforced residence at Linlithgow. As we have seen, it was the usual practice to take everything that might be required when the royal court moved from one residence to another, so the fact that Marie travelled with her great bed, entire wardrobe and contents of the royal larder and kitchens would have raised very few eyebrows as the procession made its way to Stirling. Nonetheless, as far as Marie was concerned, this was not so much a royal progress as a permanent withdrawal. She knew that as soon as she and her daughter were safely sequestered behind Stirling's formidable walls, there was no power on earth that could force them to leave again, and there was certainly no way that Henry or Arran could contrive to separate her from her daughter. Stirling was her very own castle, and within the safety of its walls she was determined that from that point forward, she would be mistress of her own fate.

Chapter 11

The Rough Wooing

Marie's baby daughter was crowned Queen of Scotland in the chapel royal of Stirling Castle on 9 September 1543 when she was just 9 months old. Although protocol had excluded her mother from attending her baptism and James's funeral, and the ambitions of others had attempted to marginalise her influence over her daughter's future, Marie de Guise had no intention of hiding in the shadows for this, one of the most triumphant moments of her life as she proudly carried her daughter, dressed in miniature robes of state trimmed with gold thread and ermine, into the chapel where Cardinal Beaton was waiting to conduct the ceremony.

It was the thirtieth anniversary of the Battle of Flodden and the death of Queen Mary's grandfather, James IV, who had been slaughtered, possibly by his own men, while facing the forces of his brother-in-law, Henry VIII. Perhaps an inauspicious date on which to crown a new Scottish ruler, but the echoes of Flodden could still be felt in Scotland and there were many men present who had been there on that fatal day and seen first hand what bloody horrors the English could wreak upon their land.

The coronation was a grand affair, even though the English spies informed Henry that it was a cheap and tawdry ceremony, devoid of the majestic splendour that attended the crowning of English Kings. The magnificent Scottish crown jewels, the 'honours of Scotland', which had been commissioned over the years by Mary's father and grandfather, were brought to Stirling to be used together for the first time. The ornate crown made for James V was obviously too large and heavy for Mary's infant head and so was held over her by Cardinal

Beaton before he anointed her with holy oil, much to her indignation for she began to scream the place down. United for once, Lord Arran and Lord Lennox took part in the solemn procession into the chapel, carrying the sword and sceptre respectively while Arran's brother-in-law, the Earl of Argyll, carried the bejewelled sword of state. After months of prevarication, Arran had finally realised that he was beaten. He had reconciled with Marie and Cardinal Beaton, repudiating the moves towards Protestantism he had implemented in Scotland in order to placate Henry, and even snubbed an offer to betroth the Lady Elizabeth, Henry's daughter by Anne Boleyn, to his eldest son.

Sitting at the high table in the enormous great hall of Stirling Castle, surveying the company eating, drinking and merry-making before her, Marie must have been satisfied to have come so far in such a short period of time. She had started the year newly widowed, the mother of a newborn baby, marginalised, isolated, ignored and disregarded. Now here she was, presiding over her daughter's coronation feast and slowly but surely coming into her own as a person of considerable influence and power. There was still a long way to go; she knew that the current harmony between the argumentative Scottish factions was transitory and unlikely to last for long but for now, at least, she could enjoy the fruits of her labours and look back on a job well done.

Shortly after her arrival at Stirling she had summoned Ralph Sadler to her presence, allegedly so that she could reassure him of her continued goodwill towards King Henry and his plans for her daughter, but really so that he could appreciate her new confident position as chatelaine of an impregnable castle. Once again Sadler was held spellbound as Marie spun her web of lies, telling him that:

she thought nothing could be more honourable for her and her daughter than this marriage, and she had good hope it would take effect, both for the above cause and for that Henry had so wisely provided to have good pledges for her daughter's delivery into England at ten years; and she would, in the mean season, look to her daughter's surety, that she might be "in good plight" to be then delivered.

After a discussion about the likelihood of insurrection against the articles of the yet-to-be-ratified Treaties of Greenwich, she changed the subject and began to extol the superior quality of the air at Stirling, which she believed was much better for her daughter's health, adding that Mary looked set to take after her mother and be of above average height. She then whisked Sadler off to the luxurious royal nursery to see the little Queen, whom he described in his dispatches as 'right fair and goodly for her age'.

However, although Marie appeared to acquiescence to plans to marry her daughter to the Prince of Wales, it's clear that she was simply playing for time and hoping that another, better option would come along before the English lost patience and forced the issue. Naturally, her first choice was always going to be a match with France but there were no available French princes of a suitable age available because the marriage of her old friend, Henri (who had become Dauphin after the death of his elder brother in 1536, and his Italian wife Catherine de' Medici), had so far failed to produce any children. There were plenty of other candidates amongst Marie's noble French relatives, but no one sufficiently grand enough to marry a girl who was already Queen of Scotland in her own right. The best policy, therefore, was to string King Henry along while hoping that the bizarre fertility aids being used by the French Dauphine would one day have a happy result.

In the meantime, secure behind the high walls of Stirling Castle, with her daughter's right to rule unquestionably upheld by her coronation, Marie decided to make the most of the unusually harmonious atmosphere at court and enjoy herself. One chronicler described that autumn's revelries at Stirling Castle as 'like Venus and Cupid in the time of fresh May, for there was such dancing, singing, playing and merriness ... that no man would have tired therein.' The state apartments commissioned by her husband were nearing completion and were a magnificent backdrop to the court entertainments, which went on into the early hours of the morning with Marie, who celebrated her twenty-eighth birthday that November, and her ladies, dressed in fashionable French black velvet and silk gowns, being the focus for the fun and flirtation that ensued. Marie was still extremely attractive and her recent troubles, particularly her near captivity in Linlithgow, had only served to make her even more alluring to the young gentlemen of the court. Marie was no damsel in distress though – she was intelligent, capable and hard working with apparently endless energy and determination.

Although she had many admirers amongst the court gentlemen, some of whom may even have cherished secret ambitions of marrying her one day, Marie only had eyes for two of the young bloods at Stirling that season and soon gossip was rife about her possible intentions towards both of them. The first suitor was Matthew Stewart, Earl of Lennox, who was just one year younger than Marie and said to be exceedingly handsome with all the polished manners and social graces one might expect from someone who had lived at the French court for several years. He had expected to marry Marie shortly after his arrival in Scotland and, although his hopes had been dashed, he still hung about her, partnered her for dances and did his best to charm her into agreeing to become his wife. His rival amongst the Scottish noblemen who had thronged to Marie's side at Stirling was Patrick Hepburn, Earl of Bothwell and hereditary Lord Admiral of Scotland, described by a contemporary chronicler as 'a young, lusty gentleman, fair and pleasant in the sight of women'. However, dashing and pleasing to the eye though Bothwell was, he had one serious drawback: he was already married with a young family. Undaunted, he made it clear that he was prepared to divorce his wife if Marie would only consent to have him but he ought to have known that she was not the sort of woman to be impressed by such blandishments, especially if they came at the high price of another woman's happiness.

Lennox and Bothwell competed for Marie's attention with the chronicler noting that:

daily these two lords pursued the court and the Queen with bravery, with dancing, singing and playing on instruments and arrayed every day in sundry garments and prided every one of them who should be most gallant in their clothing and behave themselves in the Queen's presence, sometimes in shooting, sometimes in singing and jousting and running of great horse at the lists with all other kindly games that might satisfy the Queen or do her pleasure.

Those closest to Marie were probably aware that she was stringing them both along to ensure their support. She had heard enough stories of the disasters that had ensued after her erstwhile mother-in-law's hasty remarriage to a Scottish nobleman to know that no good could ever come of such an action. It would have been foolish to raise any of these men up above the others by making him step-father of the young Queen. Marie was undoubtedly lonely and still young enough to appreciate flirting with attractive men, even dream of another marriage perhaps, but she was intelligent enough to realise that this was not really a viable option.

In some ways, her policy of stringing prospective suitors along with no intention of ever actually marrying one of them was a tactic that was later employed to great effect by Elizabeth Tudor. Power did not come easily to either woman and, thanks to the examples of others, they quickly learned that the only way to hold on to that power was to not share it. In Marie's case, the issue was forced when the mischievous Lord Bothwell let it be known that she had finally agreed to marry him, which led to Lennox departing Stirling Castle in a fit of piqued disappointment. This left the field clear for his rival who then accompanied Marie to Edinburgh and on to St Andrews where she stayed as a guest of Cardinal Beaton. Although Lennox's departure from her side was an annoyance, Marie learned that he had struck up a secret correspondence with Henry VIII and was beginning to reconsider his former loyalty to the French alliance. Delighted to have Lennox onside, and keen to exploit this unprecedented opportunity to drive a serious wedge between the different factions of the currently united Scottish court, Henry made Lennox an offer he couldn't refuse – the hand in marriage of his beautiful niece, Lady Margaret Douglas, only daughter of his sister, Margaret, and the disgraced Earl of Angus, half sister of the dead James V and aunt of the baby Queen of Scots.

For a while, Lennox did his best to appear like the perfect, loyal subject but his cover was blown in October when he intercepted a large cargo of money, which had been sent along with a consignment of artillery and 500 soldiers for Marie's use. Had it not fallen into the greedy clutches of Lennox, Marie would have welcomed this gift because the healthy coffers left behind by her husband had been denuded by the Earl of Arran and she was in great need of money. Of even more use than weapons, men and cash though were the seasoned politicians Jacques de la Brosse and Jules de Mesnage, whom François had sent to Scotland in a flotilla of seven ships to act as ambassadors and advisors to the beleaguered Dowager Queen. Their calm, intelligent advice and constant presence at her side would act as a reassuring reminder that France had not forgotten about her and she could always rely on King François for assistance. In a show of diplomatic mettle, the ambassadors informed Lennox, a naturalised French citizen, that his actions in stealing French money and ordnance were treasonable and could have grave repercussions for him. The cowed young Earl responded by handing back the purloined money and artillery. To further ensure his continued loyalty to Marie and the French alliance, the ambassadors were authorised by Marie to offer him the hand in marriage of her daughter, Queen Mary, once she was of marriageable age.

This offer kept Lennox on Marie's side long enough to give his support to the formal invalidation of the hated Treaties of Greenwich, which were declared null in December 1543 on the basis that Henry VIII had broken their terms by stealing Scottish ships. As an additional slap in the face to the English, the Auld Alliance with France was renewed a few days later to the great satisfaction of Marie and the newly arrived ambassadors. They had contributed by using the retrieved French gold to offer generous pensions to several high-ranking noblemen whose support was needed to revoke the treaty and prop up the French alliance. Marie was elated by the success of her machinations and the mood at Stirling that Christmas was buoyant as the court threw themselves wholeheartedly into the usual elaborate celebrations. The young Queen Mary had her first birthday that

December and was at the centre of the festivities, while her mother danced and played cards until dawn; on one memorable occasion she won £100 from the Earl of Arran, who was still in attendance at Stirling.

It was almost as though everyone had forgotten all about Henry VIII, who was simmering with humiliation and thwarted rage in London after being informed of the revocation of his treaties. His mood soured further still when news arrived in January 1544 that the Dauphine of France had, at last, managed to give birth to a son. Duly named François in honour of his grandfather, the boy was the answer to Marie de Guise's prayers that God would provide her with a suitable French match for her daughter.

Henry was still determined that Queen Mary would marry his own son Edward and began to look into other means by which he could secure the little Queen's person after his demands that she should be sent to England were ignored. Kidnap was always an option of course, but even Henry had to concede that any such plan was unlikely to prosper after Sadler told him how formidable the defences at Stirling Castle were.

Now that Marie was at liberty again, she was able to resume her usual correspondence with her family, which had always acted as a tonic during her darkest moments. Claude and Antoinette had been desperately worried about Marie and her daughter during the months of silence and it was an immense relief to them to be able to hear from her directly once again, although what she had to say did not always do much to ease their concerns.

'I praise God,' Antoinette wrote towards the end of 1543, 'that he has freed you and the little Queen from your long captivity, and that you are both in good health ... I have been very anxious and had almost lost hope of seeing your affairs prosper again and your father and I have often discussed the possibility of bringing you both back to France ...The King is most anxious to help, as you will soon learn for yourself now that messengers are able to get to you again. She ends with a characteristic

admonishment: Remember that whatever honour, good or victory God gives you, you must humbly acknowledge that it is due to His goodness alone and that as all prosperity and adversity are alike in his hands, he will guide you on to the best course.

Once communication channels were open again, Marie was also able to receive letters from other family members such as her uncle Antoine, Duc de Lorraine, and her younger brother, François, Comte d'Aumale, who was now in his early twenties and already a popular and respected military man, who would soon earn himself the nickname 'Balafré' (the Scarred One) after a lance pierced him through both cheeks during the Second Siege of Boulogne. The plucky Comte, an undoubted chip off the old block, rode back to camp with the lance still in place and, allegedly, bore the pain of its removal as 'easily as if it had been but the plucking of a hair out of his head'. Not a man to be crossed and definitely someone that would be an asset to any side. Even though he had not seen Marie since her departure to Scotland several years earlier, his letters make it clear that he remained devoted to her.

Another much-loved correspondent was Marie's eldest son, another François, who turned 8 in October 1543 and, like his uncle of the same name, was clearly champing at the bit to be allowed to come to Scotland to defend his mother's honour. He sent her a piece of string to show her how much he had grown and, at the end of 1546, he sent her a portrait, modestly writing that 'I think that the artist has improved upon his model.' His short but sweet letters give the impression of a charming and intelligent boy, adored by his family but still missing his mother, whom he wished was free to come back to France to be with him again. Marie must have been tempted to leave the Scottish to fight it out amongst themselves, but she made the decision to stay and, once she had decided to do something, it was her nature to see it through to the end, no matter how bitter that conclusion might be.

Although she had offered her daughter's hand to Lennox, it quickly became obvious that this would never do as a means of securing his loyalty to the French party at the Scottish court, especially as he insisted on arguing with Arran at every opportunity and was known to be corresponding with the English. He even went as far as sending passionate love letters to Lady Margaret Douglas while he continued to woo Marie de Guise. Eventually Marie, who had come to regard him as a liability, informed Lennox that she had no intention of marrying him, either to herself or her daughter, and did nothing to prevent Arran and Cardinal Beaton, in a rare moment of agreement, from laying siege to Glasgow Castle in an attempt to seize him as a prisoner. Despite their efforts, Lennox was still able to travel south to England at the end of May and, on 29 June, he was married to Lady Margaret in the presence of Henry VIII and Catherine Parr, irrevocably binding himself to the English from that point on.

The departure of Lennox, although undeniably disappointing, was generally regarded as inevitable and a good thing rather than an abject disaster. It was obvious from the start that Marie, even with all her wiles and cunning, could not have successfully strung such an ambitious man along with half-hearted promises of marriage forever. He was not much missed in Scotland, where he had managed to make himself thoroughly disliked during his short period of residence and had even managed to fall out with King François before his departure, earning a sharp reprimand from the French monarch who scathingly informed him that Marie 'has not so great an enemy or unfriend as you are' before washing his hands of him for good. As far as Marie was concerned, it was good riddance to bad rubbish, not least because she could now spend more time keeping the peace between Arran and Beaton.

At the same time as Marie was dealing with her warring nobility, she was doing her best to prepare for the inevitable English invasion, which her spies had informed her was due to begin in March. In the end, English troops surprised the Scottish by landing close to Leith at the beginning of May. Henry was preparing to invade France that summer as well and, unwilling to find himself fighting on two fronts, gave his commander, the Earl of Hertford, strict instructions not to spend longer than three weeks bringing the Scottish to heel. His orders make for terrifying reading as Hertford was told to sack Edinburgh, Leith and the surrounding area, 'putting man, woman and child to fire and sword without exception, where any resistance shall be made against you'. Particular attention was paid to the stronghold of Edinburgh Castle and the royal palace at Holyrood, both of which were to be thoroughly sacked and destroyed before the raiders moved on to do the same in the royal burgh of Fife. In a fury of rage, Henry ordered Hertford to 'put all to fire and sword, burn Edinburgh town, so razed and defaced when you have sacked and got what you can out of it as there may remain forever a perpetual memory of the vengeance of God lightened upon them for their falsehood and disobedience.'

While Arran and Cardinal Beaton set out with several thousand men to meet the invaders, Marie remained at Stirling Castle, keeping abreast of events with regular reports. She was horrified when news arrived that the English had scattered Scottish forces and marched on Edinburgh, which they proceeded to sack and burn, even setting light to Holyrood Abbey where she had been crowned and where her husband and sons lay buried. The impregnable Edinburgh Castle luckily foiled their attempts at capture but Leith, much of Fife and several towns and villages on the east coast of Scotland were not so fortunate and were decimated. The English troops came within a few miles of Stirling and Marie would have been able to see the black smoke of burning villages from the parapet of her castle. Not for the first time she must have cursed the fact that her sex made it impossible for her to ride out as her father, uncles and brothers would have done to defend her people under her own banner and with her own sword.

Once the English had withdrawn, it was time to regroup and assess the damage they had left in their wake. Although the invasion was not really Arran's fault, his limp and ineffective response to it had incurred much anger and brought into question his suitability to act as Protector of Scotland. It was the moment that Marie had been waiting for and she was quick to press her advantage, reminding everyone that she was the person most able to secure the all-important French military assistance that everything now depended upon. To further boost her cause, Sir George Douglas and the Earl of Angus, who could always be relied upon to throw their weight behind whichever side they considered most likely to win, both travelled to Stirling to offer their loyalty. Arran's protests that he had always acted in good faith fell upon deaf ears and, when he stole away from Stirling after being ordered to resign from office, his position was declared forfeit and offered to Marie instead, with a council of twelve lords being appointed to help her govern.

Unfortunately, although she was clearly the most capable person for the job, Marie found herself thwarted by the old prejudices that still riddled Scottish society even at the highest levels. As both a woman and a foreigner, she was considered doubly beyond the pale as far as many of the lords were concerned. Despite her determined efforts to get assistance from the French and seek a truce with the English, she still didn't have enough support to see off Arran when he opposed her rule and summoned a rival parliament. Cardinal Beaton was forced to intervene and in the end Marie was forced to concede defeat and allow Arran to don the mantle of Regent once again, on the understanding that she would join his Privy Council and attend its meetings and, in addition, Arran would hand his eldest son over to Cardinal Beaton to act as a pledge for his continued loyalty. It was a frustrating blow to her ambition to rule on her daughter's behalf but not an insurmountable one. She was hopeful that her new position on the council would help her gain enough support amongst the nobility, and sufficiently undermine Arran, to be able to stake another claim in the future.

Whereas the winter of 1543 had been notable for its ostentatious merry-making and romantic entanglements, that of 1544 was very different as Marie and her court braced themselves for another English assault on Scottish soil. Henry VIII was currently still preoccupied with his invasion of France, where he had scored a notable victory in managing to take the town of Boulogne, and it would be some time before he would be free to turn his attention to his northern neighbours. In the meantime the Scots had little option but to regroup and prepare themselves for the worst, while doing their best to remain united in the face of a common enemy.

In February, the Scots received an unexpected morale boost when Arran and his men scored a victory against marauding English troops at Ancrum Moor, before triumphantly returning to Stirling Castle. This humiliating defeat would result in a bloody retaliation from the English but for now, Marie and the Scottish lords were exultant and more determined than ever to snub English attempts to revive the Treaties of Greenwich as a means of ending the conflict. Another result of this well-timed show of Scottish might was that it reminded their French allies of the value of having Scotland on side; to Marie's great delight, King François finally gave in to the pressure of her family and the Dauphin Henri, who had taken great interest in her plight. Francois wrote to pledge his support, and offered to send over 500 more soldiers led by Jacques de Montgomery, Seigneur de Lorges, a captain in the French King's prestigious Scots Guard.

It would have been even better if Marie's father or brother, the Comte d' Aumale, had come to her rescue but Lorges was a welcome sight nonetheless. He arrived at Stirling Castle in June, having entirely won her heart beforehand by sending a crate of French wine having heard that she was 'ill provided with wines' in Scotland. Rather less welcome was the debased coinage that the crafty King François had sent as wages for his soldiers. The coinage fooled no one, least of all the shrewd Scots, who refused to have anything to do with them. On the whole though, the French and Scottish rubbed along together fairly well, united as they were by a common enemy: the English, who launched their second invasion that September. This time they swarmed across the border by Kelso, setting fire to the abbey there before marching on to Melrose and Jedburgh, where they carried out further atrocities before withdrawing back across the border again. Although left shell shocked, the Scots were relieved it had not been any worse.

It was the presence of King François' troops that deterred Hertford from leading his men any further into Scotland; yet more proof that the French alliance was necessary to keep the English at bay, even if there were many at court who refused to believe it, still hoping it might be possible to come to amicable terms with Henry VIII.

For his part, Henry was growing weary of the situation and decided to cut the troublesome Scots out altogether. He approached King François instead, offering to return his recent acquisition of Boulogne if François would put pressure on the Scottish to guarantee a match between Queen Mary and the Prince of Wales. The proposal was unpopular both with his son, the Dauphin and also the Guise family, who were all in favour of marrying Mary to Prince François. Nonetheless, if he agreed to help the English out in this matter, it would be a neat way of resolving several problems all at once. For now though, François did what he did best; he nodded and smiled, but committed himself to absolutely nothing.

At the same time, things were steadily going from bad to worse in Scotland where Cardinal Beaton had been sent away from court after coming to blows with the Seigneur de Lorges in front of Marie; servants had to be called to break the two men apart. It was a shameful display that only served to further isolate the already unpopular Cardinal from the other members of the council. He withdrew to his castle in St Andrews and remained there over the Christmas period when the court traditionally gathered at Stirling. He was joined by Lord Arran, whose son was still being held as a hostage in the Cardinal's household, doubtless making an awkward little gathering. Arran and the Cardinal had had their issues over the years but seem to have put that behind them at this stage as they faced another difficult year of power struggles.

The Cardinal was loathed not just by his peers, but also by the ever-increasing numbers of Scottish Protestants, who saw him as the embodiment of a venal, power hungry, arrogant Papist priest. Most disturbing was the evident pleasure he took from burning heretics, most notably the popular itinerant preacher George Wishart, who was hanged on a gibbet then burned at the stake in March 1546, after a rigged show-trial orchestrated by Beaton, who then watched the execution from his window. It was allegedly in Wishart's name that, on 29 May 1546, a small group of assassins led by Norman Leslie, eldest son of the Earl of Rothes, forced their way into the Cardinal's rooms in St Andrews Castle before stabbing him to death, ignoring his

144

screams of 'I am a priest! You cannot slay me!' The body of the hated Cardinal was then hung from the window from a knotted sheet, before being thrust into a salt-chest and thrown down inside a dungeon where Beaton had held several Protestants over the years.

Although Beaton was too unpopular to be much mourned, the savagery of his murder shocked everyone. Marie had not always seen eye-to-eye with Beaton and they had stepped on each other's toes far too often over the question of who should take over from Arran as Regent of Scotland, but she would nonetheless miss his advice and diplomatic skills. Although he managed to fall out with everyone at one time or another, he had also been a prime mover in bringing people together and negotiating truces between warring factions; Marie knew her task would be made all the more difficult by his death. In England, the news of Beaton's murder was greeted with enthusiasm by Henry, who saw him as meddlesome, devoted to the interests of the French, and chief architect of the Scottish resistance of the Treaties of Greenwich. Consequently, he had been plotting for several years to either kidnap Beaton, or have him quietly disposed of in some way. However, if Henry thought that the liquidation of Cardinal Beaton would result in a move away from the French alliance, he was sorely mistaken.

After the Cardinal's murder, his assassins remained barricaded inside St Andrews Castle, defying all attempts to get them to leave and earning themselves the nickname of 'Castilians' in the process. Worried about the fate of his eldest son, who was still trapped inside the castle, Arran mounted a half-hearted siege which looked set to drag on for several months after the 'Castilians' adroitly foiled his attempt to mine his way inside by cutting him off with a counter mine. It wasn't possible to starve them out either as the castle was easily accessible by sea. The rebels were kept well supplied with food, drink and money by Henry, who gleefully sent ships with all the necessary munitions, delighted to help a group of renegade Protestants flout Scottish authority. Amongst the 'Castilians' locked inside St Andrews Castle was a young Protestant preacher called John Knox. Although Knox had not taken part in Cardinal Beaton's murder, he had been an admirer of George Wishart and wanted to share the fate of the men who were avenging his death.

Although it was just a small group of assassins had murdered Cardinal Beaton, the brutal nature of the crime, their defiance of the Scottish authorities and the blatant support offered by the English was enough to make people fearful that there might be darker forces at play. Protestantism was not fully established as a religion in Scotland at that point and most people were still, nominally at least, Roman Catholic; even stronger than any religious faith was their hatred and suspicion of the English. It didn't matter that Beaton's murderers had been Scottish as well, their brutality and defiance were generally regarded as intrinsically 'unpatriotic' and ultimately increased support for the French alliance, which was seen as the antidote to the chaos and bloodshed enacted on Scottish soil by the English and their sympathisers.

Chapter 12

The Defence of the Realm

On the 28 January 1547, Henry VIII, that great titan who had dominated European politics for almost four decades, breathed his last in the Palace of Whitehall. He was just 55 years old but disease, lack of exercise and gluttony had wasted the shining beauty that had enraptured his subjects when he had first succeeded to the throne as a handsome, carefree boy of 17. When the news of his death arrived in Scotland, Marie could hardly believe it. Henry had been King of England for as long as she could remember and, although they had never actually met, it must have seemed to her as though their fates were intrinsically linked in some way. She may not have become his wife, despite his best efforts to make her so, but she had married his nephew, become close to his sister, and was now fiercely resisting the marriage of his son to her daughter. They were enemies, but on some level she may well have missed his demanding, arrogant, brutish presence in the background of her life, especially now that there was a new English King and an entirely new regime to get used to.

Henry's successor was his only son, Edward, who was just 9 years old and required a Regent until he reached the age of 18. Unlike his nephew James V, Henry VIII had left behind a will naming sixteen executors who were to act as Edward VI's Council of Regency during his minority with no one man having particular authority over the others. Within a few days of the old King's death this system was abandoned and Edward's maternal uncle, the Earl of Hertford, who also bestowed upon himself the title of Duke of Somerset, was declared Lord Protector, no doubt because he had greased a few fists with bribes to make it so. Although the news of Henry's death was greeted with delight north of the border, the appointment of Somerset, the man who had recently led two devastating raids into Scotland, burned their abbeys and looted Edinburgh itself, was regarded as a calamity.

Somerset made it clear to the Scots that he had no intention of forgetting about the Treaties of Greenwich and was still to forcing the Scottish to accede to the betrothal of Queen Mary to his nephew. He also continued to support the 'Castilians' barricaded inside St Andrews Castle and even welcomed three of them to court after English forces helped them to escape; a grave insult directed at the Scottish council where Lord Huntly, a supporter of Marie, had replaced Beaton as Lord Chancellor and the pro-French party was gathering increasing strength by the day.

As if the death of Henry VIII was not shocking enough, in April 1547 the news arrived in Scotland that King François had also suddenly passed away a month earlier, leaving the throne to his eldest son, Henri. Although she sincerely mourned the King, this was a massive stroke of good fortune as far as Marie was concerned. The new young King of France was a close friend of her eldest brothers François, Comte d'Aumale, and Charles, Archbishop of Reims, and had already written to offer his support to Marie, of whom he seems to have been extremely fond. Perhaps she might have felt rather less sanguine had she known that François' last words on his deathbed were to warn his son about letting the ambitious Guise family become too powerful, but for now they basked in the new King's favour and looked set to become more influential than ever.

As always there was a constant stream of letters between Marie and her family and friends in France at this time, their contents a curious mixture of endearments, gossipy chit-chat and business matters all written in that typical good humoured, frank Guise style that makes for compelling reading. The letters must have been a comfort to Marie, who often felt isolated in Scotland and relied on the correspondence for descriptions of weddings, births and funerals that she was unable to attend. Unsurprisingly, the most prolific correspondent was the Duchesse Antoinette, whose letters are full of family news, advice and updates about lawsuits and financial affairs pertaining to the Longueville estate. Other regular correspondents included Marie's brothers, Charles and François, who more than once dictated letters while recovering from battle wounds. Her cousins, François de Lorraine and his sister Anna, Princess of Orange, also wrote regularly, as did her uncles, Antoine, Duc de Lorraine and Jean, Cardinal de Lorraine, both of whom were clearly extremely fond of her. Even her formidable grandmother, Philippa of Guelders, wrote from the convent at Pont-à-Mousson, telling Marie that she would always be remembered in the nuns' prayers there.

Most precious of all though were the letters from her son, François, who turned 11 in October 1546 and was, by all accounts, growing up to be a fine, handsome boy. His proud grandparents took him everywhere with them and, as Duc de Longueville and hereditary Grand Chamberlain of France, he had grown used to mixing in the highest levels of society. Despite this, he was still excited to meet King François when he paid a visit to Joinville, informing his mother that, 'the King was very nice to me and told me to grow up big so that I can do him service; I wish for this very much but want to see you more.'

On another occasion he proudly reported that he was at Fontainebleau for the christening of the Princess Elisabeth in 1546. Almost a year later, he was back at court again for the coronation of Henri II and was pleased to inform his mother that the King had treated him very kindly, while it seems that his mistress, Diane de Poitiers, had taken him under her wing, no doubt thinking he might make a suitable husband for one of her daughters one day. The Guise family played a significant role in the coronation with Marie's young son, François, dressed in the splendid robes and regalia of Grand Chamberlain of France, leading the procession up the aisle of Reims Cathedral. Her younger brother, Charles, who would be promoted to Cardinal just a few days later at the age of just 23, performed the actual crowning itself.

It was not long before Henri II proved that his offers of assistance were more than just empty promises and sent a fleet of twenty-one galleys under the command of the celebrated naval officer Leone

Strozzi. Sailing into St Andrews, Strozzi made short work of laying siege to the castle, taking just six days of heavy-duty bombardment to force the 'Castilians' into submission and rescue Arran's son from their clutches. Many of them were immediately imprisoned but others, including John Knox who would later be ransomed by the Duke of Somerset, were set to work as oarsmen in the French galleys. Arran's relief at having his son restored to him was tempered by some embarrassment that he himself had not been able to lift the siege, which had been going on for well over a year before Strozzi came along to save the day. He was also uneasy by the display of French power and the fact that King Henri and Strozzi had both made it clear that Scotland could owe their assistance entirely to Marie de Guise and the great influence of her family at the French court. Although not the brightest of men, Arran was still intelligent enough to realise that it was only a matter of time before Marie tried to depose him as Regent once again and assume the mantle of power herself. This time, if King Henri decided to back her, she might well succeed.

The English reaction to the ending of the St Andrews' siege was predictably swift and brutal. Marie was overseeing preparations for the defence of Edinburgh when the news arrived that Somerset had brought an army of 15,000 men over the border at Berwick, and was marching north towards the capital in what was clearly intended to be another violent phase of the so called 'rough wooing' of her daughter. This time, he was free to do as he pleased and had decided that the best policy would be to forcibly occupy Scotland by means of garrisons, which could be employed to terrorise the populace into submitting to English rule. First though, he intended to teach the Scots another harsh lesson by attacking Edinburgh again. Marie had hurried back to Stirling to be with her daughter as soon as the news of the invasion came and so it was Arran who took charge of the city's defence with the 12,000 men they had managed to muster – the biggest Scottish army to date.

Marching his men down to Inveresk near Musselburgh, Arran placed them behind trenches blocking the road to Edinburgh by the hamlet of Pinkie, with marshland on one side and the sea on the other, which meant that Somerset would have to work hard to get behind them. For once it looked as though victory might be assured and for a while it seemed like the Scottish attack had the advantage until things began to go badly wrong when the Highland regiments lost their nerve in the face of heavy artillery fire. Sensing disaster with the acute antennae of the chronically self-interested, Arran turned his horse around and fled the scene, leaving his men to be slaughtered by the English. Some 10,000 Scottish soldiers died that day, amongst them Lord Fleming, one of Marie's most prominent supporters, and several members of the nobility. Another 2,000 were taken prisoner, including the Lord Chancellor, Lord Huntly. Even some English soldiers were horrified by the scale of the barbarity meted out to the Scottish, with one William Patten describing the

> ...*pitiful sight of the dead corpses lying dispersed abroad, some their legs off, some but hamstrung, and left lying half dead, some thrust quite through the body, others the arms cut off, diverse their necks half asunder, many their heads cloven, of sundry the brains pasht out, some others again their heads quite off, with other many kinds of killing.*

Marie was waiting for Arran when he finally arrived back at Stirling Castle, splattered in mud and blood, and fearful of her reaction. Messengers had been sent ahead and already appraised her of the disaster at Pinkie, but she was still shocked when Arran was shown into her presence, full of the usual excuses for his ineptitude. Yet again Marie must have wished she was able to lead her own troops into battle; for she was certain that she could do a better job than the cowering Arran, who had once again contrived to survive the slaughter when other, worthier men had died or been taken prisoner. However, Arran was not her main concern now – the defeat at Pinkie and complete disintegration of their defences meant that the road between the Duke of Somerset and Stirling Castle lay completely open. Her only thought was how to get her daughter away from danger.

Old Lord Erskine, who had lost his eldest son in the massacre at

Pinkie, offered to take the little Queen to the safety of Inchmahome Priory, which stood on an isolated small island in the middle of the Lake of Menteith, 15 miles west of Stirling Castle. The 4-year-old Queen was spirited away in the dead of night; very few knew where she had been taken so, should the unthinkable happen and Stirling fall to Somerset and his men, there was a good chance that the English would never find her.

With her daughter safely ensconced with the Augustinian friars of Inchmahome for the next three weeks, Marie was able to turn her attention to the state of emergency that now existed throughout Scotland as Somerset's men slaughtered, pillaged and destroyed all that stood in their path. Once again, Leith bore the brunt of their wrath and it was only a matter of time before they turned their attention to Edinburgh and Stirling. To Marie's great disgust, she also received reports that the disgraced Earl of Lennox had led more English troops over the border and an English fleet had managed to capture Broughty Castle, which occupied an important defensive position at the mouth of the River Tay near Dundee.

When the English finally withdrew from Scotland, leaving behind the first of the forts with which Somerset hoped to subdue the nation, Marie took stock of their tremendous losses and the terrible threat of what was still to come. She turned in desperation to her French allies for assistance, heartened by a letter from Constable Montmorency, who informed her that the news of her misfortunes had 'grieved the King and court as greatly as if they had been their own loss', while her mother, Antoinette, wrote to let her know that her brother, François 'is troubled by your anxieties and often wishes that he were there with you. I, however, wish that you were with us in France.'

Although she had long been in favour of a match with France, it was still a shock to Marie when Monsieur d'Oysel, the French Ambassador to Scotland, hinted that a deal might be brokered whereby the French would offer all the necessary assistance in return for an assurance that her daughter would be sent to the safety of France where she would one day marry the Dauphin François. Marie knew that such a match would be unpopular in Scotland but was also aware that they had been left in such a beleaguered state following the last English invasion that they had no choice but to agree.

Marie did not mention her negotiations with Oysel and his master at the next Privy Council meeting saying only that she had written to the French to request more assistance. Nonetheless, her meetings with Oysel and his return to France soon afterwards caused tongues to wag and rumours began to spread that the Dowager Queen was arranging to have her daughter spirited away by the French. When the story came to Arran's ears he was furious because, like many of the nobility, he believed it would be best if the little Queen Mary married one of their own rather than either going abroad and ruling from afar, or even worse – taking a meddlesome foreign prince as her husband. He particularly fancied his own son's chances at becoming the next King of Scotland and Marie, wishing to keep on side as much as possible, had never bothered to contradict him in this.

Similarly alarmed by the threat of French intervention and the possible spiriting away of the young Queen, the English mounted another short, brutal invasion of Scotland at the start of 1548, seizing the important and strategically placed town of Haddington in East Lothian. Alarmed by this latest threat, Marie managed to persuade Arran that she had no intention of sending her daughter to France and persuaded him to move Queen Mary to Dumbarton Castle, another impregnable fortress on the west coast of the country which had been confiscated from the Earl of Lennox after his defection to England. While there, Mary received a delightful and very touching letter from her half brother, the Duc de Longueville, in which he informed her:

I have received your letter which you were kind enough to send to me and in answer to your desire that I should come to help you, I have been practising wearing armour and tilting at the ring every day so that I may be able to help and to serve you against all of your enemies.

Perhaps more promisingly, Marie was soon to receive a flurry of family letters that informed her that Monsieur d'Oysel had arrived in

France and had done his very best for her. 'I have received your letter … which the King listened to very willingly and to which he is sending a full answer which should greatly please you and prevent you from ever thinking that you have been abandoned by your family and friends,' her brother François wrote reassuringly after his meeting with Oysel and the King. 'I will say no more other than that your affairs will always be my own.' While Constable Montmorency wrote at greater length to assure her that:

> *the King cares no less for* [your affairs] *than for his own; also you have at court two brothers and myself, your faithful servant, who will not forget you. The King ... wished, as did all the court, that every man in France could make one jump to be at your side and said that had the expedition to Scotland cost three times as much, he would hold it cheap to be of so much assistance to you.*

As soon as King Henri received Marie's agreement to a match between her daughter and his son, he ordered her brother, a military genius and already veteran of several campaigns, to begin planning their strategy for the defence of Scotland. François de Guise would not be going, much to his sister's sorrow, but he placed the campaign in the capable hands of André de Montalembert, Sieur d'Essé as well as several other officers who were trusted veterans of the Guise family's past campaigns. François de Guise instructed them to obey his sister implicitly and according to Monsieur de Brezé, commanded to 'serve the Queen as if she were their own master... as though the King in person were there.'

The only potential fly in the ointment was, as always, the Earl of Arran who resented Marie's close links to the French because he was still hopeful that she would agree to a betrothal between his son and the little Queen. Concerned by reports that he was secretly corresponding with the English, Marie and King Henri agreed to offer the disgruntled Regent the duchy of Châtelherault as well as a match between his son and the daughter of the enormously wealthy Duc de Montpensier. It was an offer that Arran, now known as the Duke of Châtelherault, could not refuse and, on 28 April, the agreement was signed and preparations began for the departure of a French expeditionary force to Scotland and the reception of Queen Mary in France.

The French troops, a veritable armada of 130 ships loaded with artillery, 5,500 infantry, 1,000 cavalry and all manner of weaponry and munitions, landed at Leith on 17 June. Their initial impressions of Scotland were not promising. Although they were as surprised as Marie de Guise had been ten years earlier that the landscape was more pleasant than they had been led to believe, were still appalled by the dejected appearance of the people and ravaged state of the countryside following the English invasions. At Marie de Guise's suggestion they began their campaign at Haddington, which was still under English control despite a concerted effort by Châtelherault to retrieve it from their clutches. Although Montalembert and his men were willing enough to do this, it proved demanding because both French and Scottish troops were difficult to muster and preferred to spend their time hanging about Edinburgh than assisting with the siege. In the end Marie was forced to visit various houses in Edinburgh to plead with the soldiers to fight, with some notable success. It had always seemed to her that if you wanted a job done properly then you should do it yourself, and from now on she was to take a more active role in the command of her troops. She still couldn't ride ahead of them into battle, but she became a constant and familiar presence in their camps where she charmed them all with the warm, friendly manner that reminded the more seasoned French soldiers of her charismatic father and brothers and inspired in them the same loyalty and devotion.

On at least one occasion she gave a speech to the men, telling them that

since the state of this realm and my service depends only on you, it is only right that your praise should come from me myself. I have given orders that you will receive certain gifts from me. Take them, I pray you, in token not of what I do now but of what I should like to do, hoping that some day I shall have the means of showing you that the greater the dangers, the inconveniences and the hazards of war, the greater will be the wages of victory.

A rousing speech that turned out to be prophetic because the dangers of war were indeed great and the death toll appalling as the French and English struggled for control of Haddington. We are told by one chronicler that Marie, so used by now to death and loss, was still touched by the death of a handsome young French nobleman, whose body was brought back to Edinburgh for burial in one of the mass graves in the Greyfriars' graveyard of the city. Horrified by the youthful promise being snuffed out thanks to the vainglorious ambitions of England, Marie was said to weep 'many tears' as she watched his body laid to rest. No wonder the English Ambassador to France noted that she harboured an 'exceeding hatred' of his countrymen, when every day brought fresh reminders of their crimes against her adopted country.

It was an immense relief to know that her daughter was not going to fall into English clutches and, on 7 July, she signed a marriage treaty agreeing that Queen Mary would marry the Dauphin François in exchange for the French King 'keeping this realm and lieges thereof in the same freedom, liberties and laws as had been in all Kings of Scotland times bypast, and shall maintain and defend this realm and lieges of the same as he does the realm of France and lieges thereof.' Devastating though it would be to part from another child, she could at least be reassured that Mary would be in safe hands and that it was now surely only a matter of time before she would be able to oust the hopeless Châtelherault for good. In the meantime she remained with the army, taking close interest in their manoeuvres and mingling with the troops. Always intrigued by military strategy, she took a group of companions to a nearby church with the intention of climbing to the top of the tower to gain a better view of the bombardment. They were just about to enter the church when it was struck by a cannon ball fired by the English artillery inside the town; excitement swiftly became confusion as Marie fainted while several of the friends and trusted servants with her were killed or maimed by the explosion. She was swiftly carried away to safety, but it would be a long time before she fully recovered from the shock of seeing her companions killed before her eyes and of almost being killed herself.

The siege of Haddington looked set to drag on for quite some time, prolonged both by French apathy and English determination not to give this precious advantage up to the enemy. Realising that it could go on very well without her presence, Marie rode to Dumbarton where everything was at last ready for her daughter's departure to France. With her were the other lords of the Privy Council and Châtelherault, whose beloved son, the focus of so much of his plotting and scheming, would also be leaving for France with the little Queen. The sizeable entourage also included two of her half brothers, the children of various noble families who were keen to have them educated in France and the usual nursemaids, attendants and servants. Like any other princess travelling to a far-off land, the 6-year-old Queen Mary was surrounded by a plethora of familiar faces that would remind her of home.

Although Marie had been bracing herself for separation from her daughter, when the moment to say goodbye finally came it proved much harder than she could have imagined. It was a great consolation that Mary was going to the French court, where Marie had enjoyed the happiest time of her life, rather than being taken off to London as the hostage of the English. Nevertheless, Marie found herself in the unhappy position of having to say goodbye to yet another child, without knowing when, or if, she would ever see her again.

Marie was a warm hearted, generous woman who had taken a great joy from being a mother. It seems exceedingly cruel that she should not be granted the pleasure of watching any of her five children grow up and especially not the daughter whom, by rights, should have remained at her side for many years.

As she tearfully kissed her daughter goodbye on 29 July 1548 and watched as she walked up the ramp to King Henri's own royal galley, Marie must have been sorely tempted to go with her and return home to the land of her birth. After all, there was a clause in her marriage contract allowing for this, not to mention several people, Arran included, who would be only too happy to see the back of her. She had made her choice when her husband died just a few days after the birth of their daughter though, and was not the sort of woman to leave a job half finished; especially when there were so many challenges still to be met.

Unable to bear the sight of her daughter's ship taking her away to her new life in France, Marie left Dumbarton for Edinburgh before the French flotilla had even departed to be greeted with the news that English ships had been spotted close to Leith.

Her sorrow at parting was now overtaken by terror that her daughter might still fall into English hands. She knew no rest until letters arrived from France informing her that, after a difficult eighteen day crossing, her daughter was with her family, who were very much taken by her although her brother, François, humorously noted that she was a little 'vain'. Châtelherault was also relieved to hear that the Scottish party had arrived safely. He had been just as keenly upset to lose his son, who had been sent as a pledge of his own continued support of the French alliance, and fell into a deep dejection after his departure. He could take comfort from the fact that his boy would be well treated at the French court though because Marie, with her usual kindness, had written ahead to her son, the Duc de Longueville, asking him to take the Scottish boy under his wing.

With their precious children now safely in France, Marie and Châtelherault could both turn their full attention to the defence of Scotland against the English. It was hard to predict how Somerset would react when he discovered that his aims had been thwarted and he had been outmanoeuvred by Marie and the French; would he give up his scheme to seize control of Scotland now that its Queen, his ultimate prize, had been taken away, or would he unleash bloody vengeance upon them all? Only time would tell.

For now though, Marie turned her attention to strengthening the defences at Stirling Castle and Leith and continued to oversee the siege of Haddington, which still showed no signs of coming to an end. The enthusiasm with which the Scots had greeted their French rescuers had long since died away and she also had the additional headache of trying to resolve tension between the townsfolk of Edinburgh and the French troops, whose marauding ways were no doubt exacerbated by their inability to cope with the much stronger and rougher Scottish alcohol. Matters reached a head in the winter of 1548 when a serious fight broke out on an Edinburgh street between French soldiers and locals, leaving several men on both sides dead or wounded, including the Provost of Edinburgh himself who had somehow become embroiled in the violence. Marie was forced to intervene and ordered the French to leave the capital city immediately and make their camp at Musselburgh instead, where she hoped they would find it easier to stay out of trouble.

The usual Christmas court at Stirling was unsurprisingly gloomy that year without the little Queen and her household to lighten the mood. Mary of Scotland was an enchanting child and her presence was very much missed at court, not least by her mother who was uncharacteristically despondent about the year's events as it finally drew to close.

Although she had hoped that the departure of her daughter would make Somerset back off from Scotland, he had recently made it clear to the French Ambassador to England that he had no intention of abandoning his nephew's claim to the Sovereignty of Scotland and would be pressing on with his plans for conquest. There was also the problem of Châtelherault, who was just as hopeless and ineffectual as ever. Marie was well aware that he was still depleting the royal coffers as fast as they filled, intent on feathering his nest and enriching his family as much as possible before he lost his position as Regent. He too had to be stopped, but how?

On Christmas Day 1548, as she sat on her dais in the great hall of Stirling, scene of so many triumphant court celebrations and festivities, Marie must have felt like the weight of the world lay on her shoulders. Her husband was dead, her children were gone, her family were far away and she had no one but herself that she could rely upon. These dismal thoughts were interrupted by the unexpected arrival of the Earl of Huntly, Lord Chancellor of Scotland, who had been captured at the battle of Pinkie and kept prisoner by the English ever since; he had effected a bold escape from his captors the previous day. All of Marie's unhappiness was forgotten as, radiant with relief to see him again, she welcomed the Earl back to court; his brave escape and determination to return to her side a timely reminder that all was not lost after all.

Chapter 13

The Homecoming

In September 1549, the beleaguered, diseased and starving English troops finally conceded Haddington to the French. Scottish troops massed outside and marched away and, although Somerset continued his posturing on the other side of the border, he was preoccupied with defending the territory that England had seized in France, dealing with his troublesome younger brother, Thomas, and quelling serious unrest in England to give his full attention to the problem of Scotland. His northern neighbours were still an annoying thorn in his side but no longer the most pressing difficulty he had to deal with and in April of the following year, the Treaty of Boulogne was signed between England, France and Scotland bringing an end to the conflict. Amongst the six French hostages sent to London as security for continued good relations between the countries was Marie's younger brother, Claude, Marquis de Mayenne, who was eleven years her junior and married to Louise de Brézé, the younger daughter of King Henri's mistress, Diane de Poitiers.

To Marie's great delight, relations between England and Scotland were amicable enough for Somerset to grant Claude a passport to visit his sister in Edinburgh and, for the first time since her arrival in Scotland in 1538, she was reunited with one of her siblings. It didn't take long to catch up with all the latest family news, including details of his marriage and their elder brother François' recent wedding in December 1548 with the Italian heiress Anna d'Este, who was the eldest daughter of Duke Ercole II of Ferrara and his wife, Princesse Renée of France (the sister-in-law of King François and aunt of the current King) and granddaughter of the notorious Lucrezia Borgia. It was a prestigious match for the Guises and one that underlined their growing influence and power on the wider European stage.

For Marie, this cessation of hostilities was a chance to lick wounds, survey the damage and regroup. Although they were free of invasion for the time being, she was all too aware that discord between England and Scotland could start up again at any time and was determined that next time they would be much better prepared to confront it. She also knew that next time war broke out between the two nations, she would like to be in supreme charge rather than Châtelherault who had been such a disappointment during the last few years. King Henri had officially recognised his position as Regent but that was not an insurmountable problem and Marie was sure that if she bided her time, she could get his support for a coup.

The main problem right now was a lack of funds. The conflict with England had been an endless drain on Scottish resources thanks to their destruction of crops and farms in the lowlands of the country, not to mention all the men that had been killed in either the raids or while defending their country. The battle of Pinkie alone had resulted in the deaths of over 10,000 Scotsmen, a significant number for such a relatively unpopulated country. There was also the matter of the royal coffers, which Châtelherault was still depleting for his own purposes thanks to an assurance by King Henri that he would not be made to repay any deficit.

Nonetheless, if Scotland was going to recover from so many years of conflict, money would need to be found from somewhere to pay for all the work needed to repair the country's defences and make it whole again. Marie's own personal jointure, while extremely generous, was not enough to do more than pay her household wages and expenses and maintain the court in a suitably regal manner.

As Scotland entered into this new period of peace, Marie found herself thinking more often about her own country of France, not just because King Henri seemed like the best bet for giving her ailing finances a boost, but also because both her surviving children were there along with the rest of her family. It was the first time in several years that her adopted country of Scotland had been at peace with their neighbour England and she wondered whether it might be time to chance a visit home. Letters still arrived as frequently as ever from her friends and relations in France, all of whom gave her updates about how healthy and handsome her son was growing up to be, and how beautiful little Queen Mary, now almost 8 years old, was. It was never going to be as good as seeing them for herself though and when the devastating news arrived of her beloved father's death on 12 April 1550, her mind was made up and she began to make plans for departure.

Claude, Duc de Guise, was much mourned throughout France where he had been regarded as a national hero and a fierce defender of the Catholic faith, although this obviously made him rather less popular with the Protestant population of the country. His funeral was a grand affair, worthy of a prince (which his father's claim to the kingdom of Sicily technically made him) and attended by all the great and good of the land. As with royal funerals, an effigy of the dead Duc de Guise, dressed in grey satin and draped in a lustrous cloak of gold cloth and costly jewels, presided over the various ceremonies, which included a feast for the poor of the district before his body was interred in a lavish tomb in the Joinville chapel. His widow, Antoinette was left well provided for, retaining beautiful Joinville for the rest of her life as well as a very handsome fortune. There had never been anyone else for her but Claude though and she spent the remainder of her days in mourning. She even commissioned her own coffin and placed it in the gallery outside her chamber so that every time she walked past it, she would be reminded of her own mortality and the fact that one day she would be reunited with her beloved husband.

There were all the usual unsavoury rumours of foul play when Claude de Guise died, it was whispered that he had been poisoned either by one of the Protestant factions that were springing up like mushrooms all over France, or their dynastic enemies and nearest rivals, the Habsburgs. When his brother, Jean, Cardinal de Lorraine, also died suddenly on 10 May, less than a month later, it gave extra credence to the suspicions of poisoning; the Guise family became convinced that the Habsburgs were behind both deaths, although without any proof all they could do was record on Claude de Guise's lead coffin that 'Here lies the high and mighty prince Claude de Lorraine, son of René de Sicily... who died by poisoning.' It was a difficult time for the Guise family, little wonder, therefore, that Marie was keen to go home and be with them.

King Henri was delighted to hear of her plans to visit and personally contacted the English Privy Council to arrange her safe passage along the coast from Scotland. Meanwhile, Marie turned her mind to more frivolous matters and wrote to her old friend, Diane de Poitiers, now her brother's mother-in-law, to ask for advice about the latest French fashions and whether it would be suitable for her to arrive in France wearing mourning for her father when queens did not usually wear mourning for anyone other than their husbands.

French etiquette was extremely strict when it came to such matters and Marie didn't want to start her visit off on the wrong foot. She was also keen to project the right impression of Scotland as a sophisticated, modern nation on a par with any other country in Europe; not the barbaric backwater that plenty of people at the French court still believed to be. It wouldn't do at all to turn up wearing last year's fashions.

She would have been gratified had she known that the French court was just excited by the prospect of seeing her again as she was about going there. Great plans were afoot for all manner of splendid receptions and celebrations in her honour. Even the christening of the latest little Valois prince, the future Charles IX who was born in June 1550, was delayed so that she could act as his godmother. However, Marie's much-anticipated departure was delayed until early September by the usual tiresome squabbling between her lords of the Scottish Privy Council. When she finally did set sail with a large retinue of Scottish nobility, most of whom were known English supporters who she wanted to impress with the magnificence of the French court and the generous pensions and cash gifts that King Henri would no doubt distribute to buy their loyalty, they were held up again by appalling storms at sea.

Marie and her retinue, the captain and sailors all wearing white damask to reflect the joyousness of the occasion, landed at Dieppe on 19 September, where they were given a rapturous welcome by her brothers. François, the eldest, had been just 19 years old when she left France to marry the King of Scotland and was now a hulking great 31-year-old with a formidable reputation as a warrior and military strategist while the next brother, 26-year-old Charles, was already Archbishop of Reims and a Cardinal who was reputed to possess one of the most brilliant minds at court, if not all Europe. They made a formidable team, the two Guise brothers, but to Marie they were simply her little brothers and most ardent defenders and she fell thankfully into their arms.

The Guise entourage made its way from Dieppe to Rouen where the entire French royal family and court had gathered to welcome her. With them was her mother Antoinette, daughter Mary and son François, now almost 15 and a far cry from the cheeky little boy she had left behind twelve years earlier.

Marie remained in France for the next twelve months, making the most of this longed for reunion with her family and friends. At the same time, she concentrated her energy on brokering an understanding with King Henri that he would financially assist Scotland's recovery from years of war and back any future claim that she might make upon the Regency. The troublesome Châtelherault had been left behind to govern in Scotland and her concern about what he might be getting up to in her absence only increased her zeal to get King Henri's support against him. The only hurdle seemed to be the fact that Henri's advisors were urging him to replace Châtelherault with a Frenchman, the prejudice against women ruling being so strong that many of them could not contemplate the thought of Marie, however clever and capable she might be, taking over the reins of power.

In the end, Marie went to Henri herself and asked him to give her the Regency of Scotland. To her relief, he willingly acquiesced, being absolutely convinced of both Marie's abilities and her loyalty to France. He cautioned her nonetheless, that it could not happen straight away and she must bide her time. As for financial assistance, again he was happy to help and there was even mention of sending more troops should she require them. He also generously greased the fists of the pro-English courtiers that she had brought in her train, winning them over with lavish pensions and other gifts.

As Marie had hoped, the King of France seemed as committed to creating a greater bond between their two nations as she was, not just because they had a common enemy in England but also because the French seemed to take an almost paternalistic interest in Scotland's growth and development. There was no finer advertisement for Scotland than the little Queen Mary, and even the most arrogant courtiers found their prejudices about the 'barbaric' northern country fade away when the pretty girl, all pink cheeks, auburn curls and huge hazel eyes, performed Scottish folk dances in her extremely fanciful 'Highland' costume of artfully sewn furs, lace and plaid.

Marie remained with the court for most of her year in France, reacquainting herself with the royal châteaux and palaces she had known in her youth while presiding over numerous fêtes, banquets, balls and other festivities being held in her honour. Real gunpowder was used during a huge fake naval battle on the Seine near Rouen to add more excitement to the explosions; unfortunately, two barrels of gunpowder accidentally ignited, destroying the ships they were on and killing the crews. These wasteful tragedies aside, it was a dazzling holiday away from the cares of governing Scotland, and she was determined to make the most of it. She also found time for personal visits, to Châteaudun, where she had been so happy with her first husband and where both he and their youngest son lay buried and also to Joinville with her appreciative Scottish entourage, where she prayed at her father's tomb. Claude de Guise may have been a lax correspondent, but his devotion to his wife and children had been genuine; the close-knit family, so committed to each other's interests and advancement, that he had left behind was a fine testimony of this. Marie may have been away for twelve years, and even committed herself to a different cause, but she would always remain a Guise, and a central part of her family no matter how far away she was.

As she wandered through the familiar, beloved rooms of Joinville with her adored son and daughter on either side of her, it must have occurred to her that it would be easy to stay where she was and let Châtelherault and the other lords deal with Scotland and its problems. It would be wonderfully easy to resume the threads of her old life in France, taking up residence at Châteaudun again with her son beside her, visiting her mother at Joinville or her brothers at their new château at Meudon, or even travelling the country with her daughter and the royal court. She could even, if she wished, take up residence in one of the convents now presided over by her younger sisters, Renée and Antoinette, both of whom had opted to take the veil even though the former was said to be the most beautiful Guise girl of them all. She knew that she would be welcomed with open arms whatever she decided and wherever she went. However, none of these plans, tempting though they must have been, had the same compelling level of challenge and satisfaction that returning to take charge of Scotland gave her. Although her children undoubtedly wanted to have her there with them, neither of them *needed* her in quite the same way as her adopted nation seemed to, and the sensation of being actually needed was one that Marie de Guise could not resist.

Having made the decision to return, Marie began to make preparations to leave in the spring of 1551, but quickly postponed them when details of a plot to poison her young daughter began to surface; the culprit being one of the dastardly 'Castilians' who had caused Marie so much trouble during the siege of St Andrews. Having been captured by the French, he somehow managed to evade his captors and join the French King's regiment of Scots Guards. His intention was to use his access to the royal kitchens in order to slip poison into the little Queen's favourite dish, frittered pears. Luckily his plan was discovered in the nick of time, but Marie was so horrified and distressed by the thought that her daughter's life was in danger, even in France, that she completely collapsed and had to remain in bed for several days.

It was September by the time she felt able to leave her children and family again and, after taking a last sorrowful farewell of her daughter Mary and the rest of her French family and friends, she set out for Dieppe, accompanied by her son, François. He was nearly 16 years old, almost a man and soon free to visit her whenever he liked. They were at Amiens when he started to feel unwell and was forced to take to his bed. Marie tenderly nursed him with her own hands and kept vigil by his side until he died in her arms on 22 September.

The entire Guise family was devastated by the news of the young Duc de Longueville's death, not least because it meant relinquishing the control that they had maintained over his vast estates and fortune, but mostly on his own account for he had been brought up by Antoinette as if he were her own son and treated like a brother by his numerous aunts and uncles. No one was more distressed though than his mother, who had been reunited with him for too short a time but at least had the consolation of being with him for his final moments. She was too devastated by his death to attend his funeral in the Sainte Chapelle of Châteaudun, where he was buried beside his father and younger brother, and chose to mourn him privately. 'I think, my lady, as you wrote to me, that Our Lord must wish me for one of His chosen ones, since He has visited me so often with such sorrow,' she wrote to her mother from Dieppe as she prepared to leave France for what was to be the last time.

In a surprising but inspired break from the original plan, Marie decided not to travel to Scotland by sea but instead to cross the Channel to Rye and progress by easy stages through England, making the most of the current peace between their two nations. As with her stay in France, this was not entirely motivated by pleasure as she planned to meet with the young King Edward and his latest Lord President of the Council, the Duke of Northumberland, who had taken power after the sudden fall of his now disgraced and imprisoned predecessor, the Duke of Somerset in October 1549. Once again the stormy autumn weather was her enemy and instead of Rye, she found herself landing at Portsmouth where she sent messengers to London to inform King Edward of her arrival. The young King responded with great pleasure, inviting her to come to him and so Marie set out on a progress across the southern counties of England where she was hosted and entertained by several noble families along the way. At Guildford in Surrey she was met by the noted diplomat and soldier, Lord William

Howard, uncle of Anne Boleyn and Catherine Howard; he accompanied her to Hampton Court Palace where a large company of courtiers greeted her.

As the Countess of Pembroke (sister of the now dead Queen Catherine Parr) and her sister-in-law, the Marchioness of Northampton, and sixty other court ladies led her through the royal apartments to the queen's rooms, Marie must have been struck by the extravagance of the palace's interior. There were countless precious carpets, beautiful paintings, richly gilded carvings and sculptures, priceless tapestries woven with gold and silver thread, enamel set furniture, gold plate and exquisite stained glass windows. There were equally fine pieces of art in the palaces of Scotland but nothing quite on this lavish scale. Marie was well aware, however, that much of England's wealth, and many of the treasures that furnished Hampton Court Palace, had been derived from the denuding and destruction of religious orders and their churches so couldn't really bring herself to envy any of it. Scotland may have less, it was true, but at least it had been bought with relatively honest coin.

That evening, Henry VIII's beautiful great hall was filled with light and colour as the courtiers gathered for a great feast followed by dancing, all presided over by Marie de Guise who sat at a high table on the dais with the Ladies of Pembroke and Northampton. It's a pity that Catherine Parr, the last wife of Henry VIII, was not still alive and able to meet her as the two women, although divided by religious belief, had much in common. Their portraits suggest that they even resembled each other and shared the same colouring. As it was, Marie went to bed that night feeling truly welcomed and heartened by the warm reception that she had received, which certainly suggested that the tensions between Scotland and England, if not entirely buried, were certainly on hold.

After enjoying a deer hunt in the palace's great park and a guided tour of its various treasures, it was time for Marie to leave Hampton Court and travel on to London, which she did in the King's own royal barge. Her first stop was Baynard's Castle, where the Duke of Northumberland welcomed her, before being escorted to the Bishop of London's palace. Here, she was lavishly entertained once again, presented with gifts of fine foods and spices from the Lord Mayor of London and received the Duke of Suffolk (Henry Grey, husband of King Edward's cousin, Lady Frances Brandon, who had recently inherited the title after the death of her young brothers) and Earl of Huntingdon, who had been despatched by King Edward with highly gratifying messages of friendship and welcome. Another notable personage who visited Marie at Fulham Palace was Lady Margaret Douglas, half sister of her husband, James V, and now Countess of Lennox. The two women, although closely connected by bonds of family, had never met before because Lady Margaret had been born and raised in England. They probably found much to talk about, not least Lady Margaret's promising 5-year-old son, Henry, who bore the courtesy title of Lord Darnley.

On the 4 November 1551, Marie travelled with great pomp and ceremony to the Palace of Westminster, where she finally met King Edward in the great hall of the palace, the very same room where Anne Boleyn had enjoyed her coronation banquet and then, just three years later, endured her trial. Although Marie seemed to have to have lived her entire life in the shadow of the Tudor monarchs, this was the first time she had come face-to-face with one; it must have been a fascinating and rather unnerving experience to meet this boy who might, under different circumstances, have been either her stepson or son-in-law. The two monarchs seemed pleased with each other as Edward formally welcomed her to his court, then did her the honour of escorting her to her apartments, which were as sumptuous as those she had enjoyed at Hampton Court Palace. Edward VI was only recently turned 14, much the same age as her son, François, which must have caused her to suffer a few pangs of sadness as they walked together through the palace. If Henry VIII had been a byword for regal magnificence, his young son was very different and seemed almost lost inside his elaborate clothes. His frail physique and pallid complexion, inherited from his mother, Jane Seymour, highlighted rather than concealed by the swaggering, ostentatious fashions of the day.

Marie and Edward dined together in the Palace of Westminster that night, sharing a cloth of state and attended by great ceremony. 'We were served by two services, two sewers, cupbearers, carvers and gentlemen,' the young King wrote in his diary about the evening.

Her Maître d'Hotel came before her service and my officers before mine. There were two cupboards, one of gold four stages high, another of massy silver, six stages. In her great chamber, dined at three boards the ladies only. After dinner when she had heard some music I brought her to the hall and so she went away.

It's not known what Marie and the young King of England found to talk about but it seems that relations were amiable enough, even if certain topics had to be tactfully avoided, for the next day he sent her two fine horses and a diamond ring worth around £1,000 as presents and tokens of his good will. Two days later, Marie left Westminster in a great procession that wound through the streets of London. At her side rode the new Lord Protector, the Duke of Northumberland, while elsewhere in their retinue rode the Countess of Lennox and several other lords and ladies, in all a great company of several hundred people. According to the Spanish Ambassador, 'many people have grumbled about this, especially about the reception given the Queen, saying that it was done rather to please the King of France than for any other reason.' He also made a point of noting that when Edward met the Queen at Westminster he came 'forward to greet her half-way down the hall of his palace' and then 'kept always to the right hand' when he parted from her at the end of the evening, both polite ways of showing her great honour and respect.

To Marie's disappointment neither of the King's sisters were present at their meeting, although both had been summoned to meet her. Lady Mary sent a polite reply claiming that her poor health made it inadvisable for her to attempt the journey to court, but history has not preserved Lady Elizabeth's excuse for not attending. It's not likely that their absence was due to personal enmity directed at Marie, but rather due to concerns about precedence, or perhaps just an unwillingness to expose themselves to the lion's den that was Edward VI's court, which was every bit as dangerous as the one his father had presided over, if not more so.

Marie travelled north back to Scotland in easy stages, seeing much of the English countryside and being entertained at each stop on her journey. At Berwick on the borders, she was met by Lord Bothwell who escorted her back to Edinburgh. Her journey was over and she was home at last. If Châtelherault was disappointed to see her return, he hid it well and gave every appearance of being delighted to see her again. Naturally Marie knew better, but spending over a year being courted and fêted by the great and good of France and England had given her a renewed sense of purpose and a fresh boost of confidence in her abilities. Châtelherault could hardly complain either, although he must have been jealous to hear of Marie's successful meetings with the two Kings and rapturous reception in both countries. Scotland's international prestige had never been higher and it was all thanks to Marie's hard work and charm. No one else could have done half as well and Châtelherault knew it.

The next eighteen months were spent relatively peacefully, restoring Scotland to full prosperity and reinforcing the country's beleaguered defences. Although her visit to France had ended badly, Marie had still returned full of enthusiasm and freshly inspired by the French way of doing things, which she was keen to implement in Scotland, determined to bring the nation up to date.

Now that they were enjoying what may prove to be a short-lived peace with England, it was time to turn their attention to the bitter fighting between the different clans and the lawlessness that prevailed in some parts of the country. To this end, Marie and Châtelherault spent a lot of time travelling around the northern counties of Scotland, dealing with disputes between the different noble families and attempting to impose some level of law and order upon the populace. In-fighting and rivalries between the different clans would continue to be a feature of Scottish life for quite some time, but Marie at least recognised that something needed to be done about it if they were to form a united front against any future threat of war from England.

For the time being though, relations between the two nations were amicable enough and from July 1553 onwards, the English had problems of their own to contend with when the 15-year-old King

Edward died suddenly without any heirs. He had been betrothed to the French Princess Élisabeth, the closest friend of Marie's daughter, but as the princess was just 8 years old, the marriage had not taken place before the young King fell ill and died. The ensuing squabbling over the succession between his putative heirs, most notably his sister, the Lady Mary Tudor, and the supporters of his cousin, Lady Jane Grey, would keep the English occupied for quite some time.

The Third Succession Act of Henry VIII had effectively disinherited the children and descendants of his elder sister, Margaret, which included both Queen Mary of Scotland and her aunt, the Countess of Lennox, in favour of the descendants of his younger sister, Mary, which included Lady Jane Grey and her sisters, in the event of his own line ending without issue. Marie had enough on her plate already and so made no mention of her own daughter's claim but in France, King Henri and the ambitious Guise brothers were both all too well aware that their young protegé, Queen Mary, was a potential heiress to the English throne. In fact, to many Catholics, her claim was far better than that of the Lady Mary, who had been deemed illegitimate after the annulment of her parents' marriage.

The Countess of Lennox was a close friend of her cousin, Lady Mary, and when the latter was finally installed as Queen, the Lennox couple naturally began to acquire even more influence at court, where the Countess was installed as the new Queen's chief favourite. One of Mary Tudor's first acts as Queen was to write to Marie to reassure her that she had every intention of maintaining peaceful relations between their nations, which was hardly surprising as they were both Catholic monarchs facing an ever-increasing tide of Protestantism in both their countries and might well need each other's support at some point.

On the other hand, Marie was worried by reports that the Earl of Lennox was planning to take advantage of his wife's closeness to the throne in order to assert his own claim to take over the Regency of Scotland once Châtelherault was ousted. Greatly disturbed by the prospect of Lennox attempting to seize power, Marie, the Lieutenant General of Scotland, Monsieur d'Oysel and her brothers in France decided it was time to make a move. After several months of discussions and bartering, they finally forced Châtelherault to agree to hand the Regency of Scotland, along with Edinburgh Castle and Holyroodhouse Palace, both of which he had used as his own residences, over to Marie in exchange for several generous financial incentives.

Marie de Guise was formally proclaimed Queen Regent of Scotland on Thursday, 12 April 1554 at a meeting of the Scottish Parliament in Edinburgh. After Châtelherault had regretfully tendered his resignation, Marie triumphantly entered the chamber dressed in her ermine lined robes of state to be crowned by Monsieur d'Oysel and handed the sceptre and sword of state. It was the moment that she had hoped and schemed for since the death of her husband eleven years earlier, and she was determined to make the most of it.

Chapter 14

Queen Regent

Marie threw herself into her new task with aplomb, delighted to be free of Châtelherault at last and finally able to put her own plans for Scotland into operation without interference. Although the French undoubtedly had ambitions to make Scotland a satellite state, subject to their own laws and government, Marie had very different ideas for her adopted land. She wanted to make Scotland entirely independent, the very model of an advanced and prosperous Renaissance state just as her husband and his father had planned to do before they were cut off in their prime. She would base her style of government on the French model and always seek to strengthen the alliance between the two countries as much as possible, but she had no intention of allowing her daughter's inheritance to slip out of her hands.

Although relations between Scotland and England were amicable enough for now, Marie was aware that they could deteriorate at any time, especially as hostilities between England and France seemed set to resume thanks to Mary Tudor's loyalty to her cousin, the Emperor Charles V, and the pro-Habsburg policies she espoused as a result. By marrying the Emperor's son, Philip II of Spain, in July 1554, she effectively bound England even closer to his family's aims and, most significantly, their quarrels, particularly with France. It was only a matter of time before England and France were at each other's throats once again and in Scotland, Marie watched and waited for war to return to her doorstep.

As expected, Châtelherault had not just cleaned out the royal coffers, but also left Marie with a sizeable deficit of £30,000 with which to begin her reign. She still had her own jointure revenues but they often arrived late and, although generous enough to provide for the household of an aristocratic widow, were not nearly enough to pay for an entire country. Money, specifically the lack of it, would be a serious problem for Marie from now on and she was forced to put an end to the renovation of the royal palaces, sell her belongings and practise economies within her own household. Not that she really minded – the days of frivolity, dancing and flirtation were long gone and now work was the one and only focus of her energies. She removed Châtelherault's supporters and the more pro-English members of the court from positions of authority and replaced them with men who were either loyal to her or could be bribed to toe the line.

The long years of war had left Scotland troubled and poor and Marie was determined to do something about both issues; turning her attention first to the incessant fighting between the different families, particularly those in the far north of the country. The greatest families held enormous authority in their areas resulting in blood feuds that could go on for generations; legal and administrative systems became localised, while those in power felt themselves answerable to no one. It was Marie's plan to enforce a more centralised form of government that would impose law and order upon the country as a whole rather than allowing several families to employ their own interpretations of it. This, she believed, would make Scotland a more unified and modern nation, better able to withstand external threats. Too many battles had been lost because of in-fighting between the different clan chiefs – this would have to end if they were to have any hope of survival. She decided to revive her husband's policy of making clan chiefs liable for the wrong doings of their followers and informed them that they would face severe sanctions if they did not bring felons to justice.

When it came to country's parlous economic state, Marie oversaw several legislations in Parliament which were designed to boost the failing economy and ensure that the Scottish people had sufficient resources. Harsh penalties were imposed on poachers and anyone one who was caught stealing beehives or committing other criminal acts that might damage the food supply. Farmers were encouraged to increase their flocks and, as sheep were in particularly short supply, they were forbidden to sell them at market or slaughter lambs for three years in order to increase numbers, while the export of meat was strictly controlled and that of animal by-products, like wool and leather, was prohibited completely.

Marie was also aghast by the destructive results of warfare on the once magnificent Scottish forests. Trees had been cut down in their thousands to provide timber for the navy and Marie gave orders that, from then on, they were to be protected and allowed to grow. She couldn't return Scotland to its original state, too many men had died and too much water had flowed under the bridge for that, but she could do her best to restore a sense of national pride and, more importantly, normalcy to the lives of its people.

In order to oversee the meting out of justice and to ensure that she was a familiar sight to the Scottish people, Marie spent a great deal of time travelling about the country; she attended justice ayres in places as far away as Forres in Morayshire, where local grievances were debated and wrongdoers put on trial. Apparently, no local issue was too trivial, no court case too mundane to be of interest to the Queen Regent and she saw the whole spectrum of Scottish life brought before her during these sessions, dealing with each one with her characteristic intelligence, sympathy and sense of fairness. She did not shy away from pronouncing death sentences on those who deserved it, but could also be relatively merciful as in the case of Henry Wynd of Dysart, who should have been condemned to death by burning for his crime of debasing the coinage but had his sentence changed to beheading at Marie's request. Usually though, she preferred to avoid the death sentence altogether and instead impose fines, which had the additional bonus of bringing more money to the country's empty coffers.

Like Elizabeth Tudor, Marie learned from the mistakes of others. In a misogynistic and patriarchal society that resented the existence of capable, outspoken women like herself – and even believed that their being in power was against the will of God – it was inadvisable for a woman who wished to maintain her authority to ever share her power with someone else. The misadventures of her mother-in-law, Margaret

Tudor, had been a perfect illustration of this, and now it seemed as though Mary Tudor was intent on making her country a mere chattel of Spain, always blindly obedient to the Habsburg party line. It was not an easy path to follow though and although Marie had decided it was better to be alone, she did not expect her daughter to do the same – even if she couldn't help but worry about what would happen to Scotland should Queen Mary or the Dauphin die.

Although she was surrounded at all times by ladies in waiting, counsellors, courtiers, visitors and advisors, Marie must have been lonely at least some of the time, when her exhausting workload was pushed aside at the end of the day and she was left alone in the candlelit gloom of her bedchamber. Unlike Elizabeth Tudor, there were never any rumours of illicit affairs, secret husbands or romantic entanglements about Marie de Guise. Even John Knox, who was gaining influence among the ever-increasing ranks of Scottish Protestants, couldn't find anything more credible to throw at her than a rather pathetic insinuation that she had been the lover of Cardinal Beaton. It really does seem that her daughter, and the work she had taken on in Scotland on her behalf, were her only passions in life and that she had genuinely resigned herself to being alone; a sad situation for a woman in her mid-thirties to be in.

As always, there were plenty of letters from France to lighten her spirits during these years. Her mother and brothers wrote regularly to keep her up to date with family news, court gossip and business matters concerning her jointure. Their own careers were going from strength to strength as the Guise brothers became ever more powerful at court and indispensable to King Henri, who was also a frequent correspondent. Above all, they kept her up-to-date with news of her daughter, who turned 15 in December 1557 and was, by all accounts, a pretty and charming young girl who delighted everyone with her intelligence and gracefulness. She was, as Marie was repeatedly informed, 'the most perfect princess' and, although she must have suffered many a pang of sorrow that she was unable to see Mary grow up, she felt enormous pride that her daughter was so admired and adored by both the royal family and the Guises.

King Henri's wife, Catherine de' Medici, might not have been fond of her future daughter-in-law, but as the French court was dominated by her husband's mistress, a great friend and ally to the Guises and their young Queen, no one really cared what she thought about her opinion on the matter.

Less pleasantly, the letters from France often included polite requests for money as Marie was expected to fund her daughter's household expenses. These became increasingly hefty as the years passed and the young Queen's tastes in clothes, jewels and horses became more extravagant and her household more sizeable. Her Guise uncles encouraged Queen Mary in her ostentatious spending, telling the impressionable girl that as a reigning Queen in her own right, it was her duty to project a majestic appearance at all times. They would not, however, pay for any of it themselves and so Marie, already worried enough about the abysmal state of the Scottish economy, was forced to find enormous sums of money to pay for her daughter's upkeep. Most of the money came from her precious jointures but it wasn't enough to assuage the flood of letters from her brothers, daughter and her daughter's chief attendant, Mademoiselle de Parois, all complaining about the lack of money and resultant indignities suffered by Queen Mary and her household, who could not always afford to travel with the court.

This all paled into insignificance though next to their concerns about Queen Mary's health, which had never been entirely robust. She had been prone to mysterious collapses ever since girlhood and often complained of stomach pains, headaches, nausea and an overwhelming sense of lassitude and depression. It's possible that the young Queen was suffering from nothing more serious than an anxiety related disorder but these could also have been symptoms of more serious conditions such as porphyria, which would affect her descendant, George III. In 1556, Mary became quite seriously ill and there were persistent rumours in Scotland that she was at death's door, which led to fears that King Henri might override the marriage treaty and seize control of Scotland anyway. Marie was kept up-to-date with the progress of Mary's illness and knew it wasn't too serious; even so she,

she struggled to reassure her subjects that they were not in danger of being invaded by the French, particularly as the country was still seemingly full of French troops.

In July 1557, the long expected hostilities between England and France flared up as Queen Mary Tudor gave in to her husband's demands that she send an invasion fleet across the Channel. To everyone's surprise, the combined English and Spanish forces then scored a decisive victory against the French at Saint Quentin, where Marie's old correspondent, Admiral de Montmorency, was captured. Her brother, François, had been fighting a dismal campaign in Spain at the time but returned to court as soon as news arrived of the French defeat. King Henri invested him with the position of Lieutenant-General of France and instructed him to take back Calais, the last piece of English territory on French soil, in revenge for the humiliation of Saint Quentin. François de Guise was doubtful that an attempt on Calais could be successful but, like his sister, he was not one to turn down a challenge and so obediently began to gather his troops and lay plans. In the event, it turned out to be well worth the gamble because he managed to take back Calais in January 1558. This almost impossible feat made him one of the most fêted war heroes that France had ever known and significantly increased his family's prestige and power at court.

Meanwhile, King Henri decided that it was time for François' sister, Marie, to prove her commitment to the French alliance and send her troops to attack the English. Although she was unwilling to imperil the fragile cordiality between the two nations, she had no choice but to give in and gave orders for all men between the ages of 16 and 60 to be mustered to supplement the existing Scottish and French troops, the latter of which were being brought up from Eyemouth by Monsieur d'Oysel. Despite Mary Tudor's protestations of friendliness, the English raids across the Scottish borders had never really abated and so Marie found it easy enough to justify military action by exaggerating the potential for another English invasion in the near future. To further bolster morale, she accompanied the troops to Hume Castle near Kelso before instructing her army to cross the border and besiege Wark Castle. It should have been an easy victory for Marie's forces but to her great dismay, Oysel quickly returned with the news that Scottish troops, unwilling to give up their lives for the sake of someone else's quarrel, had picked arguments with the French commanders and deserted before they had even reached the border, deliberately flouting her orders and humiliating her in the eyes of the French.

To add to her annoyance, the Scottish Parliament, which had been seriously alarmed by the reports of Queen Mary's poor health, had begun pressing Marie on the subject of her daughter's marriage which, they believed, ought to have taken place by now. The French match was not universally popular but with the increasing threat of war with England, the lords did not feel secure with an unmarried Queen at the helm and wanted to see Mary married as soon as possible, despite baulking at the prospect of her French husband being crowned King of Scotland. Marie might have privately laughed at the thought of the Dauphin François – who was two years younger than her daughter and of a sickly disposition – being regarded as the manly saviour of the Scottish people, but she had to concede that their position would never be secure until the marriage was accomplished and France and Scotland officially joined as allies.

To this end, she urged her brothers to use their influence to bring the match about, telling Charles that:

> *my daughter's illness has put many things in doubt, and, to keep nothing back from you, men's minds have been so changeable and in such a state of suspense that those from the most I have found more estranged than I have ever seen them, not just since I have ruled them but since I came to Scotland.*

Despite beginning her regency with such high hopes, Marie was now dismayed to find the Scottish people were beginning to turn against her; it was obvious that no matter what she did, her sex and nationality would always count against her as far as they were concerned.

God knows, brother, what a life I lead, she wrote sadly to her brother Charles. *It is no small thing to bring a young nation to a state of perfection and to an unwonted subservience to those who wish to see justice reign. Great responsibilities are easily undertaken but not so easily discharged to the satisfaction of God. Happy is he who has least to do with worldly affairs. I can safely say that in twenty years past I have not had one year of rest and I think that if I were to say not one month I should not be far wrong, for a troubled spirit is the greatest trial of all.*

King Henri was eager to reward the Guise family by accepting their request that the marriage between his son and Queen Mary of Scotland should take place as soon as possible. The royal wedding took place at Notre Dame in Paris on 24 April 1558 with the bride's Guise uncles almost stealing the show with the lavish amounts of largesse that they distributed amongst the enormous crowds that had gathered to see Mary of Scotland enter the beautiful gothic cathedral in a gown of white satin encrusted with pearls and diamonds. Amongst those in Paris to take part in the wedding festivities was Mary's 27-year-old half brother, Lord James Stewart, the son of her father, James V, and his favourite mistress, Lady Margaret Erskine.

Lord James could never quite forget that he might have been King of Scotland if his father had gone ahead with his original plan to marry his mother; despite this, he got on well with Marie de Guise and became a favourite of hers. At one point, there had even been the suggestion that she planned to make James Regent of Scotland instead of herself, thinking it might be a more popular move with the Scots than seizing power for herself. This seems unlikely, not least because he was known to be sympathetic to the Protestant religion and a supporter of the burgeoning Scottish Reformation. However, it's clear that he was certainly trusted enough by her to form part of the Scottish delegation sent to Paris to oversee her daughter's marriage to the Dauphin.

What Lord James and his fellow Scottish wedding guests didn't know was that at the palace of Fontainebleau, only a few weeks before the wedding, Queen Mary had betrayed them all by secretly signing two documents that bequeathed her kingdom of Scotland, and all important place in the English royal succession, over to France should she die without any heirs. The documents also guaranteed King Henri the vast sum of one million crowns from the strained Scottish crown revenue to repay the sums that he had spent defending her country and providing for her maintenance and education in France.

The third document was a prenuptial agreement between Mary and the Dauphin François with an additional sting hidden amongst its ornate language: the nullification of any future agreements or contracts made by the Scottish Parliament that might prejudice the other two agreements. This was a brilliant but unethical move by the Guise brothers who had relied upon their niece's youthful naïvety and, worse still, absolute trust in their good faith not to alert her to the fact that she was signing away her inheritance. It is perhaps telling that they did not inform their sister, Marie, of what they had induced her daughter to do, undoubtedly aware that she would have been horrified. The agreement would do irreparable damage to her reputation and increasingly difficult hold upon authority if the Scottish people became aware of Mary's betrayal.

Mercifully ignorant of her brothers' cynical exploitation of her daughter's youth and inexperience, Marie presided over the Scottish celebrations of the marriage, which included cannon fire from Edinburgh Castle and other festivities. Although she allowed herself to enjoy this moment of triumph, she knew that anti-French feeling was on the rise throughout Scotland, exacerbated by the Protestant groups whose numbers were swelled by refugees from the persecution of Mary Tudor across the border. Marie de Guise may have shared her neighbour Queen's sincere and deep Catholic faith, but the similarity ended there. Marie had no taste for persecution, martyrdom or bloodshed. This was an unusual stance for such a prominent member of the notoriously hard-line Roman Catholic Guise family to take, but Marie had learned that God moves in mysterious and often terrible ways, and it was not for her to question the different paths that took people to Him. Like Elizabeth Tudor, she had no desire to make windows into men's souls.

Senseless destruction, however, was a very different matter and she became concerned about the increasing incidents of iconoclasm by Protestant mobs, egged on by the likes of John Knox, who was residing in Geneva but would return to Scotland in May 1559, when he and his friends destroyed the famous life-sized effigy of Saint Giles that was traditionally carried through Edinburgh on his feast day. To Marie, this presaged something more threatening than a mere difference of religious opinion and she was determined to nip it in the bud.

As to the statue of Saint Giles, Marie hastily commissioned a smaller version and personally attended its procession through the streets on 1 September, which began well before descending into chaos and violence when a Protestant mob seized the statue and threw it to the ground. Dispirited and alarmed by this, Marie began to reconsider her neutral stance, even though it was obvious that, as with modern day terrorists, the mobs had little to do with the religion they espoused and merely used it as an excuse to cause havoc and disharmony. Marie sincerely pitied the ordinary, every day Protestants caught up in the trouble but still could not afford to give in to their demands for greater religious freedoms. She believed that giving them permission to organise meetings to pray and hear the Bible in the vernacular, along with other relatively harmless sounding concessions, was merely the thin edge of the wedge and would lead to greater, more divisive demands.

Matters went from bad to worse when Mary Tudor died in November 1558 and was succeeded by her younger half sister, Elizabeth, a known supporter of the Protestant faith. Almost immediately, Marie's hope that they could continue the amicable relationship maintained throughout her sister's reign was threatened by the reaction of her brothers in France. The indisputable royal lineage and Catholic faith of Mary Tudor had protected her from any aggressive assertion of the counter claim by the Stuart line descended from Henry VIII's sister, Margaret. Elizabeth, the Protestant daughter of Henry's rather more patrician second wife, was a very different matter, however.

Cardinal de Lorraine wasted little time before proclaiming his niece, Mary of Scotland, the rightful Queen of England and began to lobby the Pope and other ruling houses of Europe to support her claim. The arms of England were added to those of France and Scotland on Mary and François' plate and other household goods. As the months went by, further embellishments were added, all designed to enhance Mary's claim to the English throne by fundamentally making her a rival Queen. However, the ambitious Guise brothers faced unexpected opposition from Philip of Spain, who was keen to marry his former sister-in-law, Elizabeth Tudor; consequently, he saw no value in supporting a rival French-Scottish claim to her throne and put pressure on the Pope to reject the Guise pretensions.

There was a further blow later in 1559 when King Henri, who had originally colluded with their assertion of his daughter-in-law's claim to the English throne, started to realise how risky this policy was and began to lose his nerve. He had already spent vast sums of money on building up and maintaining the defences of Scotland and had no appetite for further warfare against the English, who would almost certainly retaliate should the Guise family continue to push the issue of Mary's claim to the throne. To this end, he made it clear to Duc François and Cardinal Charles that they had gone too far and began to negotiate treaties with Elizabeth of England and Philip of Spain. The result was the Treaty of Cateau-Cambrésis, which promised peace between England, France, Spain and Scotland and was sealed by the usual merry-go-round of royal marriages.

Isolated in Scotland, Marie could do very little but watch this drama unfold, irritated by her brothers' meddling and apprehensive for her daughter, whom she had quickly realised was an innocent pawn in the schemes of her elders. She could only hope that Elizabeth Tudor, who by all accounts had endured more than her own fair share of exploitation by unscrupulous elders during her tempestuous youth, realised this too and would not lay the blame for the whole debacle at Mary's door.

Closer to home, Elizabeth's succession to the English throne gave a definite boost to the activities of the more militant Scottish Protestants who believed that they could now rely on English support in their quest to rid Scotland of what they regarded as the interlinked evils of France and the Roman Catholic faith. Attacks on churches and clergy increased in 1559, a year which began with the so-called 'Beggars Summons' being nailed to every monastery door, ordering the monks to hand their assets over to the poor or face the consequences. The reappearance of John Knox in a blaze of glory and publicity less than a week later, at the same time as Queen Elizabeth made an official return to the Protestant religious policies of her brother, Edward VI, only added to Marie's headache. In an attempt to maintain order she invited the Protestant ringleaders to meet her at Stirling Castle, hoping that she could win them over. Unfortunately, their suspicion and dislike of everything she represented to them was too great and her request resulted in even more violence as their followers threatened to come with them, hinting that they didn't trust Marie not to have them all imprisoned or worse.

This was the final straw and Marie retaliated by ordering that the agitating Protestant preachers should be immediately arrested and deported from Scotland. The response to this unusual miscalculation was swift and brutal; Knox began to whip up support against her with a series of sermons that denounced both Marie and the French alliance and extolled his listeners to 'cleanse the temple' by removing all symbols of idolatrous Papistry. His sermon at St John's Kirk in Perth on 11 May ended with a full scale riot as the crowd, inflamed beyond reason by Knox's rabble rousing speech, desecrated the interior of the church before rioting in the streets and looting the local monasteries, attacking and driving out the monks, many of whom had been there for decades. This wave of anti-clerical violence rapidly began to sweep across the country, initially restricted to the places where Knox was preaching but eventually spreading further and becoming increasingly brutal; the perpetuators were becoming less of a disorganised, rancorous mob and more of a small army by the day.

Aghast by this turn of events, Marie mustered the support of Châtelherault and her stepson, Lord James Stewart, despite the fact that both men were well known to be supporters of the Protestant faith. Like Marie, however, they both realised that this was not so much a religious revolution as an attack upon the state itself and although Lord James in particular was in favour of the Scottish Reformation gaining influence, he was clever enough to realise that this was not the way to go about it.

Determined to frighten the Protestant forces with a show of force, Marie and Châtelherault led an army of mixed French and Scottish troops to meet them, prepared to do battle if necessary but probably relieved to be able to withdraw when a truce was agreed between the two sides on 29 May. It was only to be a temporary solution, however, because the Protestants, now calling themselves the Congregation, continued to gather strength and Marie lost the support of her stepson, Lord James, when he switched sides. Châtelherault looked certain to follow him, especially as it was rumoured that his beloved son, now Earl of Arran, was on his way back from France to join the Protestant cause. 'You can never know here who is the friend or the enemy,' her French advisor Oysel wrote to the French Ambassador to England, 'for he who is with us in the morning is with them after dinner.'

Heartened by these high-profile new supporters, the Congregation forces continued to increase their numbers and their policy of savage iconoclasm continued throughout the summer, culminating in the looting of the great cathedral at St Andrews, along with every other church and religious house in the town. Horrified by this and other acts of sacrilege, Marie mustered her troops once more, sending a French army to St Andrews, and other forces under the command of Châtelherault and Oysel to meet with the Protestants, who were camped near Cupar. If Marie, who had fallen ill with a stress-related illness and was forced to remain at Falkland Palace, had been confident of victory, this was a serious error of judgement because the Congregation army was far larger than that of Châtelherault, so he and Oysel were forced to concede defeat. They came to an agreement with the Protestant leaders that Marie's French troops would withdraw from Fife and that she would give in to their demand for complete religious freedom.

Alarmed by the withdrawal of her troops and realising that Falkland Palace was ill-equipped to rebuff an attack, Marie responded by retreating to Edinburgh Castle. There she remained while the Protestant forces marched on Perth and then on to Stirling, looting and destroying churches and religious buildings and harassing members of the clergy and monastical orders, before turning their attention to the capital. Forewarned of their advance, Marie and a group of companions managed to slip out of the castle at night and rode to Dunbar Castle in East Lothian, a formidable fortress overlooking the North Sea. Her departure from Edinburgh was in the nick of time as Protestant forces overran the city only a few days later on 30 June and ransacked its churches and religious buildings. If Marie had remained in residence, she would have found herself trapped inside Edinburgh Castle and even more isolated – at least at Dunbar she would be able to communicate with her family and friends in France and could even escape by ship if need be.

Feeling altogether more secure in her clifftop eyrie, Marie issued a proclamation that, as the Protestant rebels were clearly motivated by a desire to flout and usurp her authority, she had no alternative but to order them to immediately disband and leave Edinburgh within six hours. She had never believed in their protestations that all they wanted was the legal freedom to practise their religion in peace as, unlike Mary Tudor, she had never made any move to persecute them and, even when she did graciously offer to consider their requests, they responded with violence and rebellion. No, it was obvious to her and her advisors that the Congregation's alleged pursuit of religious freedom was being used as an excuse for altogether more sinister motives; namely the dissolution of Marie's regency and the end of the French presence in Scotland.

Chapter 15

And Still it Stands

On 30 June 1559, King Henri of France donned his gilded armour, picked up his lance and prepared to take part in a special joust being held in the Palais des Tournelles in Paris to celebrate both the signing of the Peace of Cateau-Cambrésis and the marriage of his eldest daughter, Élisabeth, to Mary Tudor's widower, Philip II of Spain.

The roars of excitement from the enormous crowd as the King charged his horse towards that of Gabriel de Montgomery, a French captain in his Scots Guards, turned to screams of panic as Montgomery's lance smashed against the King's helmet, knocking Henri to the ground. Ten days later the King of France was dead, killed by septicaemia caused by splinters of wood from his opponent's lance entering his eye. His son, François, had succeeded to the throne with his wife, Mary of Scotland, as the Queen of France.

Marie was still in Dunbar Castle, desperately waiting for word of assistance from France when the news of King Henri's accident and subsequent alarming condition arrived. On a personal level, she was devastated and dumbfounded by the prospect of losing someone who had been one of her oldest friends and admirers, but more dispassionately she was aware that this was a stroke of luck for her family because it was well known that their aggressive enforcement of her daughter's claim to the English throne had driven a wedge between the Guise brothers and their King. Now though, they were likely to become the beloved and most trusted uncles of the new Queen of France and, better still, were completely hero worshipped by her mediocre and malleable young husband.

Promising though this situation must have been from Marie's point of view, she had doubts about how it would be regarded in Scotland where Mary was virtually unknown after all her years of absence and whose husband had never shown his face there and was yet to be crowned as King.

As she had suspected, the Congregation leaders saw the possible death of King Henri as a victory for their cause and a harbinger of increased French weakness. After all, no one knew better than the Scots what discord and instability could be fermented by having a juvenile monarch on the throne and they were determined to take advantage of this unexpected chink in the French armour. On 21 July, they ransacked Holyrood Palace and seized control of the country's coining irons, which were used to mint the currency, a serious act of rebellion that struck straight at the heart of Marie's authority. Infuriated by what was clearly intended as a challenge, she summoned together her council and once again sent Châtelherault and the faithful Oysel at the head of her army, this time to Edinburgh. Again outright battle was avoided by the drawing up of an agreement, whereby the Congregation agreed to desist from harassing religious buildings and their occupants, return Holyrood Palace and the coining irons to Marie, and swear to obey her authority along with that of her daughter and her husband, in return for the freedom to worship as they pleased and without any harassment.

Heartened both by the end to the conflict and the expectation that she could soon expect to receive a large number of troops from France, Marie left Dunbar and returned to Edinburgh where she was relieved to see that, although the city was somewhat battered and bruised about the edges, things had more or less returned to normal. It was there, on 7 August 1559, that she received the sad news of King Henri's death and the succession of her son-in-law and daughter to the throne of France. As she had expected, the news gave the still muttering Congregation members an additional boost and, slowly but surely, dissension began to rise up again as they preached against the continued French presence in Scotland and attempts by Marie to transform their country into a French satellite state, wilfully misinterpreting her desire to improve and modernise their antiquated old legal and administrative systems in order to make Scotland a more up-to-date and independent country. Wearily accepting that it was only a matter of time before conflict broke out again, Marie quietly began to reinforce the defences at Stirling and prepare for the inevitable.

Meanwhile, Elizabeth Tudor, despite blithely pretending that she had nothing but admiration and feelings of friendship for Marie and absolutely no intention of assisting her rebellious subjects against her, had sent Sir Ralph Sadler, that redoubtable survivor of several Tudor monarchs, up to Edinburgh. He had secret orders to do everything he could to strike at the very heart of Marie's regime and sow discord amongst her subjects with the aim of forcing her to sign a treaty with the English and getting the French out of Scotland once and for all. He was to use the Earl of Arran as a lever to separate his father, Châtelherault, from the Queen Regent's service and then persuade him to have the troublesome Oysel arrested. Shortly afterwards, Arran was secretly despatched from London back to Scotland having been primed by Elizabeth and her advisor, Sir William Cecil, to act as an agent for English interests at the Scottish court.

The arrival of Arran, and his reunion with his father, Châtelherault, was to completely change everything and struck a death knell for any hopes that Marie might have had that it was still possible to achieve peace between herself and the lords of the Congregation. She had already guessed that their ultimate aim was to oust her from the position of Regent and replace her with one of their own, so it didn't come as a surprise when she heard that either Arran or her step son, Lord James, were being mooted as a possible replacements and that Châtelherault, whose loyalty had always been fluid and unreliable, was almost certainly going to switch sides and stand against her. In desperation, Marie renewed her pleas for assistance from France, even asking her son-in-law to freeze the French assets of Châtelherault and his family in an attempt to bring them to heel. In the meantime she gave orders that the fortifications at Leith should be reinforced in case she and the other French occupants of Scotland had need to withdraw there.

When news arrived that Châtelherault had finally thrown in his lot with the Congregation leaders, Marie wrote yet another despairing letter to her son-in-law, King François.

This is to tell you that the Duke of Châtelherault has wasted no time after his son's arrival in declaring himself chief and leader of your rebels. For this he has found no better cover than to say that I am fortifying Leith and on this news he and all the said rebels who have assembled in his house ... have written me a letter of menace and defiance of which I enclose the translation. And they are now leaving to go and gather their men with all diligence for the purpose of interrupting our enterprise, defying me and your men if they can, and at least interfering with us in every way they can by cutting off our supplies and fuel as well as by circulating rumours to win over more and more people and alienate them from you, saying, Sire, that you and the French wish to subvert all their laws and place them in extreme servitude ... I beg you must humbly, Sire, to have pity on us and help us with good forces and money as quickly as possible, not doubting that the said Duke and his accomplices will do all that they can as soon as possible.

Her accompanying letter to her brothers was even more troubling, informing them that without money and assistance from the French she would be forced to barricade herself in Leith with very little in the way of food and other resources and concluding:

I beg you to send help for I make no doubt that our need is greater than ever. They are secretly helped by the English and they will do all they can to ruin both the Queen and her mother which will, I think, touch your heart, for it is not for my own cause that I suffer so many evils.

Her suspicion that it was English gold that was supporting the Scottish rebels was accurate and the knowledge that they could rely on Elizabeth Tudor for protection, even if she was still publicly protesting that she would have nothing to do with them, gave both Châtelherault and Lord James the courage to rebuff Marie's attempts to bring them back to her side. In October, the Congregation lords renewed their complaints about what they perceived as a French occupation of Scotland and demanded that all French troops leave the country immediately, before massing troops and marching on Edinburgh hoping to seize, or at least seriously frighten Marie, whom they believed was in residence at Holyrood Palace.

However, she had been forewarned of their arrival and managed to escape to Leith. Undaunted, the rebels, who were aware of how poor her resources were, prepared to lay siege while Marie sent increasingly frantic letters to France begging for whatever help they could muster and letting them know that her support in Scotland had all but vanished.

Little did she know that her daughter and brothers were caught up in a struggle of their own against their enemies at the French court and that there was little hope of help from that quarter at present. They were also concerned about reports of Marie's failing health and had been considered having her brought back to France, replacing her as Regent with her youngest brother, René, Marquis d'Elbeuf. René may have offered a suitable compromise to the lords of the Congregation because his wife, Louise de Rieux, was known to have Protestant sympathies, a drawback that was more than amply compensated for in Guise eyes by the fact that she was one of the wealthiest heiresses in France.

On 21 October, Marie's situation became all the more desperate when the lords of the Congregation proclaimed that they were suspending her Regency with immediate effect and that, from now on, all of her previous authority would be given to Châtelherault and a specially appointed Council, all of whose members would be entirely sympathetic to their own cause and members of the anti-French party in Scotland. Marie rebuffed both this threat to her authority and an attempt to lay siege to Leith, which ended with her own troops, led by Oysel, routing those of the Congregation and forcing them to retreat back to Edinburgh and then on to Linlithgow, leaving the capital free for Marie to make a triumphant return.

However, despite the relief of this temporary respite, Marie was feeling far from triumphant as she rode down the Royal Mile of Edinburgh towards Holyrood. The seemingly endless conflict had had a deleterious effect on her health, causing her to have anxiety attacks and worsening an already existent heart condition to the extent that she was now often weak of breath and subject to frightening attacks of palpitations and dizziness. It was probably during this period that her doctor wrote a memorandum about her health, detailing her various symptoms, which included hot flushes, a feeling of heaviness and a sense of depressed lassitude which was quite unlike her usual buoyant good humour and optimism. He recommended that she rest more and spend less time worrying about the cares of office, but this was advice that Marie could not afford to take.

She took to her bed as soon as she arrived back in her apartments in the palace but still continued to work, drawing on her last reserves of energy to direct her few remaining supporters in their attempts to disperse the rebel forces from the royal strongholds of Linlithgow and Stirling.

Rumours spread through Scotland that the redoubtable Queen Regent, who turned 44 in November 1559, was close to death and even Ralph Sadler reported back to England that she could not be much longer for this world, even if her enemies amongst the Congregation lords whispered that the devil himself could not kill this woman they saw as a scourge upon their land.

The news that Marie's youngest brother, René, Marquis d'Elbeuf, had been despatched from France with official papers that named him King François' Lieutenant General in Scotland, England and Ireland spurred both the lords of the Congregation and Elizabeth Tudor into action. Despite Marie's protestations that her daughter had not been directly involved in the proclamations of her right to rule England, Elizabeth had not forgiven this great impertinence, so when she was informed that the Guises were once again claiming they had a right to govern England as agents of the French monarchy, she decided that the time had come to act against the French regime in Scotland.

The notoriously poor weather conditions in the North Sea during the winter succeeded in driving René de Guise back to Dieppe, although almost a thousand of his men managed to reach their destination, and Elizabeth's navy did the rest, sailing up the Firth of Forth to blockade Leith and intercept further attempts to send aid and munitions to the French troops garrisoned in Scotland. A clear declaration of war that even Elizabeth could not deny, try though she might.

Desperate now to avert disaster, and fast losing hope that her brother would arrive in time to save the day, Marie fruitlessly tried once more to regain the support of Châtelherault, Lord James and even the Earl of Lennox. She also gave orders that all able bodied men of fighting age should ready themselves immediately for war – orders that were mostly ignored as few were willing to take arms against their fellow countrymen to defend the rights of a Queen who lived abroad and her foreign mother.

Alarmed by what this disobedience presaged, Marie made the decision to move from Holyrood Palace up to the more secure royal apartments in Edinburgh Castle, a residence she had never been overly fond of, but which offered her greater security and protection during these challenging times. She began to negotiate with Lord Erskine, the Keeper of the Castle, who was torn between his loyalty to the crown and his sympathies with the Congregation's cause and so did not immediately agree to let her take up residence.

Her decision to protect herself from her people was justified shortly afterwards in February 1560, when Lord James and other lords of the Congregation made a journey to Berwick to meet in secret with the Duke of Norfolk, Elizabeth Tudor's cousin and envoy. The result was the Treaty of Berwick in which Elizabeth promised to send English troops and weaponry into Scotland and help expel the French thereby forcibly ending Marie's Regency and the Auld Alliance between Scotland and France. In exchange for this, she was assured by the lords of the Congregation that they would aid the English army in every way possible; that their troops would in future come to England's aid should the French invade, and that from then on, all enemies of England would be Scotland's enemies also. When news of the treaty came to Marie's ears, she fired off a letter to her brothers declaring it 'shameful' as the various articles agreed by Elizabeth and the Scots lords sought to destroy everything she had worked so hard to achieve.

The threat of imminent English invasion made it imperative that Marie leave the vulnerable Holyrood Palace and take up residence in Edinburgh Castle and, to her relief, Lord Erskine gave way on 1 April and opened the fortress gates to her and her small group of remaining supporters, including the Archbishop of St Andrews, half brother of Châtelherault and uncle of the rebel Earl of Arran. She had never much liked Edinburgh Castle, finding it dank, cheerless and gloomy; in her enfeebled state it must have depressed her spirits even further to know that there was every chance that she would die within its impregnable stone walls. For the time being though, she would ignore her failing health and weakening body and continue to fight on against the lords and their English allies.

The situation looked desperate indeed, with English ships lying in the Firth of Forth and English troops swarming across the border, but Marie had not given up hope and so, when a messenger arrived from the English commander Lord Grey with a request to open negotiations, she accepted with alacrity.

She knew that the English troops at Leith had insufficient ordnance to effectively lay siege to the port and were probably looking for an honourable way to call off the whole sorry affair. What she didn't know, however, was that Grey was considering transferring his attention to Edinburgh instead, and laying siege to the castle, which he had been wrongly informed would be much easier to take. Luckily for Marie and the populace of Edinburgh, the Duke of Norfolk forcibly dissuaded him from this course. Norfolk foresaw that no good could come of it, and that Queen Elizabeth would almost certainly be displeased by a direct attack upon Marie de Guise. Suitably chastised, Lord Grey arranged to send his envoys to Edinburgh Castle to talk with Marie, probably mindful that he was sending them to deal with a woman so famously charming and charismatic that her enemies, the lords of the Congregation, refused to send men to talk to her face-to-face lest they be turned by her womanly wiles.

Even desperately ill, lame, exhausted and swollen almost beyond recognition by the symptoms of what was known at the time as 'dropsy' (nowadays known as congestive heart failure), Marie retained much of her old kittenish charm and, despite themselves, the two English envoys, Sir George Howard and Sir James Croftes, were impressed by her as she formally greeted them in a splendid silk marquee erected in the grounds of the castle. She was much less impressed by the demands they presented her with, which involved the dismissal of all French troops still remaining on Scottish soil. The negotiations fell apart and the tense stand off between the two sides resumed again; this time with the additional threat of the English laying siege to Edinburgh Castle at the behest of Elizabeth Tudor. Elizabeth was beginning to realise that there was no other way to displace Marie from power, especially as her troops appeared to be gaining very little ground at Leith, which was still in the hands of a sizeable French garrison commanded by Oysel.

High up in her fortress, perched on volcanic rock and surrounded by thick stone walls, the desperately ailing Marie felt cut off from what was happening in the outside world. She continued to write to her brothers and son-in-law to request immediate assistance but without any real hope that anything would ever come of it. She also tried to keep up a surreptitious, cyphered correspondence with Monsieur d'Oysel who was similarly trapped inside Leith, but with little success of keeping her missives out of English hands. Attempts to re-open negotiations with the Congregation lords and the English also floundered when her envoys, Lord Findlater and Master Spens, were insulted by Lord Grey and Châtelherault who insinuated that their continued loyalty to Marie made them traitors to their country and, yet again, insisted that all capitulation on their part was dependant on the French troops being sent away from Scotland and Leith being returned to Scottish hands. Initially Marie refused, but then changed her mind when Châtelherault and thirty of his fellow Congregation lords signed the Treaty of Berwick on 10 May, officially confirming their alliance with England.

A few days later Marie was finally granted her wish of a meeting with her estranged stepson, Lord James, and a selection of his fellow rebel lords. They entered Edinburgh Castle in order to present Marie with a great list of demands and grievances, all adamant that she had tried to impose France's will on Scotland in order to turn their country into a vassal state of the French. As always, her efforts to impose improvements upon her adopted country were wilfully misconstrued by the resentful Scottish as an attempt to erase their national identity. Even her attempts to improve the nation's resources of food and forestry were suspiciously interpreted as an attempt to boost Scottish income and supplies to make it more economically viable to the rapacious French.

Marie protested in vain that she had only ever acted in what she had believed to be the best interests of the Scottish people. Indeed, she felt she had devoted her life to the protection of their nation's independence, an assertion misconstrued as a defence of her daughter's rights and the French alliance. Although she agreed to dismantle the fortifications at Leith and send most of the French troops home, retaining only two garrisons, she was still to be disappointed by the lords' refusal to end their alliance with English, which she believed could only end in ruination and disaster for Scotland and would certainly leave them worse off than through any association with the French. She did not know about her daughter's foolish signing over of her kingdom and its resources to the French should she die without issue and, luckily for Marie, no one else in Scotland knew about this either.

Marie's health problems worsened severely over the next few weeks to the extent that she struggled to eat, was constantly thirsty, found it difficult to breathe when lying down and her mind began to wander. On the 27 June, she sat down and composed her final letters to the faithful Oysel, who was still trapped in Leith, and her brothers in France who had failed to come to her assistance despite all of their grand promises. As always her letters were full of talk about politics and her current difficulties with the still recalcitrant rebel lords with very little mention of her own personal troubles other than an almost dismissive, 'my health has been quite good until two days ago, when

197

I had a relapse and for two nights now have had a return of the fever. I do not know what will happen.'

She almost certainly knew by now that she was mortally ill, but she was determined to keep working for as long as she could and still keep up-to-date with the regular reports that were coming in from her intelligence network. By the start of July, it was obvious to everyone that she was dying; despite this, a request by Lord Erskine that she be allowed a visit by her friend, the Bishop of Amiens, was rejected by the vindictive Châtelherault even though all the other opposition leaders agreed to it.

Now completely unable to lie down and sleep properly, Marie spent long hours seated and it was thus that the lords of the Congregation found her when they were summoned to her presence on 7 June for one final attempt to persuade them to reject their alliance with England. Châtelherault, that great hypocrite, openly wept when he beheld her pitiful state while the others maintained a respectful silence as she addressed each one in turn, beseeching them to put their trust in the French and reiterating that she had been motivated only by her love of Scotland and its people, not by any loyalty to France.

After warning them about the dangers of throwing in their lot with the English, she reminded them that their true loyalty must always lie with Mary and her husband, clearly fearful that the rejection of the French alliance might ultimately result in an attempt to depose her daughter from the throne of Scotland. She then began to cry, which in turn made several of the rebel lords start weeping too as she took each by the hand to bid him farewell and beg their forgiveness for any offence she had caused them since her arrival in Scotland twenty-two years earlier and assured them that she forgave them for everything they had done to her.

The sombre procession of lords, many of whom were genuinely distressed by their last audience with the Queen Regent, left Edinburgh Castle and returned to Leith shortly afterwards. Only Lord James and William Keith, the Earl Marischal, remained with Marie at her request for she wished them to bear witness to her final will and testament, which was drawn up and signed the following evening after she had met with Châtelherault and his son, the Earl of Arran, both of whom looked noticeably upset when they left her presence.

Now that Marie's end was drawing near, her enemies realised there was no benefit at all in maintaining hostilities and, although she had none of her own family there with her during her final days, she had the consolation of knowing that she and the rebellious Scottish lords were at peace with each other. It didn't matter that Knox and his more fiery cohorts were preaching against her in the streets of Edinburgh as she was dying in her bedchamber of the castle above their heads; none of that could touch her now. However, it was Knox's deputy at St Giles' Church, the Protestant preacher John Willock, who came to her side and, with admirable gentleness, gave whatever spiritual comfort he could as she lost the power of speech and slowly, silently slipped from one world to the next.

Marie de Guise died just after midnight on 11 June 1560, with her stepson, Lord James, and the Earl of Argyll, two of the most prominent members of the Congregation, at her side. That two of her greatest enemies should have been the only people on hand to offer support and comfort as she died is perhaps the greatest tribute imaginable to Marie de Guise's famously irresistible charm.

Afterword

For several months after her death, the embalmed body of Marie de Guise rested in its coffin on a bier in the tiny chapel of St Margaret perched at the very top of Edinburgh Castle. News of her death did not reach France until 18 July and then was kept from her daughter for another ten days due to fears that the highly-strung 16-year-old Queen of France would have a total breakdown when she learned that the mother she had idolised was dead.

These gloomy predictions turned out to be true, and Mary was forced to withdraw to her apartments for several weeks to recover from the blow. She wore heavy mourning for quite some time after she emerged, pale, red-eyed and wan, to resume her place by her husband's side. It was while dressed in this mourning for her mother that she was painted by Clouet for his famous *Dieul* portrait of the young Queen, looking sombre yet still beautiful and the living image of her deceased mother in the stark white mourning veils traditionally worn by Queens of France. Perhaps pointedly, Mary decided to send the finished portrait as a gift to Elizabeth Tudor, whose machinations had done nothing to improve her mother's situation during her final months and might even have hastened her death.

The French alliance that Marie had worked so hard to maintain, and which she died believing was the very best hope for Scotland's future prosperity, rapidly disintegrated after her death. The French troops she had once so desperately begged for were sent home for good in the wake of the Treaty of Edinburgh, which cemented the accord between Scotland and England, while at the same time upholding the peace between France and England that had been agreed in the Treaty of Cateau-Cambrésis. Both French and English troops were consequently withdrawn from Scotland and their fortifications destroyed, leaving the country in the hands of the Congregation lords.

In the midst of all this, no one spared much thought for the body of the dead Queen Regent, which lay undisturbed in the chapel beneath a pall simply embellished with a single white taffeta cross. When the subject did arise, the lords decided that she could not be accorded a Catholic funeral and would not interred beside her husband, their sons and his first French wife in Holyrood Abbey, where she must have expected to be buried.

The heart of her sister, Louise de Guise, Princesse de Chimay, had been returned to Joinville for burial after her death in 1542 and perhaps Marie had hoped that she too would be allowed the same honour. It was not to be. Finally, after many months of negotiation, on 16 March 1561, the body of Marie de Guise was secretly taken from the precincts of Edinburgh Castle, transported to Leith and placed on a ship bound for France, where she was finally laid to rest in the Convent of St Pierre in Reims, where her younger sister, Renée, was Abbess of the order. The ornate and beautiful tomb erected in her memory, surmounted with a brass life sized statue of the dead Regent, was sadly destroyed during the French Revolution, but there remains an equally fitting, albeit more modern, memorial to Marie within the precincts of Edinburgh Castle, reminding visitors that:

Mary of Lorraine, Queen of James V and mother of Mary Queen of Scots and Regent of Scotland from 1554-1560 died here 11th June 1560. "A lady of honourable conditions, of singular judgement, full of humanity, a great lover of justice, helpful to the poor."

Bibliography

Wood, Marguerite, *Foreign Correspondence with Marie de Lorraine: the Balcarres Papers*, Edinburgh, Scottish History Society, 2 vols 1923, 1925.

Cameron, Annie I., *The Scottish Correspondence of Mary of Lorraine*, Edinburgh, Scottish History Society 1927.

Sedgwick, Henry Dwight, *The House of Guise*, Indianapolis, Bobbs-Merrill 1938.

Williams, Hugh Noel, *The Brood of False Lorraine*, London, Hutchinson (1918).

Thomas, Andrea, *Princelie Majestie: The Court of James V of Scotland*, Edinburgh, John Donald 2005.

Thomas, Andrea, *Glory and Honour: The Renaissance in Scotland*, Edinburgh, Birlinn 2013.

Ritchie, Pamela E., *Mary of Guise in Scotland, 1548–1560: A Political Study*, Edinburgh, Tuckwell Press 2002.

Merriman, Marcus, *The Rough Wooings*, Edinburgh, Tuckwell Press 2000.

Perry, Maria, *Sisters of the King*, London, Andre Deutsch 1998.

Dunbar, John G., *Scottish Royal Palaces*, Edinburgh, Historic Royal Scotland 1999.

Dunlop, Ian, *French Royal Palaces*, London, Hamish Hamilton 1985.

Knecht, R.J., *Francis I*, Cambridge, Cambridge University Press 1982.

Marshall, Rosalind K., *Mary of Guise: Queen of Scots*, London, Collins 1977.

Marshall, Rosalind K., *Queen Mary's Women*, Edinburgh, John Donald 2006.

Marshall, Rosalind K., *Mary Queen of Scots: In My End is my Beginning*, Edinburgh, NMSE 2013.

Dunn, Jane, *Elizabeth and Mary: Cousins, Rivals, Queens*, London, Harper 2004.

BIBLIOGRAPHY

Graham, Roderick, *An Accidental Tragedy: The Life of Mary Queen of Scots*, Edinburgh, Birlinn 2012.

Wellman, Kathleen, *Queens and Mistresses of Renaissance France*, New Haven, Yale University Press 2013.

Porter, Linda, *Crown of Thistles: The Fatal Inheritance of Mary Queen of Scots*, London, Pan 2013.

Carroll, Stuart, *Martyrs and Murderers: The Guise Family and the Making of Europe*, Oxford, Oxford University Press 2009.

Guy, John, *My Heart is My Own: The Life of Mary Queen of Scots*, New York, Harper 2004.

Guy, John, *The Children of Henry VIII*, Oxford, Oxford University Press 2013.

Frieda, Leonie, *Catherine de Medici*, London, Weidenfeld and Nicholson 2003.

Scarisbrick, J.J., *Henry VIII*, New Haven, Yale University Press 1997.

Starkey, David, *Six Wives: The Queens of Henry VIII*, London, Chatto & Windus 2003.

Warnicke, Retha M., *The Marrying of Anne of Cleves: Royal Protocol in Tudor England*, Cambridge, Cambridge University Press 2000.

Fraser, Antonia, *The Wives of Henry VIII*, New York, Vintage 1994.

Fraser, Antonia, *Mary Queen of Scots*, London, Weidenfeld and Nicolson 1969.

Weir, Alison, *Henry VIII: King and Court*, London, Jonathan Cape 2001.

Weir, Alison, *The Six Wives of Henry VIII*, London, Bodley Head 1991.

Borman, Tracy, *Thomas Cromwell*, London, Hodder and Stoughton 2014.

Harrison, John G., *Ladies in Waiting: Marie de Guise at Stirling*, (PDF), Kirkdale Archaeology/Historic Scotland 2008.

Harrison, John G., *Rebirth of a Palace: The Royal Court at Stirling Castle*, Edinburgh, Historic Scotland 2011.

Index

Aickenhead, James, 54
Amboise, 18, 45
Amiens, 51-2, 167
Amiens, Nicolas Pellevé, Bishop of, 198
Ancrum Moor, Battle of, 143
Angus, Archibald, 6th Earl of, 55, 71, 91-2, 95, 109, 119, 123, 126, 136, 141
Anjou, René, Duc d', 13, 23
Anjou, Yolande d' *see* Lorraine, Duchesse de
Anne Boleyn, 25, 46-8, 54, 96, 133, 168-9
Anne of Cleves, 41, 96, 101
Antigay, Renée d', 74
Arcadelt, Jacques, 21
Argyll, Archibald, 4th Earl of, 122, 133
Argyll, Archibald, 5th Earl of, 199
Arran, James Hamilton, 2nd Earl of, *see* Châtelherault, Duke of
Arran, James Hamilton, 3rd Earl of, 158, 186, 190, 195, 199
Aumale, Duc d', brother of Marie de Guise, *see* Lorraine, François de
Aumale, Anna d'Este, Duchesse d', 160

Balcomie Castle, 75-6, 78
Balliol, John, 53
Bar-le-Duc, 17-19
Bassett, Anthony, 113
Baynard's Castle, 168
Beaton, Cardinal David, 61, 64, 67, 70, 75, 97, 100, 108, 114, 119, 122, 124-5, 128-30, 132-3, 136, 140-2, 144-6, 148, 177
Beaugency, Château de, 51
Berwick, 115, 150, 171, 194
Berwick, Treaty of, 194, 196
Bethune, Elizabeth, 91
Bidassoa, River 30
Black Band, 18, 31, 36,
Blois, 15, 45, 57
Bothwell, Patrick, 3rd Earl of, 125-6, 135-6, 171
Bonnivet, Admiral, 30, 31
Bontel, Ambroise, 74
Boulogne, 46-7, 139, 142, 144
Boulogne, Treaty of, 160
Bourbon, Anne de France, Duchesse de, 34, 41
Bourbon, Suzanne de Bourbon, Duchesse de, 34-5, 41
Bourbon, Charles de Bourbon, Duc de and Constable of France, 34-6, 41
Bourbon, Marie de, 54-5, 57, 88

Brosse, Jacques de la, 137
Broughty Castle, 152
Bryan, Sir Francis, 67
Burgundy, Charles the Bold, Duc de, 13-14, 19

Calais, 46-7, 88-9, 179
Carlisle, 115
Castillon, Louis de Perreau, Sieur de, 63-5, 67, 70, 72-3
Cateau-Cambrésis, Treaty of, 184, 188, 200
Catherine de Medici, 26, 47-8, 52, 54, 134, 138, 178
Catherine of Aragon, 46, 49
Catherine Howard, 108, 113, 168
Catherine Parr, 140, 168
Cecil, Sir William, 190
Champagne, 30, 36, 37
Chapuys, Eustace, 114, 120
Charles V, Holy Roman Emperor, 28-30, 36-7, 40, 73, 174
Charles de Valois, Prince of France and Duc d'Angoulême, 163
Charlotte de Savoie, Queen of France, 16
Châteaudun, 50-1, 59-60, 65-6, 68-9, 70, 72, 74, 88, 165-7
Châtelherault, James, Duke of (formerly 2nd Earl of Arran), 76-7, 95, 106, 122-31, 133, 137-8, 140-5, 150-1, 153-9, 161, 164, 166, 171-5, 185-6, 189-92, 194-6, 198-9
Chatellerault, François de Bourbon, Duc de, 18
Christina of Denmark, Duchess of Milan and Duchesse de Lorraine, 54, 70, 96, 104
Claude de France, 16, 40, 46-7
Clouet, Jean, 55
Clouet, François, 200
Cluny, Hôtel de, 45, 57
Conciergerie, Paris, 43
Condé, château de, 14
Colonna, Prospero, 18
Croftes, Sir James, 196
Cromwell, Thomas, 62, 64-5, 69, 98
Cupar Castle, 80
Curel, Mademoiselle de, 74, 111
Custines, 15

Darnley, Lord Henry Stewart, 169
Dieppe, 164, 166-7, 194
Dingwall Castle, 71
Douglas, Sir George, 123, 125, 141

INDEX

Douglas, Lady Margaret, Countess of Lennox, 109, 136, 140, 169, 170, 172
Dumbarton Castle, 100, 128, 153, 157-8
Dunbar Castle, 187-9
Dundee, 102, 152
Dunois, Jean d'Orléans, Comte de, 49

Edinburgh, 10, 80, 83-5, 87, 90, 97-8, 115-16, 125-6, 129, 136, 141, 148, 150, 152, 155-6, 158-60, 171, 173, 182-3, 187, 189-90, 192-201
Edward I, 53
Edward IV, 54, 86
Edward VI, 12, 124, 138, 147, 167, 169-72, 185
Elbeuf, Marquis d', 192-4
Eleonore of Austria, 40, 42-4, 46, 48-9
Elisabeth de Valois, 149, 172, 188
Elizabeth I, 26, 34, 48, 133, 136, 170, 176-7, 182-5, 190-1, 193-6, 200
England, 12, 26, 28, 37, 53-5, 62, 65, 67, 69-70, 72, 78, 87, 92, 104, 108-109, 113-16, 119, 121-6, 129, 133, 138, 140, 145, 147, 153, 156, 159-62, 165, 167-71, 174, 179-80, 184, 186, 193-4, 196, 198, 200
Erskine, Lady Margaret, 181
Erskine, John, 5th Lord, 130, 151
Erskine, John, 6th Lord, 194-5, 198
Essartz, Mahout d', 74
Étampes, Anne de Pisseleu d'Heilly, Duchesse de, 43
Eyemouth, 179

Falkland Palace, 10-11, 71, 80-2, 94, 102-103, 109, 116-18, 121, 126, 186
Ferat, jester to Marie de Guise, 74
Ferdinand of Aragon, 28
Ferrara, Ercole II, Duke of, 160
Ferrara, Renée de France, Duchess of, 16, 29, 160
Fife, 71, 80, 115, 141, 186
Findlater, Lord, 196
Fleming, Malcolm, 3rd Lord, 151
Flodden, Battle of, 12, 53, 82, 97, 116, 132
Fontainebleau, 45, 149, 181
Forres, 176
Forth, River, 81, 96, 194-5
Fouvert, Ada, 18
France, 11-12, 14-20, 26, 28-31, 35-8, 40-3, 45, 47, 49-50, 53-5, 59-60, 62-4, 67, 69-75, 77, 79, 82, 85-6, 88-90, 92-3, 98, 107-109, 111-12, 117, 123-5, 127, 130-1, 134, 137-40, 142, 148-9, 152-8, 160-7, 169-72, 174, 177-80, 182-90, 192-4, 197-8, 200-201

François I, 15-20, 28-31, 33, 35-7, 40-8, 50-9, 61-5, 67-70, 72-3, 77, 88, 91, 101, 108, 114, 121, 124, 128, 137-8, 140, 143-4, 148
François II, 138, 152, 156, 177, 180-2, 184, 188, 191, 193, 198
François de Valois, 40, 43, 134
Fuenterrabia, 30
Fulham Palace, 169
Furstemburg, Duke of, 32

Gardiner, Stephen, Bishop of Winchester, 58, 62, 63
Geneva, 183
Glamis Castle, 102
Glasgow, 140
Graham, Patrick, 4th Lord, 130
Grey, Lady Jane, 172
Grey, William, 13th Baron of Wilton,195-6
Greenwich, Treaties of, 129, 134, 137, 143, 145, 148
Guildford, 167
Guillet, Jean, 74
Guise, Antoinette de Bourbon, Comtesse then Duchesse de, 11, 16-20, 22-6, 28, 31-2, 34, 39, 41-4, 48, 50-2, 57-8, 60-2, 68, 88, 95, 101-102, 111, 138, 148, 152, 162, 164, 166-7
Guise, Claude, Comte then Duc de, 14-26, 28, 30-2, 35-8, 41, 46-50, 52, 54, 56, 62, 64, 68, 70-1, 75, 78, 111, 124, 128, 138, 162-3, 165
Guise, François, Duc de, see Lorraine, François de, Duc d'Aumale
Guise, Marie de,
    Appearance, 10, 44, 50, 58, 61, 63, 65, 69, 76, 87, 89-90, 93, 97, 127, 135
    Personality, 11-12, 32, 34, 42, 44-5, 51-2, 62-3, 75, 79, 83, 87, 89, 100, 108, 119, 127, 129, 135-6, 140, 155, 157, 195
    Religious views, 22, 172, 182-3, 185, 187
    Birth, 17
    Childhood 11, 17-41
    At the French court, 42-60
    Marriage to the Duc de Longueville, 49-50
    Birth of François de Longueville, 52
    Widowed for the first time, 60
    Birth of Louis de Longueville, 60
    Wooing by Henry VIII, 62-71
    Marriage to James V, 72
    Arrival in Scotland, 75-79
    Coronation, 96-98
    Birth of James Stuart, 99-100
    Birth of Robert Stuart, 104
    Death of her sons, 104-107
    Birth of Mary Stuart, 117-118

Widowed for the second time, 118
Coronation of her daughter, 132-133
Departure of her daughter to France, 157-8
Visit to France, 161-167
Death of Louis, 167
Visit to the English court and meeting with Edward VI, 167-170
Becomes Queen Regent of Scotland, 173
Final illness and death, 193-199
Burial in France, 201

Haddington, 153, 155-8, 160
Hamilton, John, Archbishop of Saint Andrews, 195
Hamilton, Sir James of Finnart, 103
Hampton Court Palace, 120, 168-9
Henri II, 40, 43, 47, 134, 143-4, 148-50, 154, 157, 160-1, 163-, 172, 177-9, 181-2, 184, 188-9
Henry VIII, 10, 12, 28, 37, 46-8, 53-5, 57-8, 62, 64-5, 70, 72, 74, 86, 88, 91, 96, 98, 101-104, 106, 108, 112, 114, 116, 120-1, 123-5, 127-9, 132, 134, 136-8, 140, 142-4, 147-8, 168-9, 172, 176, 183
Herpon, Jacques, 74
Hertford, Earl of, see Somerset, Duke of
Hoby, Philip, 70
Holyrood, Abbey of, 84-6, 96-7, 106, 121, 141, 201
Holyroodhouse, Palace of, 59, 85, 92, 125-6, 141, 173, 189, 192-5
Howard, Lord William, 62-3, 167
Howard, Sir George, 196
Hume Castle, 179
Huntingdon, Francis, 19th Earl of, 169
Huntly, George, 4th Earl of, 90, 122, 126, 128, 148, 151, 159

Inchmahome Priory, 152
Inveresk, 150
Italy, 17-18, 29-30, 36-37, 41

James II, 14, 76, 80
James IV, 12, 54, 80-3, 856, 89, 92, 116, 121-2, 132
James V, 11-12, 53-9, 61, 67-8, 70-8, 80-3, 85-7, 89-100, 102-19, 121-4, 126, 132, 136, 147, 169, 181, 201
James, Prince of Scotland, Duke of Rothesay, 100-102, 104-105
Jane Seymour, 62, 100, 169
Janequin, Clément, 21
Jedburgh, 143
Jeanne d'Arc, 32, 49

Joinville, 15, 17, 19-22, 24, 26, 28, 31-32, 39, 41, 46, 50, 72, 82, 95, 112, 149, 162, 165-6, 201

Kelso, 114, 143, 179
Knox, John, 145, 150, 177, 183, 185, 199

Le Havre, 74, 75
Leith, 59, 140-41, 152, 155, 158, 190-2, 194-8, 201
Lennox, Countess of, see Douglas, Lady Margaret
Lennox, Matthew Stewart, 4th Earl of, 77, 106, 124-5, 128-31, 133, 135-7, 139-40, 152, 153, 172, 194
Leslie, Norman, Master of Rothes, 144
Lindsay, Sir David, 77
Linlithgow, 10-12, 83, 92, 94, 97, 116-18, 120, 122-5, 127, 129-31, 135, 192-3
Lisle, John, Viscount, 120, 123
Loire, 15, 45, 50-51, 56, 59, 80
London, 12, 49, 114, 116, 120, 138, 157, 160, 167-70, 190
Longueville, Claude d'Orléans, Duc de, 49
Longueville, François d'Orléans, Duc de, 12, 52, 59-60, 68, 71-2, 88, 139, 149, 153-4, 158, 164-5
Longueville, Joan of Hachberg Sausenberg, Duchesse de, 49, 96
Longueville, Louis d'Orléans, Duc de, 49
Longueville, Louis d'Orléans, Duc de, 40, 42, 49-51, 57, 59-61, 66-7, 165
Longueville, Louis de, 60, 66-7, 165-7
Lorraine, 13-15, 17, 20, 42
Lorraine, Hôtel de, 45
Lorraine, Anna de, Princess of Orange, 41, 70, 88, 104, 149,
Lorraine, Antoinette de, Abbess of Faremoutiers, 166
Lorraine, Antoine, Duc de, 14, 15, 38, 41-2, 44, 70, 95-6, 139, 149
Lorraine, Charles de, Archbishop of Reims, Cardinal de Guise then Lorraine 148-9, 164, 166, 172, 177-8, 180-4, 188, 191-2, 195-7
Lorraine, Christina of Denmark, Duchesse de, see Christina of Denmark
Lorraine, Claude de, Marquis de Mayenne, 160
Lorraine, François de, Comte de Lambesc, 15, 33, 36
Lorraine, François de, Duc de Lorraine, 41, 44, 96, 149
Lorraine, François de, Duc d'Aumale, later Duc de Guise, 19, 21, 42-3, 47, 139, 148-9,

152, 154-5, 158, 160, 164, 166, 172, 177-84, 188, 19-2, 195-7
Lorraine, Jean de, Bishop of Metz, later Cardinal de Lorraine, 15, 17, 34, 42, 45, 47, 57-8, 101, 123, 149, 162
Lorraine, Jeanne d'Harcourt, Duchesse de, 14
Lorraine, Louise de, Princesse de Chimay, 20, 70, 73-4, 78, 88, 96, 102, 104, 114, 201
Lorraine, Marie de, *see* Guise, Marie de
Lorraine, Nicolas de, cousin of Marie de Guise, 41
Lorraine, Philippa of Guelders, Duchesse de, 11, 14-17, 20, 33-4, 39, 44, 80, 95, 149
Lorraine, René, Marquis d'Elbeuf, 72, 192-4
Lorraine, René, King of Sicily and Duc de, 13-15, 41
Lorraine, Renée de Bourbon, Duchesse de, 18, 34, 41-2, 95
Lorraine, Renée de, Abbess of St Pierre at Rheims, 166, 201
Lorraine, Yolande d'Anjou, Duchesse de, 13
Louis XI, 13
Louis XII, 15-18, 34
Louise de Savoie, Duchesse d'Angoulême, 15, 31, 35-6, 41
Louvre, the, 50
Luxembourg, Marie de, *see* Comtesse de Vendôme
Lyon, 56, 71

Madeleine de Valois, 42, 52, 54-7, 59, 61-2, 67, 71-2, 74, 76, 84-6, 103, 121
Madrid, Treaty of, 40
Manson, André, 99, 103
Margaret Tudor, 12, 53-4, 71, 80, 83-4, 86-7, 98-100, 103, 106, 109-10, 119, 121, 127, 136, 172, 176, 183
Marguerite de Valois, 42, 52, 56, 61, 63-4
Marguerite d'Angoulême, 40, 44, 52, 55
Marguerite d'Anjou, 13
Marischal, William Keith, 4th Earl of, 198
Mary of Guelders, 14, 76, 80
Marignano, Battle of, 18-19, 31, 36
Marne, River, 20
Marseilles, 47, 48
Mary I, 170, 172, 174, 177, 179, 182-3, 187-8
Mary Tudor, 32, 86, 172
Mary, Queen of Scots, 11, 15, 24, 75, 120-9, 132, 134, 137-8, 144, 148, 153, 155-7, 159, 162, 164-6, 172, 177-8, 180-2, 184, 188-9, 198, 200-201
Maximilian I, Holy Roman Emperor, 28, 29
Maxwell, Robert, 5th Lord, 71, 72, 75, 115-16
May, Isle of, 96

Mayenne, Louise de Brézé, Marquise de, 160
Meine, Henri le, 74
Melrose, 143
Mesnage, Jules de, 137
Methven Castle, 109
Meudon, Château de, 166
Meuse, River, 32
Mewtes, Sir Peter, 65, 69
Michelson, Andrew, 100
Milan, 18-19, 28, 36
Milan, Bona de Savoie, Duchess of, 16
Milan, Christina of Denmark, Duchess of, *see* Christina of Denmark
Montalembert, André de, Sieur d'Essé, 154-5
Montgomery, Gabriel de, 188
Montgomery, Jacques de, Seigneur de Lorges, 143
Montmorency, Anne de, Constable of France, 101, 152, 154, 179
Montpensier, Duc de, 154
Moray, Lord James Stewart, Earl of, 122, 181, 185-6, 190, 192, 194, 197-9
Musselburgh, 113, 150, 159

Nancy, 13, 20, 41-2, 70
Naples, 13, 28
Navarre, 30, 40
Netherlands, 14, 29, 30
Neufchâteau, 32, 33
Norfolk, Thomas Howard, 3rd Duke of, 115
Norfolk, Thomas Howard, 4th Duke of, 194, 195
Normandy, 60
Northampton, Elisabeth Brooke, 6th Marchioness of, 168
Northumberland, John Dudley, 1st Duke of, 167, 168, 170
Notre Dame Cathedral, 57, 181

Orkney, 71
Orléans, 14
Orléans, Henri de Valois, Duc de, *see* Henri II, King of France
Oysel, Henri Cleutin, Seigneur d', 152-4, 172-3, 179-80, 186, 189-90, 192, 196-7

Paris, 15-17, 42-3, 45, 55-8, 61-2, 181, 188
Parois, Mademoiselle de, 178
Pasquiere, Jeanne, 74
Pavia, 33, 36-8, 41, 43, 47, 49
Peebles, 113
Pembroke, Anne Parr, Countess of, 168
Perth, 110, 185, 187
Peronne, Château de, 60

Picardy, 55, 60
Pieddeser, Jeanne, 74
Pinkie Clough, Battle of, 150-2, 159, 161
Philip II, King of Spain, 174, 184, 188
Philippa de Guelders, *see* Lorraine, Duchesse de
Philippe IV, King of France, 53
Pizzighettone, 36
Poitiers, Diane de, 21, 41, 43, 52, 149, 160, 163
Pont-à-Moussonm, 33-4, 38-9, 41-2, 45, 95, 149
Pope Clement VII, 47, 48, 52
Pope Julius III, 184
Pope Leo X, 29, 30
Portsmouth, 167
Puiguillon, Gilbert de Beaucaire, Seigneur de, 68, 71

Rainville, Jeanne de la, 74
Reims, 1489, 164, 201
Robert, Prince of Scotland, Duke of Albany, 104-105, 107
Roches, 46
Rothes, George Leslie, 4th Earl of, 144
Rouen, 51, 60, 61, 74, 164-5
Rouen, Treaty of, 53
Rome, 30, 41, 98
Rye, 167

Sadler, Sir Ralph, 98, 109, 126-30, 133-4, 138, 190, 193
Saint Andrews, 75-8, 80, 94, 99, 100, 102, 105, 136, 144-5, 148, 150, 166, 186, 195
Sainte Chapelle, 43
Saint Denis Cathedral, 42
Saint-Germain-en-Laye, 45
Saint Giles Church, 84-5, 183, 199
Saint John's Kirk, 185
Saint Margaret's Chapel, 200
Saint Michael's Church, 120
Saint Nicolas Basilica, 19
Saint Paul's Church, 17
Saint Pierre's Convent, 201
Saint Quentin, 179
Saverne, 38
Savoie, Anne of Cyprus, Duchesse de, 16
Scotland, 12, 53-6, 59, 62, 69, 71-2, 74, 76-9, 82-3, 87, 90-1, 94-5, 108-109, 111-15, 118, 120, 121, 122-3, 125-33, 135, 137, 139-41,

143-4, 146-8, 150, 152-6, 158-61, 163-8, 171, 174-8, 180, 182-5, 187-90, 192-4, 196-8, 200-201
Strozzi, Leone, 150
Seine, River, 165
Seton, George, 4th Lord, 91
Seton, George, 5th Lord, 128
Seton, Marie Pierres, Lady, 91
Sicily, 162-3
Sinclair, Janet, 120
Sinclair, Sir Oliver, 90, 115-16
Solway Firth, 115
Solway Moss, 10, 115-17, 119
Somerset, Edward Seymour, Duke of (formerly Earl of Hertford), 140-1, 143, 147-8, 150-2, 158, 159-60, 167
Somerville, Hugh, 4th Lord, 90
Spain, 28, 29, 30, 177, 179, 184
Stewart, Lady Jean, 91
Stirling, 71, 81-2, 94, 97, 99, 103-106, 126, 130-8, 141-4, 150-2, 158-9, 185, 187, 190, 193
Suffolk, Richard de la Pole, Duke of, 37
Suffolk, Charles Brandon, Duke of, 31, 32
Suffolk, Mary Tudor, Duchess of, *see* Mary Tudor
Suffolk, Henry Grey, Duke of, 169
Suffolk, Lady Frances Brandon, Duchess of, 169

Tay, River, 157
Touche, Françoise de la, 74
Tournelles, Hôtel de, 16, 45, 188
Threave Castle, 71

Vaudémont, Frédéric, Comte de, 13
Vendôme, François de Bourbon, Comte de, 16
Vendôme, Princesse Marie de Luxembourg, Comtesse de, 16-17, 20, 26, 42
Vendôme, Charles de Bourbon, Duc de, 40, 54
Vial, Michel, 74, 94

Wark Castle, 180
Westminster, Palace of, 169-70
Wharton, Sir Thomas, 115
Whitehall, Palace of, 147
Willock, John, 199
Wishart, George, 144, 146

York, 108, 109